The Exploits of Baron de Marbot

SMYTHE LIBRARY

Stamp this label with the date for return.
Contact the librarian if you wish to renew this book.

.-7 JUL 2005		
-7 JUL 2005		

The Exploits of Baron de Marbot

Selected and Edited by C.J. Summerville

You may call the feeling which urged us love of
glory, or perhaps madness; it was an imperious
master and we marched without looking back.
                                        Marbot, Memoirs

CARROLL & GRAF PUBLISHERS, INC.
New York

Carroll & Graf Publishers, Inc.
19 West 21st Street
New York
NY 10010-6805

First published in the UK by Robinson Publishing 2000

First Caroll & Graf edition 2000

Copyright collection and introduction © Constable & Robinson Ltd 2000

ISBN 0-7867-0801-8

Printed and bound in the EU

940.27092

R38204

Contents

Editor's Preface

'. . . the human, the gallant, the inimitable Marbot! His book is that which gives us the best picture by far of the Napoleonic soldiers.'[1] So wrote Sir Arthur Conan Doyle in 1907 and his statement is, I feel, as true now as it was then. *The Memoirs of Baron de Marbot* (published in Great Britain for the first time in 1892, and translated from its original French by A.J. Butler) is a classic, well known and well loved by *aficionados* of the Napoleonic period. References to Marbot's reminiscences may be found in the bibliographies of scores of history books; and when Conan Doyle needed inspiration for his fictional hussar-hero, Brigadier Gerard, it was to General Jean-Baptiste-Antoine-Marcellin de Marbot's book that he turned. Long out of print, I felt the time was ripe to re-introduce this *raconteur par excellence* to a new generation of readers. This present volume, featuring the most colourful of the Baron's adventures, is the result.

Marbot's original work sprawled over three volumes in its native French, and two volumes in Butler's English translation. By concentrating, however, on those events in which Marbot was directly involved – his exploits – I have endeavoured to present a more concise and accessible single-volume edition. The text upon which I have relied is that of Longman & Company's Silver Library edition of 1900; and I acknowledge my debt to A.J. Butler, its translator and first English editor. Some changes have been made: occasional lapses in continuity have been noted, and corrections suggested; typographical errors, where found, have been remedied; obscure and obsolete words have been replaced; the punctuation has, here and there, been modernized; dates, numerals, names, titles, have been consistently rendered; and place-names, where appropriate, have been given in their native form (e.g. Zaragoza instead of Saragossa). My aim throughout has been a fluent, consistent text, accessible to both the specialist and the general reader alike. In a book of this size it has been necessary, of course, to edit some passages; and a dedicated student of the original work will, no doubt, detect the omissions. As far as possible, however, the anecdotes which form the body of this book are given in their entirety. It must be emphasized, however, that I have selected these anecdotes from the many which make up Marbot's *Memoirs*; and that the present work represents a severe abridgement of the original.

Having decided at the outset to concentrate on those episodes which feature Marbot himself as the main protagonist, I also wanted to present an unfolding story: the rise of Marbot from trooper to colonel; the glories and follies of the marshals to whom Marbot was aide-de-camp; and the journey of Napoleon Bonaparte, from victor to vanquished. In order to fill in some gaps, and to provide background information for the general reader, I have included some extras which are absent in the Butler edition: each chapter has been furnished with a short introduction, a title, and a quotation from one of Marbot's contemporaries – more often than not Napoleon himself, whose opinions and musings form a kind of sub-text to the action; I have also provided a glossary of military terms, and a select bibliography; further information, as well as the sources for all quotations (the material quoted in the chapter introductions, unless otherwise indicated, is taken from Butler, A.J., *Memoirs of Baron de Marbot*, London 1900) may be found in the endnotes; a map has also been included for the reader's convenience.

As for Marbot himself, I can do no better than quote from Butler's original preface: 'On the whole the author's fairness is conspicuous. Though attached to Napoleon, he is by no means a blind partisan, and when he thinks the Emperor in the wrong, does not scruple to say so . . . He was not writing history, still less criticism; nor does he, as a rule, lay any claim to special knowledge in regard to matters which did not fall under his personal observation.'[2] Marbot was loyal, dutiful, patriotic; but he also had an eye for the quaint and the absurd: his *Memoirs* tell the story of his own spectacular career, while providing some of the most colourful accounts ever penned of Napoleon, his marshals and his campaigns. In a nod to Sir Arthur Conan Doyle's indefatigable Gerard, I have called this present work *The Exploits of Baron de Marbot*.

I would like to take this opportunity to thank those who have guided, helped and supported me during this project: my parents, John and Sylvia Summerville; my friend, Antonia Evans; and at Constable Publishers, Carol O'Brien and James Wickham.

C.J. *Summerville*
York 1999

NORTH SEA

London

Brussels
Mons • • Waterloo
Paris
R.Loire
R.Seine
R.Rhine
Frankfurt •
Hanover
Leipzig
Auerstädt •
Jena •
Hanau •
Ratisbon •
Ulm •
Zürich •
Münich •

BAY OF BISCAY

La Coruña
R.Douro
Valladolid • Tudela
Almeida •
Agreda •
Ciudad Rodrigo •
Lisbon
R.Tagus
R.Guadiana
Bayonne
Toulouse
Zaragoza
R.Ebro
Madrid •

Lyons •
Marengo •
Savona •
Nice •
Milan •
Venice •
Genoa

Elba

CORSICA

SARDINIA

Rome •

MEDITERRANEAN
SICILY

Algiers

0   100   200   300   400   500
miles

Stockholm

St. Petersburg

BALTIC SEA

R. Volga

R. Dvina

Polotsk

Borodino •Moscow

Tauroggen

Vitebsk

Königsberg Tilsit

Vilna Borisov •Smolensk

Friedland Smorgon •Mogilev

Danzig Eylau Minsk

R. Niemen

R. Beresina

•Berlin

R. Vistula

Warsaw

R. Oder

Kiev

•Dresden

R. Dnieper

Prague Brünn

R. Dniester

Wagram •Austerlitz

R. Bug

Vienna •Pressburg

R. Danube

BLACK SEA

ADRIATIC SEA

•Naples •Constantinople

SEA

Chronology of Major Events

The Napoleonic Wars grew out of the War of the First Coalition; as the sovereigns of the *Ancien Régime* sought to stifle the new French Republic, born of the Revolution of 1789. However, what had started as an attempt to restore the Old Order in France by military intervention, eventually exploded into a general European conflagration. When the First Coalition collapsed in October 1797, and the war had been brought to an end by the Treaty of Campo Formio, not only had the Revolution been saved, but France was left in control of Belgium, northern Italy and the Rhineland. A series of startling victories had brought this about, powered by Revolutionary fervour, mass conscription and the genius of a young Corsican general: Napoleon Bonaparte. Within the space of eighteen months, however, France was beset by social unrest, economic and political turmoil, and a new coalition of foreign armies. Bonaparte, meanwhile, was in Egypt: his dreams of Oriental conquest dashed by Nelson at the Battle of the Nile, and Sydney Smith at the Siege of Acre.

1799

1 March: War of the Second Coalition begins. France's enemies are Austria, Britain, Naples, Russia and Turkey. The main theatres of conflict include Egypt, Holland, Italy, the Rhine and Switzerland.

26 September: Second Battle of Zürich. The French under Masséna defeat a Russian invasion force, causing Tsar Paul to quit the Coalition.

9 October: Having left the Army of the Orient to its fate in Egypt, Bonaparte returns to France.

4 November: Championnet's Army of the Alps is defeated by the Austrians under Von Melas; 18,000 French soldiers seek refuge in the port of Genoa.

9 November: Bonaparte seizes power in the coup of 18 *Brumaire.* Having disposed of the Directory, he establishes the Consulate with himself as First Consul.

1800

20 April: Siege of Genoa begins, ending six weeks later in defeat for the French garrison.

14 June: Battle of Marengo. Having crossed the Alps with his Army of the Reserve, Bonaparte defeats the Austrians in northern Italy.

3 December: Battle of Hohenlinden. General Moreau's Army of the Rhine decisively defeats the Austrians who sue for peace.

1801

9 February: Treaty of Lunéville. Bonaparte brings the War of the Second Coalition to a successful conclusion: securing territorial gains in Belgium, Italy and the Rhineland.

1802

25 March: Peace of Amiens. Hostilities between Britain and France are brought to a temporary close.

2 August: Bonaparte is made Consul for life. He now turns his attention to a projected invasion of Britain.

1804

21 March: Execution of the Duc d'Enghien. Weary of Bourbon threats on his life, Bonaparte orders the kidnapping and execution of the young – and undoubtedly innocent – Bourbon *émigré*. Europe is outraged and a Third Coalition is formed by Austria, Britain, Russia and Sweden.

18 May: Bonaparte becomes Napoleon I, Emperor of the French. His imperial status is confirmed by plebiscite.

2 December: Coronation of Napoleon at Notre Dame.

1805

20 October: Capitulation of Ulm. Having taken the initiative in the War of the Third Coalition, Napoleon encircles an Austrian army at Ulm in Bavaria.

21 October: Battle of Trafalgar. Nelson destroys the combined fleets of France and Spain, at the cost of his own life.

2 December: Battle of Austerlitz. Napoleon crushes the combined Austro-Russian army, thus successfully concluding the War of the Third Coalition.

26 December: Treaty of Pressburg. Napoleon strips Austria of her Venetian, Balkan and German territories; rendering the Holy Roman Empire defunct. Meanwhile his allies, Bavaria and Würtemberg, are recognized as independent kingdoms.

1806

12 July: The pro-French Confederation of the Rhine is formed by Napoleon from the southern states of Germany.

6 August: Emperor Francis II abdicates as Holy Roman Emperor, becoming Francis I of Austria.

9 August: Prussia mobilizes for war against France.

6 October: A Fourth Coalition is formed by Britain, Russia and Prussia.

14 October: Battles of Jena-Auerstädt. Napoleon crushes the Prussian army and occupies Berlin. King Frederick William flees, seeking sanctuary from the Russians.

21 November: Berlin Decrees. Napoleon initiates an economic war with Britain by closing European ports to British goods: it is the start of his ruinous Continental System.

16 December: The French enter Warsaw in an attempt to head off a Russian force marching to the aid of the Prussians.

1807

8 February: Battle of Eylau. A costly and inconclusive clash with the Russian and Prussian armies, claimed as a victory by Napoleon.

14 June: Battle of Friedland. Napoleon defeats the Russian army in detail, causing Tsar Alexander to sue for peace.

7 July: Peace of Tilsit. Napoleon dismantles Prussia, creating new French satellites: the Grand Duchy of Warsaw; and, for his brother Jerôme, the kingdom of Westphalia. Russia joins the Continental System. The Fourth Coalition is dissolved.

27 October: Treaty of Fontainebleau. Napoleon secures the assistance of his Spanish allies in a projected invasion of Portugal. It is, however, merely the first step in a plan to dominate the whole Iberian Peninsula.

1808

16 April: Conference of Bayonne. With Portugal and much of Spain occupied by French troops, the Spanish royal family are obliged to surrender their throne to Napoleon, who gives it to his brother Joseph.

2 May: Dos de Mayo. Public outrage at Napoleon's actions sparks a violent anti-French uprising in Madrid, marking the start of the Peninsular War: Napoleon's 'Spanish Ulcer'.

15 June: First Siege of Zaragoza begins. The French launch several unsuccessful attempts to take the city.

22 July: Battle of Bailén. A French army under Dupont is defeated by the Spanish. An enraged Napoleon marches on Madrid.

21 August: Battle of Vimeiro. The French army in Portugal is defeated by a small British expeditionary force under Sir Arthur Wellesley, later 1st Duke of Wellington.

4 December: Napoleon enters Madrid at the head of a veteran army, determined to crush all Spanish resistance, retrieve Joseph's throne and drive the British into the sea.

20 December: Second Siege of Zaragoza begins.

1809

1 January: The British begin their retreat to La Coruña and a successful evacuation of Spain. A small force remains in Portugal to protect Lisbon.

20 February: Zaragoza falls to the French.

9 April: War of the Fifth Coalition begins. Austria invades Bavaria, Napoleon's ally.

22 April: Battle of Eckmühl. Napoleon defeats the Austrians who retreat across the Danube.

23 April: Storming of Ratisbon. Napoleon takes this Austrian stronghold on the Danube, but the Austrian army makes good its escape.

13 May: Napoleon enters Vienna.

21 May: Battle of Aspern–Essling. Having elected to pursue the Austrian army eastwards, Napoleon receives his first defeat in one of history's bloodiest battles.

6 July: Battle of Wagram. Napoleon inflicts a decisive defeat on the Austrians. An armistice follows.

28 July: Battle of Talavera. A victory over the French in Spain for the recently returned British under Wellesley.

14 October: Treaty of Schönbrunn. An ultimatum from Napoleon forces Austria into making peace: thereby losing territory to France and her allies. The War of the Fifth Coalition is over; but Britain and France remain at war.

1810

2 April: Having divorced the Empress Josephine, Napoleon marries the Archduchess Marie-Louise of Austria for dynastic reasons.

21 August: Bernadotte, Napoleon's disgraced marshal, is elected Crown Prince of Sweden.

27 September: Battle of Busaco. The French under Masséna are checked by Wellington, who, expecting to be outflanked, heads for the safety of Lisbon.

10 October: Masséna's pursuit of Wellington is halted at the Lines of Torres Vedras.

1811

5 March: No longer able to feed his army due to Wellington's 'scorched earth' policy, Masséna begins his retreat from Portugal.

20 March: Napoleon's only legitimate son is born. He is given the title, King of Rome.

5 May: Battle of Fuentes de Oñoro. Masséna is narrowly defeated by Wellington.

1812

24 June: Napoleon invades Russia. A Sixth Coalition is formed by Russia and Britain.

22 July: Battle of Salamanca. Wellington achieves a decisive victory over the French in Spain.

17 August: Battle of Smolensk. The French take the city; but the Russians successfully evacuate, drawing Napoleon's army deeper into Russia.

18 August: Battle of Polotsk. French forces under Saint-Cyr defeat a Russian force under Wittgenstein.

14 September: Napoleon enters Moscow. The city is torched by Russian incendiaries; meanwhile Tsar Alexander refuses to treat with Napoleon.

19 October: With the onset of winter imminent, Napoleon orders the evacuation of Moscow.

24 October: Battle of Maloyaroslavets. A strategic victory for the Russians who block Napoleon's southern line of march; forcing his retreating army through territory devastated by the invasion of the previous summer.

26 October: Napoleon formally orders the Grand Army to retreat via the main Smolensk road.

4 November: Winter begins in earnest with the first snowfall. Harassed by the Russians, the Grand Army begins to disintegrate.

25 November: The remnants of the Grand Army reach the River Beresina, the last major obstacle before quitting Russian territory.

5 December: Napoleon takes his leave of the Grand Army and returns by fast coach to Paris.

9 December: The Russians under Kutusov give up their pursuit of the French at the River Niemen on the Polish border.

30 December: Convention of Tauroggen. The Prussian contingent of the Grand Army defects.

1813

28 February: The Treaty of Kalisch. Prussia joins the Sixth Coalition: Tsar Alexander agrees to help Frederick William recover territory taken from him at Tilsit.

16 March: Prussia declares war on France. The War of German Liberation begins.

2 May: Battle of Lützen. Napoleon seizes the initiative in Germany and defeats the Prussians and their Russian allies. Another victory follows at Bautzen on 20 May.

12 June: The French evacuate Madrid.

21 June: Battle of Vitoria. Wellington routs the French in northern Spain and marches on the French frontier.

12 August: Austria joins the Sixth Coalition.

27 August: Battle of Dresden. Napoleon defeats a combined

force of Austrian, Prussian and Russian troops, forcing them to retire.

7 October: Wellington crosses the River Bidassoa into southern France.

16 October: Battle of Leipzig. Called 'the Battle of the Nations', Napoleon is decisively beaten by a vastly superior Coalition force and forced to quit Germany.

30 October: Battle of Hanau. Napoleon defeats an Austro-Bavarian army attempting to cut his line of retreat.

1814

1 January: The Allies cross the Rhine and the invasion of France begins.

11 January: Murat, Napoleon's brother-in-law, defects to the Allies.

29 January: Battle of Brienne. Napoleon leads an army of raw conscripts to victory against the invading Allies.

10 February: Battle of Champaubert. Napoleon defeats an Allied force advancing on Paris. Within the space of a week, Napoleon reaps further victories at Montmirail, Château-Thierry and Vauchamps.

1 March: Treaty of Chaumont. The Allies of the Sixth Coalition agree not to make separate deals with Napoleon; and declare their joint aim of toppling the Emperor, and breaking French influence in Switzerland, the Netherlands, Spain and Italy.

9 March: Battle of Lâon. Hopelessly outnumbered, Napoleon is defeated by the Allies.

21 March: Battle of Arcis-sur-Aube. Outnumbered by almost three-to-one, Napoleon is defeated and forced to retreat.

25 March: Battle of La Fère-Champenoise. A French force under Marmont is defeated and Napoleon is unable to stop the Allied armies from concentrating and marching on Paris.

30 March: Action of Montmartre. The Allied armies converge on Paris and the fight for the suburbs begins. The following day the victorious Allies enter Paris.

6 April: Napoleon abdicates for the first time at Fontainebleau.

3 May: Louis XVIII enters Paris, escorted by Allied troops.

4 May: Napoleon lands on the island of Elba, his first place of exile.

30 May: First Treaty of Paris. With Napoleon in exile the peace process begins.

1 November: Congress of Vienna. The Allied powers set about reshaping the map of Europe.

1815

26 February: Napoleon escapes from Elba and returns to France.

14 March: The Allies outlaw Napoleon.

20 March: Napoleon enters Paris in triumph, Louis XVIII flees to Ghent.

25 March: A Seventh Coalition is formed. The Allies mobilize.

12 June: Napoleon marches on Belgium in a bid to split the Allied armies there and seize Brussels.

16 June: Battles of Ligny and Quatre Bras. Napoleon defeats the Prussians under Blücher; while Wellington fends off Marshal Ney, and retreats to prepared positions at Waterloo.

18 June: Battle of Waterloo. Napoleon is decisively beaten by the Allied armies under Wellington and Blücher.

22 June: Napoleon abdicates for the second time.

7 July: Allied occupation of Paris begins.

15 July: Napoleon surrenders to the British.

17 October: Napoleon lands on St Helena, his final place of exile.

20 November: Second Treaty of Paris. France is reduced to her boundaries of 1790, forced to pay an indemnity of 700 million francs, and occupied by Allied troops for a period of five years.

1821

5 May: Death of Napoleon on St Helena.

1 Hurrah For Bonaparte!

France, September–October 1799

I had found my vocation; from that moment I
was a soldier, I only dreamt of combats, and I
disdained any other career.

Philippe-Paul de Ségur[1]

*Jean-Baptiste-Antoine-Marcellin de Marbot was born on 18
August 1782 at Larivière in the department of Corrèze, in
central France. He was the second of four sons: Adolphe, the
eldest, joined the army in 1800, surviving the wars to become
a major general; Theodore and Felix, the third and fourth sons
respectively, both died in tragic circumstances before reaching
adulthood. The family background was noble and genteel:
'We lived on our own income, without adding to it by any
profession or trade.' Marbot's mother was the daughter of a
gentleman of 'small means but old family'; and his father, 'a
splendid man – very tall and strongly built', had been an
officer in the bodyguard of Louis XV. When the 'storm of
revolution' broke in 1789, Marbot's father welcomed the
changes, freeing his peasants and becoming a local adminis-
trator. On the outbreak of the Revolutionary Wars, when
almost every nation in Europe sought the destruction of the
new Republic, he returned to the colours, quickly rising to the
rank of general. Marbot, meanwhile, was hidden away from
the worst excesses of the Revolutionary Terror in a girls'*

school at Turenne. His mother, alarmed by the ugly turn of events, left the family home to seek refuge with her uncle at Rennes; and Marbot, too ill to travel, was left in the care of a friend, Mademoiselle Mongalvi, headmistress of the school. Upon his father's return from the front in 1793, the sensitive young boy, spoiled and petted by the young ladies, was put into military college, 'for a more masculine education.'

When Marbot left the college of Sorèze at the age of sixteen and a half, the War of the Second Coalition was in full swing. The First Coalition against France had collapsed in October 1797 with the meteoric rise of the young General Bonaparte, whose ragtag army had kicked the Austrians out of their Italian provinces, and even marched on Vienna itself. The Treaty of Campo Formio had followed; but the desire of the Republic to export the Revolution and create a series of sister republics along France's frontiers – not to mention Bonaparte's invasion of Egypt – had provoked a backlash. By May 1798 a second anti-French Coalition, dominated by Austria, Britain and Russia, was firming up and war was declared on 17 March. Once more, Italy was to be the main theatre of operations. This time, however, with Bonaparte stuck in Egypt (Nelson had sunk his fleet on 1 August at Aboukir Bay), the French suffered one setback after another. To make matters worse, the government of the day, the Directory, was teetering on the brink of ruin: corrupt and ineffective, it was threatened from the outside by financial collapse, civil unrest and a ring of foreign armies; and from the inside by its scheming president, Emmanuel Sieyès and his conspirators. In Italy the French suffered a string of defeats at the hands of the legendary Field Marshal Suvarov, whose Austro-Russian army, impervious to losses, rolled the French back upon the Riviera.

Marbot's father, meanwhile, having been for some time commandant of the Paris garrison, had become weary of the hothouse atmosphere of political intrigue in the capital. A coup d'état was in the offing, and General Jean de Marbot, being an honourable man, and having sworn to defend the constitution, wanted no part in the coming events. He therefore resigned his Paris command and asked for a division on active service. Sieyès, who was secretly plotting the downfall of his own government, needed the co-operation of the army. He particularly needed the help of an ambitious general; and as the upright General de Marbot did not fit the bill, he was only too glad to be rid of him and posted him to the Italian front.

TRIFLING CAUSES often influence human destiny. My father and mother were very intimate with Monsieur Barairon, the Registrar General. One day they were going to breakfast with him and took me with them. The conversation turned on my father's posting to Italy and on the good conduct of my two younger brothers. Finally, Monsieur Barairon enquired, 'And what is Marcellin to be?' 'A sailor,' answered my father, 'Captain Sibille is going to carry him off to Toulon.' Whereupon good Madame Barairon (I have always been most grateful to her for it) remarked to my father that the French navy was utterly disorganised, that the finances were in a deplorable state, and that, moreover, its inferiority to the English fleet would keep it shut up in the ports indefinitely. She wondered that he, a general of division, should put his son in the navy instead of in a regiment where his father's name and services would be sure to make him welcome. She ended by saying, 'It would be better for you to take him to Italy than send him to be bored to death on some boat blockaded in Toulon harbour.' My father then turned to me, saying, 'Well, will you come to Italy with me and serve in the army?' I threw my arms around his neck and accepted with joy. My mother was equally glad, for she had always been opposed to my father's original plan.

In those days the only way to enter the army was in the ranks. My father took me straight to the Place Beauvau and enlisted me in the 1st Regiment of Hussars, which formed part of the division which he was about to command in Italy; the date was 3 September 1799. He next took me to a tailor and ordered for me a complete uniform and equipment: thus I became a hussar. I was beside myself with joy, made all the more complete by the thought that it would increase the vexation of my brother Adolphe, who was two years older than I and was still stuck at college like a child. I decided that I would tell him of my enlistment and at the same moment inform him that I was going to spend in his company the month which would pass before my departure. I therefore begged my father to allow me to settle myself near Adolphe at Sainte-Barbe until the day when we should have to set out for Italy. He understood the motive of my request and the next day he took me himself. You may imagine my entry into the college! It was recreation time, but all games ceased on the spot and pupils young and old crowded round me, contending for the honour of touching my uniform. The hussar was a complete success. When the day of my departure came, I took leave of my mother and my three brothers with grief, tempered though it was by my delight at entering upon a career of arms.

Soon after my father had accepted a command in Italy, a vacancy occurred in that of a division of the Army of the Rhine. He would have preferred to be there, but an inevitable destiny drew him towards the country where he was to find a grave. He had a friend from his own province, Monsieur Lachèze – his evil genius, I might say – who had long been consul at Leghorn and Genoa, and had personal business interests in those parts. This infernal man was always setting before my father the most exaggerated pictures of the beauties of Italy, and pointing out how much was to be gained by restoring victory to an army that had been unfortunate, and how little chance of obtaining glory with the prosperous Army of the Rhine. My poor father let himself be captured by these arguments, thinking that where the danger was greatest, most credit was to be gained, and adhered to his purpose of going to Italy. My mother opposed in vain. She had a secret presentiment that it would be better if my father was on the Rhine: a presentiment that was fulfilled, for she never saw him again.

Besides Captain Gault, my father took another aide-de-camp, Major R—— who had been passed on to him by his friend General Augereau.[2] This officer, who belonged to a Maintenon family, possessed talents and education of which he made little use; for by a whim not uncommon at that time, he thought fit to adopt the style of a swashbuckler. For ever swearing, damning and threatening to split people's heads, this bully had only one good point: he was always most carefully dressed. My father was soon sorry that he had accepted him for his aide without knowing him better, but he could not be dismissed without offending his old friend. As however, he did not care to have the company of Major R—— on a long journey, he had given him the duty of bringing his carriages and horses from Paris to Nice. Our old groom Spire (a faithful servant), accustomed to looking after stablemen, was put under his orders. Major R—— started a month before us, in command of a numerous caravan: fifteen horses belonging to my father, besides those of the staff, the baggage wagons and so on.

In my father's carriage travelled Monsieur Lachèze, Captain Gault and I. Colonel Ménard, the chief-of-staff, with one of his aides, followed in a postchaise. I had at this time a very smart forage cap which I liked to wear. One night, being troubled with my old enemy travel sickness, I was putting my head out of the window when my cap fell off. The carriage was going at the best pace of six stout horses and I did not dare to stop it. My cap was lost. I was much distressed but did not mention it for fear of the banter which would ensue as to the little care which the new recruit took of his uniform!

After staying a day at Mâcon with an old friend of my father's, we pushed on towards Lyons. When we were changing horses at Limonest – very near to that town – we noticed that all the houses were adorned with tricoloured flags. On asking the cause of this display we were told that Bonaparte had just arrived at Lyons.[3] My father, thinking he knew for certain that Bonaparte was at the other end of Egypt, treated this piece of news as a joke. His astonishment then was great when, on questioning the postmaster he was told, 'It is true! Bonaparte is at Lyons, at the Hotel——. His brother Louis,[4] and Generals Berthier,[5] Lannes[6] and Murat[7] are with him; also many other officers – and a Mameluke!' This seemed like positive evidence. Still, the Revolution had given rise to so many impostures and so much ingenuity had been shown in conjuring stories to serve party purposes, that my father was still in doubt as we entered Lyons by the suburb of Vaise.

The houses were all illuminated and beflagged and fireworks were being let off; our carriage could hardly make its way through the crowd. People were dancing in the open spaces and the air rang with cries of, 'Hurrah for Bonaparte! He will save the country!' This evidence was irresistible: my father said, 'Of course I thought they would bring him but I never suspected it would be so soon. They have played their game well and we shall see what great events come to pass.' With that he fell into deep thought as we tried to make our way through the crowds to our hotel.

Arrived there, we found it hung with lanterns and guarded by grenadiers. They had given General Bonaparte the apartments ordered a week ago for my father. Quick-tempered though he was, he said nothing; and when the landlord made somewhat confused apologies to the effect that he had been compelled to obey the orders of the town council, my father made no answer. On hearing that a lodging had been taken for us in a hotel of the second class, he confined himself to bidding Captain Gault order the postillions to drive there. When we arrived, we found our courier had kicked up the devil's own row on learning that the apartments engaged for his master had been given to General Bonaparte. The aides-de-camp, hearing this fearful uproar and learning the cause of it, went to let Bonaparte know that General Marbot had been thrown over for him. At the same moment Bonaparte himself, through his open window, perceived my father's two carriages standing before the door. Up to then he had known nothing of his landlord's shabby behaviour towards my father; and seeing that General Marbot – recently commandant of Paris and at that moment the head of a division in the Army of Italy – was too important a man for any offhand treatment, ordered one of his officers to go down and invite my father to come and share his lodging, soldier-fashion. However the carriages had moved off before the aide could speak, so Bonaparte started at once on foot in order to come and express his regret in person. The cheers of the crowd which followed him as he drew near our hotel might have given us notice, but we had heard so much cheering since we entered the town that it occurred to none of us to look out into the street. We were all in the sitting room and my father was pacing up and down, plunged in meditation, when suddenly a waiter threw open both folding doors and announced General Bonaparte.

On entering, he ran up to my father and embraced him; my father received him courteously but coldly. They were old acquaintances and between persons of their rank a few words were sufficient to explain matters with regard to the lodging. They had much else to talk of, so they went alone into the bedroom where they conferred together for more than an hour. Meanwhile the generals and officers who had come with

Bonaparte from Egypt chatted with us in the sitting room. I could not help studying their martial air, their faces bronzed by the eastern sun, their strange costumes, and their Turkish sabres, slung by cords. I listened attentively to their tales of the campaigns in Egypt and the battles fought there. I enjoyed the repetition of the celebrated names: Pyramids, Nile, Cairo, Alexandria, Acre and so forth. But what delighted me most was the sight of the young Mameluke, Roustam.[8] He had waited in the antechamber and I went there more than once to admire his costume which he was pleased to show me. He could already speak French pretty well and I was never tired of asking him questions. General Lannes remembered how he had let me fire his pistols in 1793 when he was serving under my father at the camp of Le Miral. He was very good-natured to me and neither of us suspected then that I should one day be his aide-de-camp, or that he would die in my arms at Essling. General Murat had been born in our own neighbourhood and, as he had been shopboy to a haberdasher at Saint-Céré in the days when my family used to spend the winter there, he had often come with goods for my mother. My father, too, had done him several kindnesses, for which he was always grateful. He kissed me and reminded me how he had often carried me when I was a baby.

General Bonaparte and my father returned to the sitting room and introduced to each other the members of their respective staffs. Lannes and Murat were old acquaintances of my father's and he received them very cordially. He was somewhat cold towards Berthier, whom he had seen in the old days at Marseilles when he was in the bodyguard and Berthier an engineer. General Bonaparte asked me very courteously for news of my mother, and complimented me in a kind manner on having taken up the military career so young. Then, gently pinching my ear – the flattering caress which he always employed to persons with whom he was pleased – he said, addressing my father, 'Here will be a second General Marbot some day.' His forecast has been verified, though at that time I had little hope of it. All the same, his words made me feel proud all over – it doesn't take much to awaken the pride of a child.

2 A Hussar of the Old School

With the Army of Italy, October–November 1799

There was one named Robin, who had a silver-mounted carbine with a fantastic inscription; declaring that he, single-handed, had rescued 400 prisoners, escorted by 200 Austrians. This Robin was a regular brigand, and looked like one; he had committed pillage, rape, murder, and this to the knowledge of the whole Regiment. The rest of the company was pretty well supplied with men of this stamp, and the stories they told of an evening made one's hair stand on end. But among all these were also admirable instances of their bravery, which they boasted of much less than their misdeeds.

Colonel de Gonneville[1]

By the time Marbot and his father reached Nice, there had been something of a turnaround in French fortunes: Suvarov had been defeated in the mountain passes of Switzerland by General André Masséna (having been diverted – against his better judgement – from an invasion of southern France); a Russo-British expedition to the Netherlands had been repulsed; and Bonaparte was back in Paris. The consequences of these events amounted to the salvation of the Republic: Suvarov was dismissed by a disillusioned Tsar Paul, who promptly quit the Second Coalition; and Bonaparte joined Sieyès' projected coup d'état. Having left his Egyptian army to its fate,[2] *Bonaparte had dodged the British naval blockade and returned to France with a handful of loyal officers – his future acolytes. Sieyès, still looking for a suitable general to be his sword-arm, offered the job to Bonaparte, who seized the opportunity for political power. It was Sieyès' intention that this popular hero should be no more than a figurehead, a rallying-point; but when the coup finally came off on 9 November, it was Sieyès and his co-conspirators who were marginalized, while Bonaparte became First Consul and de facto dictator of France. The little General had succeeded in outmanoeuvring or simply shunting aside at bayonet-point all opposition.*

Marbot, meanwhile, had joined his new regiment as a trooper. In most armies of the period the son of a general would simply have purchased an officer's commission; but in France the Revolution had swept away such privileges and Marbot had to start at the bottom. The shy young boy, brought up in a girls' school, had joined the ranks of the hell-raising hussars, epitomized by the swaggering Sergeant Pertelay.

THE TOWN OF NICE was full of troops, among them a squadron of my regiment, the 1st Hussars. In the Colonel's absence the regiment was commanded by Major Müller, a brave officer, father of the poor adjutant of the 7th Hussars who was wounded at my side by a cannon-ball at Waterloo. On learning that the divisional commander had arrived, Major Müller waited on my father and it was settled that after a few days' rest I should begin my service in the 7th Troop. Kind as my father was to me, I held him in such awe that in his presence I was extremely shy: he used to say that I ought to have been a girl, and often called me 'Miss Marcellin'. This vexed me a good deal, especially now that I was a hussar. It was in order to overcome this shyness that my father wished me to serve with my comrades. Although it was impossible to enter the army except through the ranks, my father might have attached me to his personal service; but he wanted me to learn how to saddle and bridle my own horse and to clean my own accoutrements. If he had allowed his son to enjoy any privileges it would have produced a bad effect on the troop. I had already been favoured in getting admitted to the regiment without a long and wearisome apprenticeship at the dépôt.

When the time came for me to join, my father directed Major Müller to send him Sergeant Pertelay. Now you must know that there were in the regiment two brothers of this name, both sergeants, but quite unlike each other both morally and physically. You might have thought that the author of *Les Deux Philibert*[3] had taken his characters from these two men: the elder Pertelay being the wicked Philibert, the younger Pertelay the virtuous Philibert. It was the latter whom the Colonel had intended to recommend as my mentor, but being in a hurry he had omitted to add the word 'junior'. Major Müller, therefore, supposed that it was the elder brother whom the Colonel had named to my father; and that this wild fellow had been selected in order to take the nonsense out of a mild and shy lad like myself: so he sent us Pertelay senior. This typical hussar of the old school was a hard drinker, a brawler, always ready for a quarrel and a fight; but brave to the point of rashness. He was absolutely ignorant of everything that did not concern his horse, his equipment, or his service in the field. Pertelay junior, on the other hand, was gentle, well-mannered, and highly educated; and being also a very handsome man and every whit as brave as his brother, he would certainly have got on fast had he not been killed, while still young, on the field of battle.

However, to return to the elder. He came to my father's house and what did we behold? A jolly ruffian – very well set

13

up, I must admit – with his shako over his ear, his sabre trailing, his florid countenance divided by an enormous scar and moustaches half a foot long, waxed and turned up to his ears. On his temples were two long locks of hair, plaited, which came from under his shako and fell on his breast.[4] What an air the fellow had! A regular rowdy air, heightened still further by his words, jerked out in the most barbarous French-Alsatian gibberish. This last peculiarity was no surprise to my father, for he knew the 1st Hussars were the old Bercheny Regiment[5] consisting formerly of border dwellers from Alsace-Lorraine. Indeed, down to 1793 the word of command used to be given in German, which was the language of most of the officers and the troopers, who were nearly all born in the provinces on the banks of the Rhine. What was a surprise however, was the demeanour, the answers and the swaggering manner of my mentor. Later on I learned that my father had hesitated in entrusting me to the hands of this fellow; but as Captain Gault pointed out, Colonel Picart had specified him as the best non-commissioned officer in the squadron: so he resolved to give him a trial.

Accordingly I followed Pertelay, who took my arm in an offhand way, came to my room, showed me how to pack up my things, and brought me to a poky barrack establishment in an old convent occupied by a squadron of the 1st Hussars. He made me saddle and unsaddle a handsome little horse which my father had bought for me. Then he showed me how to dispose of my cloak and accoutrements. He showed, in short, all that was to be shown. When he had explained everything, he bethought him that it was time to go to dinner; for my father, wishing me to take my meals with my mentor, had allowed us extra pay for this item. Pertelay brought me to a little inn, where the dining room was full of hussars, grenadiers and soldiers of all arms. Our dinner was served and on the table was placed an enormous bottle of the strongest and roughest red wine, of which Pertelay poured me out a bumper.

We clinked our glasses and my friend emptied his. I set mine down without putting it to my lips, for I had never drunk unmixed wine and I did not like the smell of this. I confessed as much to my mentor, who straightaway shouted in a thunderous voice, 'Waiter! Lemonade for this lad, he never drinks wine.' Shouts of laughter rang through the whole room. I was much abashed, but I could not bring myself to taste the wine, nor did I dare to ask for water: so I dined without drinking.

The apprenticeship of a soldier's life is at all times pretty rough; it was especially so at the time of which I am writing and I had some disagreeable moments to pass. But what seemed to me intolerable, was to be obliged to share a bed with another man, for the regulations at that time only allowed one between every two: non-commissioned officers alone had a bed to themselves. The first night which I passed in barracks I had just got into bed, when a strapping great soldier (who had come in an hour after the others) came up to the bed and, seeing someone there already, unhooked the lamp and shoved it under my nose to obtain a better look. As I watched him undressing I had no idea that he proposed to take his place beside me; but I was soon undeceived when he said roughly, 'Make room, recruit!' Therewith he got into the bed, lay down so as to take up three-quarters of it, and set to work snoring in a high key. I found it impossible to sleep, chiefly by reason of the horrible smell which emanated from a great bundle placed by my comrade under the bolster to raise his head. I couldn't imagine what it could be. In order to find out, I slipped my hand gently towards the object and discovered a leathern apron well impregnated with cobbler's wax: my amiable bedfellow was one of the regimental shoemaker's assistants. I was so disgusted that I got up, dressed, and went to the stable to sleep on a truss of straw. Next day I imparted my misfortune to Pertelay who reported it to our sub-lieutenant – a man of good breeding – and understanding how disagreeable it must be to me to sleep with a shoemaker, ordered me a bed (to my everlasting gratitude) in the non-commissioned officers' room.

Although with the Revolution military costume had become slovenly, the 1st Hussars had always preserved theirs as correct as in the days when they were the Bercheny. Save, therefore, for the physical dissimilarities imposed by nature, all the troopers were bound to get themselves up alike. Hussar regiments at that time wore not only a pigtail but also long 'lovelocks' on the temples and had their moustaches waxed and turned up. And so it was that everyone belonging to the corps was expected to follow this fashion; but as I possessed none of these items, my mentor took me to the regimental barber, where I purchased a sham pigtail and locks and these were attached to my hair. I was embarrassed at first by this make-up, but in a few days I got used to it: now I had the air of an old hussar! With regard to moustaches the case was different: of them I had no more than a girl; and as a beardless face would have spoilt the uniformity of the squadron, Perte-lay, in conformity with the practice of the regiment, took a pot of blacking and with his thumb made two enormous hooks covering my upper lip and reaching almost to my eyes. At that time the shakos had no peak, so it happened that during reviews (or when I was doing *vedette* duty and was bound to remain perfectly motionless) the scorching rays of the Italian sun pouring down on to my face would suck up the liquid in the blacking, drawing my skin in a most unpleasant way. Still, I did not so much as wink: I was a hussar. The very word had a magical effect on me and, besides, when I entered on a military career I thoroughly understood that my first duty was to conform to the regulations!

Before my father left Nice, news arrived of the overthrow of the Directory on the 18 *Brumaire*[6] and the establishment of the Consulate. My father's opinion of the Directory had not been such as to make him regret its fall, but he feared that in the intoxication of power, Bonaparte, when he had restored order to France, would not content himself with the modest title of consul and predicted that before long he would want to make himself king. He was only wrong as to the title: in four years' time Napoleon made himself Emperor. Whatever his presentiments may have been, my father rejoiced at being absent from Paris on the 18 *Brumaire*; if he had been there I think he would have vigorously opposed Bonaparte's enterprise. But being on service, at the head of a division in face of the enemy, he felt able to take refuge in the passive obedience of a soldier. He rejected the proposals which several generals and colonels made to him to march on Paris at the head of their troops. 'Who,' he asked, 'will defend the frontier if we desert it? And what will become of France if the miseries of a civil war are added to our war against the foreigner?' By this caution he kept the excitement in check, but at the same time, he nonetheless felt very strongly on the subject of the recent *coup d'état*. He adored his country and would have wished to see her saved without being brought under the yoke of a tyrant.

My father's chief motive, as I have said, in making me go through my service in the ranks, was to get rid of my rather foolish schoolboy air, which my short stay in Paris had not removed. He succeeded beyond his hopes; for living in the middle of the boisterous hussars and having for my tutor a kind of Pandour who laughed at all my follies, I learned to suit my conduct to my company and became a perfect daredevil. I was not, however, as yet qualified to be admitted into a sort of brotherhood, which, under the name of 'the Gang', drew its initiated from all the squadrons of the 1st Hussars. The Gang was composed of the most reckless soldiers of the regiment; its members supported each other against all comers, especially in the presence of the enemy and were to be known by means of a notch made in the first button of the row on the right side of the *pelisse* and jacket. The officers knew of the existence of the Gang, but as its greatest crimes were limited to the occasional

17

looting of sheep and fowls, the chiefs winked at it. Feather-brain that I was, I was eager to be admitted into this society of roysterers, for it seemed to me that it would give me a respectable position among my peers. It was, however, all very well to frequent the fencing school, to learn foil and broadsword, pistol and carbine, to elbow out of the way everyone I met, to let my sabre trail and wear my shako over one ear: the members of the Gang looked upon me as a child and refused to admit me. That is until an unforeseen adventure brought about my unanimous election in the following way.

At that time the Army of Italy was occupying Liguria,[7] extended on a front more than sixty leagues[8] in length – its right on the Gulf of Spezia beyond Genoa, the centre at Finale and the left on the River Var – that is, the French frontier. We had, therefore, the sea in our rear and were fronting towards Piedmont,[9] which was occupied by the Austrian army. It was a false position, for the French army was exposed to be cut in two – which actually happened some months later – but I will not anticipate. My father had been ordered to concentrate at Savona and established his headquarters in the Bishop's palace. The 1st Hussars had come from Nice and were bivouacking in a plain called La Madona. The enemy's outposts were at Dego, four or five leagues from us, on the reverse slope of the Apennines. Our bivouac would have been delightful if provisions had been more plentiful but there was no high road from Nice to Genoa: the English cruisers held the sea and the army had to live on supplies brought by mules along the *corniche* or landed from such small coasters as could slip along unperceived. These precarious methods barely sufficed to provide the grain necessary for the daily bread of the troops. Happily, the country produces plenty of wine, which served to keep up the soldiers' spirits and made them bear their hardships more cheerfully. One lovely day, as I was walking along the shore with friend Pertelay, he spied a tavern in a garden full of orange trees and olives. Under these were tables at which soldiers of all arms were sitting, and he proposed that we should go in. I had not been able to get over my dislike of wine but out of friendship I followed him.

I may mention that at this time a cavalry soldier's belt had no hook, so that when he went on foot he had to hold the scabbard of his sword in the left hand, letting the point trail on the ground. This made a clatter and gave a roystering air which was quite enough to make me adopt the fashion. But behold, as I entered the garden, the end of my scabbard touched the foot of a gigantic horse-artilleryman who was taking his ease stretched out on a chair, his legs in front of him. The Horse-Artillery had been formed at the beginning of the Revolutionary Wars of volunteers from the grenadier companies, and the opportunity had been taken to get rid of some of the more disorderly soldiers from the regiments. 'The Gallopers' were therefore renowned for their courage and for their love of a quarrel no less.

The man whom my sabre had touched said to me in a loud and majestic tone: 'You hussar, your sword trails far too much.' I was going on without taking any notice when friend Pertelay, touching my elbow, whispered in a low tone: 'Answer him, "Come and pick it up."' I, to the gunner: 'Come and pick it up.' 'That is easily done,' replied he. Pertelay, prompting me again: 'We have got to see that.' Thereupon the gunner – the Goliath I might say, for he was all six feet high – sat upright with a threatening air. My mentor dashed between him and me. All the artillerymen in the garden at once took their comrade's part but a crowd of hussars ranged up alongside of Pertelay and myself. Tempers grew hot. Everyone shouted and spoke at once. The whole place was in such a terrible uproar I thought there would be a riot. The hussars, being two to one, were the calmer and the artillerymen perceived that if swords were drawn they would get the worst of it. So at length, the giant was brought to see that in touching his foot with the point of my sword I had in no way insulted him: between us two, things need go no further.

But in the tumult an artillery bugler some twenty years old had been saying rude things to me; and in my anger I had pushed him so roughly that he had fallen head foremost into a muddy ditch. It was agreed by all that for the sake of honour, this lad and I should fight with sabres; and we left the garden, followed by all present. Behold us then, close to the water's edge, ready for a bout with the steel. Pertelay knew that I was fairly good with the sabre but still gave me advice as to the best method of attack, and fastened my sword-hilt to my hand with a large handkerchief, which he wrapped around my arm.

Here I may mention that my father had a horror of duelling, based not only on his views as to the barbarism of the practice, but also on a recollection of his youthful days in the body-guard, when he acted as second to a much-loved comrade who had been killed in single combat in a most futile cause. For whatever reason, his first step on assuming command was to order the *gendarmes* to arrest and bring before him any soldiers whom they might catch crossing swords. The artillery bugler and I were well aware of this order; nonetheless we had thrown off our jackets and stood sabre in hand. I had my back to the town of Savona; my adversary faced it. Just as we were about to begin our fence, I saw the bugler leap to one side, catch up his jacket and bolt: 'Running away, coward?' I shouted, and was about to pursue him when a grip of iron seized my collar from behind. I turned and found myself in the hands of eight or ten *gendarmes*. I knew then why my antagonist had fled. The spectators had done the same and were making off as fast as their legs could carry them, Master Pertelay among the number, in dire fear of being arrested and brought before the General.

There I was, disarmed and a prisoner! I slipped on my jacket and followed the *gendarmes* with a hangdog expression. I did not give my name and they brought me to the Bishop's palace where my father lodged. He was at that moment with General (afterwards Marshal) Suchet, walking in a gallery open to the court. The *gendarmes* brought me up without a notion that I was the General's son and the corporal explained the reason for my arrest. My father, in his most severe manner, gave me a sharp reprimand at the end of which he said to the corporal, 'Take this hussar to the citadel.' I retired without a word and without a suspicion on the part of General Suchet, who did not know me, that the scene to which he had been a witness had passed between father and son. On reaching the citadel, an old relic of the Genoese standing near the harbour, I was shut up in a vast room lighted by a dormer looking towards the sea.

Gradually I got over my excitement and felt that I had deserved my reprimand but at the same time I thought more of having given pain to my father than of having disobeyed my commanding officer. I spent the rest of the day gloomily enough; and in the evening an old pensioner of the Genoese army brought me a jug of water, a piece of bread and a truss of straw. I flung myself on it, unable to eat. Nor could I sleep: first, because I was too much upset and further, by reason of the evolutions of some big rats who soon took possession of my bread. I was in the dark, brooding over my sorrows, when towards ten o'clock I heard the bolts of my prison drawn and behold, my father's faithful old servant, Spire. From him I learned that after I had been sent to the citadel Colonel Ménard, Captain Gault and all my father's officers had interceded on my behalf and secured a pardon for me. Spire had been sent to fetch me and to bear the order for my liberation to the governor of the fort. I was taken before this governor, General Buget, an excellent man who had lost an arm in battle and who had a great regard for my father. He returned me my sword and thought it his duty to give me a long lecture. I listened patiently enough but with the thought that I was sure to have another, much more severe, from my father. This I did not feel I had the courage to endure and resolved to escape it if I could.

Well, we were escorted past the gates of the citadel, and as the night was dark, Spire walked in front with a lantern. As we made our way through the narrow streets, the good man, in his delight at bringing me back, enlarged upon all the comforts that awaited me at headquarters: 'But you know,' he added, 'you may expect a fine scolding from your father!' This last remark fixed my resolution and in order to leave time for my father's wrath to cool, I decided to return to the bivouac at La Madona and to keep out of his presence for several days. I could, no doubt, have got away without playing any trick on poor Spire but I was afraid that he might pursue me by the light of his lantern, so with a kick I sent it flying and ran for my life. As the good man groped about I could hear him exclaim, 'You little scamp, I'll tell your father! I'm blessed if he was not quite right to put you with those Bercheny rascals. A fine school for a scapegrace!'

I wandered for a while through the deserted streets and at length found the road to La Madona. My comrades thought I was still in prison; but as soon as I was recognised by the firelight they came round me, asking questions and shouting with laughter when I related how I got away from the trusty servant charged to bring me to the General. The members of the Gang were especially delighted with this sign of resolute character and unanimously agreed to admit me into their society. They were just planning an expedition for that very night: to go to the gates of Dego and carry off a herd of cattle belonging to the Austrian army. The French generals were obliged to feign ignorance of the excursions which the soldiers made beyond the outposts, since there was no other way of procuring a regular supply of victuals. Thus in every regiment the bravest men had formed marauding bands, who had a wonderful knack of discovering the places where the enemy's victualling went forward and of getting hold, by cunning or boldness, of his stores.

A scoundrelly horse-dealer had given information to the

Gang that a herd of cattle which he had sold to the Austrians was parked in a meadow a quarter of a league from Dego. Accordingly, sixty hussars, armed only with their carbines, started to lift them. We went for several leagues through the mountains by side roads of the most fearful kind, so as to avoid the highway, and surprised five Croats, who were on guard over the herd, asleep in a shed. Lest they should give the alarm to the garrison, we tied them up and left them there, carrying off the cattle without having to strike a blow. By the time we got back to our bivouac we were tired but highly pleased at the smart trick we had played the enemy; to say nothing of having got food for our starving stomachs. I have told this story to show the state of destitution into which the Army of Italy had fallen, and how desperate troops may become when left to themselves by officers who not only tolerate expeditions of this kind, but who also profit by the plunder so obtained; affecting all the while to be ignorant whence it has come.

3 The Parfait Partisan

North-West Italy, December 1799

What is war? It is the trade of barbarians.

Napoleon[1]

Italy at this point in time did not exist as a nation; rather, it consisted of a hotchpotch of states, kingdoms and republics. Before the French Revolution of 1789 the country was largely divided up into the Kingdom of Naples and Sicily in the south, the Papal States (ruled by the Vatican) in the centre, and a patchwork of small territories in the north: hereditary possessions of the Habsburgs, rulers of the Austrian Empire. After Bonaparte's successful Italian campaign of 1796, Austrian influence was greatly reduced as the French founded a series of satellite republics: the Roman Republic in the south; the Cisalpine Republic in the centre; and the Ligurian Republic in the north-west, with its capital at Genoa. By November 1799 most of these fledgling republics had been reconquered by the Allies, led – after Suvarov's fall from grace – by the Austrian general, Michael von Melas. The French army in Italy, commanded by General Etienne Championnet, after six months of defeat, found itself cooped up in a pocket around the Gulf of Genoa. Starved of food, forage, supplies – and back pay – morale was low and desertion rife. The seventeen-year-old Marcellin de Marbot, however, still attached to romantic notions of the excitement and chivalry of war, was only seeking a chance to prove himself.

WITH THE GOOD FORTUNE which attended my military career, I avoided altogether the rank of corporal, passing from trooper to sergeant in a leap. It happened like this. To the left of my father's division was stationed that of General Séras, with its headquarters at Finale. This division occupied that part of Liguria where the mountains are steepest and consequently consisted of infantry only, there being no room for cavalry to move, save in small detachments. General Séras, having received orders from the commander-in-chief, General Championnet, to push a reconnaissance into the valleys beyond Monte San Giacomo, wrote to my father begging the loan of fifty hussars. My father naturally agreed and appointed Lieutenant Lesteinschneider to command the detachment, of which my section formed a part. The Lieutenant, however, happened to dislocate his foot in consequence of a fall from his horse; and the next in rank to him was Sergeant Canon, a fine man, apparently possessing plenty of ability and still more assurance. On the following day General Séras led his force over Monte San Giacomo where we bivouacked in the snow. We were certain the next day, if we advanced, to come in contact with the enemy: but in what strength should we find him? The General had no notion. His orders were to reconnoitre the position of the Austrians but on no account to engage if he found them in force. It had struck him that in advancing his infantry through the mountains, where a column cannot be perceived until one comes face to face with it at the turn of a gorge, that he might be drawn into a serious action against superior forces and obliged to execute a perilous retreat. He resolved, therefore, to march cautiously, sending forward his fifty hussars to explore the country. As the ground was very much broken, he handed a map to our sergeant and gave him full instructions in the presence of the detachment. Two hours before daylight he sent us off, repeating that we must march without fail until we touched the enemy's outposts, from which he was exceedingly anxious that we might bring away some prisoners.

Sergeant Canon's dispositions were perfect. He sent out a small advance guard, covered his flanks with scouts, and took, in short, all the precautions customary in guerrilla warfare. Two leagues from camp we came to a large inn; our sergeant questioned the innkeeper and was informed that a good hour further on we should find an Austrian corps, the strength of which he could not state. He knew, however, that the leading regiment was one of very ill-conditioned hussars who had maltreated sundry of the inhabitants. With this information we continued our march; but we had hardly gone a few hundred paces when Sergeant Canon began to writhe on his horse, saying that he was in horrible pain and that he could go no farther but must hand over command to Sergeant Pertelay, the next in seniority to himself. Pertelay promptly remarked that being an Alsatian, he could not read French and would be unable, therefore, to make any sense of the map or the General's written instructions and he flatly refused to take command. The other sergeants – all old Bercheny men – also refused on the same grounds.

In vain did I offer to read aloud the General's instructions and point out the route on the map to any sergeant who would take command; but instead, to my great surprise, these veterans answered: 'Take command yourself!' And as the whole detachment were in agreement, it became clear to me that if I declined we should get no farther and that the honour of the regiment should suffer – for in some way or other the order of General Séras would have to be executed or his division might be in serious trouble – so I accepted the command, after having first asked Sergeant Canon whether he felt fit to resume it. On this he renewed his complaints, left us, and returned to the inn. I must admit that I believed him to be really indisposed; but the men, who knew him better, indulged in some very insulting banter.

I may, I think, say without boasting that nature has allotted to me a fair share of courage; I will even add that there was a time when I enjoyed being in danger, as my thirteen wounds and some distinguished services prove, I think, sufficiently. When, therefore, I took command of the fifty men who had come under my orders in such unusual circumstances – a mere trooper as I was and only seventeen years old – I resolved to show my comrades that if I had not yet much military experience, I at least possessed pluck: so I resolutely put myself at their head and marched in what I knew was the direction of the enemy.

We had been some time on the way, when our scouts perceived a peasant trying to hide himself: they quickly captured him and brought him to me for questioning. It appeared that he came from four or five leagues off and swore that he had not met any Austrian troops. I was sure that he was lying – through fear or cunning – for we must be very near the enemy's cantonments. I remembered having read in the *Parfait Partisan*, of which my father had given me a copy, that in order to get information from the inhabitants of a country which one is passing through in time of war, one must sometimes frighten them; so I put on a big voice, and trying to give my youthful countenance a ferocious air, I cried: 'What, you scamp! You have just come through a country occupied by a strong Austrian army corps and you pretend to have seen nothing? You're a spy. Here, shoot him on the spot!' I ordered four hussars to dismount, giving them a sign that they were to do the man no harm. The man, seeing himself in the hands of troopers who had just cocked their carbines, was in such a fright that he swore to tell me all he knew. He was the servant of a convent and was charged with a letter to some relations of the prior. He had been ordered, if he met the French, not to tell them where the Austrians were; but since he was forced to confess, he informed us that at a distance of a league, several of the enemy's regiments were quartered, while there were a hundred Barco Hussars in a hamlet nearby. When questioned as to the kind of guard which the hussars kept, the peasant replied that they had in advance of the houses, a grand guard consisting of a dozen dismounted men posted in a garden surrounded by hedges.

Having got this information, I made my plans at once. I would avoid passing in front of the grand guard, who, being entrenched behind their hedges, were safe from a cavalry attack; while the fire from their carbines might kill some of my men and give warning of our approach. I must therefore turn the hamlet and fall upon the enemy unawares. But how was I to get round unperceived? I ordered the peasant to guide us, promising to let him go as soon as we were at the other side of the hamlet. He was, however, unwilling to march; so I made one hussar take him by the collar while another held the muzzle of a pistol to his ear and he did as he was told. He guided us very well and our movement was masked by the high hedges. We turned the village successfully and perceived at the edge of a little pond, the Austrian squadron quietly watering their horses. All the troopers had their arms with them (as is customary with outposts) but the officers had neglected a very essential precaution: namely, to allow only a certain number of horses to be unbridled and drink at once, sending them into the water in succession, so that half may always be on the bank ready to repulse an enemy. Trusting in the distance of the French and the vigilance of the outpost placed in advance of the village, the enemy's commander had thought it unnecessary to take this precaution. It was fatal to him.

At 500 paces from the little pond I let our guide go and he

made off as fast as his legs could carry him. Meanwhile I, sabre in hand, dashed at full gallop on the enemy's hussars. They did not catch sight of us till just before we reached the edge of the pond. The banks were almost everywhere too steep for their horses to climb, the only practicable approach being at the spot where the villagers drew their water; but here the enemy troopers were massed, bridles over their arms and their carbines in the buckets, so perfectly at ease that some were even singing. Their surprise may be imagined when I first attacked them with a carbine-fire which killed several, wounded many, and knocked over a great number of horses. They were thrown into utter confusion!

The Austrian captain proceeded to rally the men who were near the bank, forcing his way out and opening up on us a fire which wounded two men. Then they charged. But Pertelay slayed the captain with a sabre-cut, while his men were rolled back into the pond. Some, in their efforts to escape our fire, reached the other bank but many lost their footing and were drowned. Those of the Austrians who got across from the other side of the pond, not being able to get their horses up the bank, abandoned them and fled across the fields: but we met them with the sabre. Meanwhile, some thirty of the enemy were still in the water, but fearing to urge their horses forward, they called out their surrender – which I accepted – and as they came ashore I made them lay down their arms. Most of the men and horses were wounded, but wishing to take away a trophy of our victory, I chose seventeen troopers and horses who were not much injured and placed them in the middle of my detachment. Then I left the other Barcos to themselves and made off at a gallop, turning the village again.

It was just as well that I did retreat promptly, for as I had foreseen, the fugitives had given the alarm and half-an-hour later there were more than 1,500 cavalry on the banks of the little pond, with infantry close behind: but we were far away.

We halted a moment on the top of a hill to dress wounds and we laughed a good deal to see in the distance several columns starting on our tracks. We knew quite well that they would not catch us because, fearing a possible ambush, they were feeling their way forward very slowly. I told Pertelay to take our two best mounted hussars and gallop forward to tell General Séras the result of our mission; then I dressed my detachment carefully and with the prisoners well guarded, I trotted easily along the road to the inn. It is impossible to describe the joy of my comrades; and the congratulations which they addressed to me can be summed up in the words which to their minds expressed the height of eulogy: 'You deserve to belong to the Bercheny Hussars, the first regiment in the world!'

What, meanwhile, had been passing at San Giacomo? After waiting for some hours General Séras, impatient for news, perceived from the heights some smoke on the horizon. His aide-de-camp, laying his ear on a drum placed upon the ground, was able to hear the sound of distant musketry. The General became uneasy and, feeling sure that his cavalry must be engaged with the enemy, took a regiment of infantry and went forward as far as the inn. There he saw a hussar's horse in the shed, hitched up to the rack: Sergeant Canon's in fact. The innkeeper appeared and from him the General learned that the sergeant in command of the hussars had got no farther than the dining room. The General entered and found Sergeant Canon asleep by the fire with a huge ham, two empty bottles, and a cup of coffee in front of him. The poor sergeant was roused from his slumbers and tried once more to plead the excuse of a sudden indisposition; but the accusing remains of the mighty meal he had just eaten destroyed all belief in his malady. General Séras was pretty rough with Sergeant Canon and his wrath was increased by the thought that a detachment of fifty cavalry, entrusted to a common trooper, had probably been destroyed by the enemy.

At precisely that moment Pertelay appeared, galloping up and announcing our triumph and immediate return with seventeen prisoners. In spite of this happy result, the General continued to heap reproaches on Sergeant Canon, putting him under arrest and degrading him on the spot, having his stripes torn off in presence of the regiment; then, turning to me he said: 'You have performed admirably a duty which is usually entrusted only to officers. I am sorry that as a general of division, I have not the power to appoint you sub-lieutenant.[2] I will, however, ask for your promotion to that rank of the commander-in-chief. Meanwhile, I make you a sergeant.'

He ordered his aide-de-camp to announce my promotion to the detachment. In order to do this, the aide had to ask my name and then General Séras learned for the first time that I was the son of his colleague General Marbot. I was very glad of this adventure because it would prove to my father that favour had nothing to do with my promotion.

The information which the General got from the prisoners having determined him to advance the next day, he sent orders to his division to descend from the heights of San Giacomo and bivouac that same night near the inn. The prisoners were forwarded to Finale, while their horses, by right, were now the property of the Bercheny Hussars. These horses were all excellent beasts, but according to a custom established to benefit ill-mounted officers, a prize horse was never sold for more than five *louis*. It was an established price and always paid in cash. The sale began as soon as the tents were pitched and General Séras, his staff officers, and the colonels and majors of the regiments, soon carried off our seventeen horses; which brought the sum of eighty-five *louis*. This was handed over to my comrades, who had received no pay for six months and were delighted with this windfall. I had some pieces of gold on me, so in order to pay my footing as a sergeant, I not only refused to take my share of the prize-money, but also bought from the inn-keeper three sheep, a gigantic cheese and a cask of wine. This was one of the happiest days of my life: it was the 10 *Frimaire*, year 8.

4 A Quarter of a Pound of Horseflesh

The Siege of Genoa, April–June 1800

Everyone was repeating the answer made to Berthier by the quartermaster-general of the Austrian army: 'The battle of Marengo was not lost here, but before Genoa;' and this famous answer, which passed from mouth to mouth, confirmed the opinion already current that the defenders of Genoa were the saviours of the country.

Baron Thiébault[1]

Marbot's days as a sergeant were to be shortlived: within a month he had been promoted to sub-lieutenant, having captured – with the aid of his fellow hussars, including the brothers Pertelay – a battery of Austrian guns before the very eyes of General Championnet. Despite the successes of Marbot's private war, the fortunes of the Army of Italy continued to decline: a sortie into Piedmont failed and the French were pushed back into Liguria; Championnet died, broken by the cares of command within weeks of handing Marbot his commission; and the cavalry had to be sent home for want of forage. Marbot's father, being the senior divisional general, became temporary commander-in-chief; and taking Marbot for his aide-de-camp, returned to his headquarters at Nice. Arrived there, General de Marbot was relieved to learn that he was to be transferred, after all, to the Army of the Rhine. Despite the enthusiastic arguments of his friend, Lachèze, he had found little honour and no glory in Italy. Accordingly, he ordered his staff – Colonel Ménard, the boorish Major R——, Captain Gault and Marbot – to prepare for Germany. Meanwhile he awaited the arrival of his successor, General Masséna, Bonaparte's 'Spoilt Child of Victory'.[2]

MASSÉNA ARRIVED to find the shadow of an army. The troops, unpaid, almost unclad and unshod, were receiving only quarter rations and dying of starvation or sickness: the result of privations. The hospitals were full and medicine was lacking. Bands of soldiers, even whole regiments, were every day quitting their posts and making for the bridge over the Var. They forced their way into France and scattered about Provence, declaring themselves ready to return to duty if they were fed. The generals had no power against such a mass of misery; every day their discouragement grew, and they were all asking for leave or resigning on the ground of illness. Masséna had, indeed, hoped to be joined in Italy by several of the generals who had been taking part in the defeat of the Russians in Switzerland: among them Soult,[3] Oudinot[4] and Gazan. But none of these had as yet come, and the pressing need must be met.

Masséna, who was born at Turbia, a township in the little principality of Monaco, was the wiliest of Italians. He was not acquainted with my father but at first sight judged him to be a man of magnanimous nature, above all things patriotic. In order to get him to stay, therefore, he approached him on his most sensitive side, appealing to his generosity and love of his country, and pointing out how much more to his honour it would be to stay with the Army of Italy in its misfortunes than to go to the Rhine, where things were prosperous. He offered, moreover, if my father would stay, to take upon himself all responsibility for his neglect of orders. My father was persuaded and, not liking to leave the new commander-in-chief while things were in confusion, agreed to stay. He made no doubt that Colonel Ménard, his friend and chief-of-staff, would follow his example and decline to serve on the Rhine; but here he was mistaken. Colonel Ménard, although assured that there would be no difficulty in getting the order revoked, held himself bound to obey it, and lost no time in reaching Paris, where he obtained the post of chief-of-staff to General Lefebvre. My father felt this defection keenly. The post he had held was filled by Colonel Sacleux, an excellent man and good soldier, of a kindly but grave disposition. His secretary was a young man named Colindo, son of one Trepano, a banker at Parma, who became an excellent friend of mine. Spire was left at Nice with the bulk of the baggage and my father repaired to Genoa, to take up the command of the three divisions composing the left wing. He lodged in the Centurione Palace until the end of the winter 1799–1800.

At the beginning of the following spring, my father learned that Masséna had given the command of the right wing to Soult, who had just arrived. At the same time he received orders to return to Savona and resume the command of his old division, the third. Although sorely hurt at this supersession by an officer much his junior, he complied with the new arrangements. Meanwhile great events were preparing in Italy. Masséna had received reinforcements, and re-established some measure of order in the army. The famous campaign of 1800, which led to the Siege of Genoa and the Battle of Marengo, was about to open.

As soon as the snow had melted on the mountains which lay between the two armies, the Austrians attacked. At the commencement of hostilities my father and Colonel Sacleux sent all non-combatants to the city of Genoa for safety. For my part, I was both excited and happy. The animating sight of troops on the march and the clatter of the artillery roused the desire which is always in the heart of a young soldier: to take part in the adventure of war. I was far from suspecting just how terrible a war this would be, and how costly to myself.

My father's division, briskly attacked by a superior force, held for two days the famous position of Cadibona[5] and Montenotte; but finally, being in danger of having its flank turned, it was forced to retreat on Voltri, and then on Genoa, where, with the other two divisions of the right wing, it was shut up. I could hear the generals (who knew the state of the case) deploring the necessity of separating ourselves from the centre and the left wing; but at that time I knew so little of the principles of war that it in no way affected me. I understood well enough that we had been beaten, but as I had with my own hands captured an officer of the Barco Hussars and fastened his plume to the headstall of my horse, I felt as if this trophy gave me some resemblance to a knight of the Middle Ages, coming home laden with the spoils of the infidels.

My boyish vanity was soon brought down by a terrible catastrophe. During the retreat, just as my father was giving me an order to carry, he was hit by a ball in the left leg. The shock was so great that he would have fallen from his horse had he not leaned upon me. I got him away from the field of battle and watched his wound being dressed. When I saw his blood I began to cry. He tried to soothe me, and said that a soldier ought to have stronger nerves. We carried him to Genoa and placed him in the Centurione Palace, which he had occupied the previous winter. Our three divisions entered the city while the Austrians blockaded the place by land, and the English by sea.

The courage fails me to describe what the garrison and population of Genoa had to suffer during the two months which this memorable siege lasted. The ravages of famine, war, and typhus were enormous. Out of 16,000 men, the garrison was to lose 10,000 and every day 700–800 corpses – of every age, sex and class – were picked up in the streets and buried in an immense trench, filled with quicklime, behind the church of Carignan. The total number of victims reached 30,000, most of which starved to death. Neither rich nor poor had the means of obtaining bread; the small quantity of dried vegetables and rice which was in the hands of the dealers had been bought up at enormous prices at the very beginning of the siege. The troops alone received a miserable ration of a quarter of a pound of horseflesh and a quarter of a pound of something which was called bread – a horrible compound of bad flour, sawdust, starch, hair powder, oatmeal, linseed, rancid nuts, and other nasty substances, to which a modicum of solidity was given by a little cocoa. Each loaf, moreover, was held together by shavings of wood, without which it would have simply disintegrated. General Thiébault, in his journal of the siege,[6] compares this bread to peat mingled with oil.

For five-and-forty days neither bread nor meat was publicly sold; the richest inhabitants were able – but only during the first part of the siege – to obtain a little codfish, figs and other dried provisions, as well as some sugar. Oil, wine and salt never failed; but of what use are these without solid food? All the dogs and cats in the town were eaten. Rats fetched a high price. At length the misery grew so terrible that whenever the French troops made a sortie, crowds followed them outside the gates, and there rich and poor, women, children and old men, set to work to cut grass, nettles and leaves, which they then boiled with salt. The Genoese government had the grass which grew on the ramparts mown, and afterwards cooked in the public squares and distributed to the sick, who were not strong enough to get this coarse food and cook it themselves. Our troops used to boil nettles and all kinds of plants with their horseflesh; the richest and most eminent envied them their meat, disgusting as it was, for nearly all the horses were ill for want of forage, and the flesh of even those which had died of consumption was distributed.

During the latter part of the siege, the exasperation of the populace became a serious danger. They were heard to exclaim that in 1746 their fathers had massacred an Austrian army,[7] and that they ought to get rid of the French in the same way. Decidedly it was better, they said, to die fighting than to see their wives and children succumb and then starve themselves. These symptoms of revolt were the more terrible in that, if they had come to anything, the English and Austrians would undoubtedly have hastened to join the insurgents in the effort to overwhelm us. In the middle of dangers so imminent and calamities so various, Masséna remained calm. To prevent any attempt at a rising, he proclaimed that the French troops had orders to fire on any groups of four men or larger. Our regiments continually bivouacked in the squares and in the principal streets, the approaches to which were defended by guns loaded with cannister; and the Genoese, being unable to assemble, found it impossible to rise.

It may seem surprising that Masséna should have clung so obstinately to the defence of Genoa but the place weighed heavily just then in the balance of the fate of France. Our army was cut in two: the left and centre had retired behind the River Var; while Masséna, shut up in Genoa, detained a portion of the Austrian army before that place and thus prevented it from invading Provence in full force. Masséna knew that at Dijon, Lyons, and at Geneva, Bonaparte was collecting a reserve army with which he proposed to cross the Alps by the Great St Bernard Pass and to surprise the Austrians by falling on their rear while they were preoccupied with the siege. It was, therefore, of immense importance to hold out for as long as possible. The First Consul had given orders to that effect, and his foresight was justified by events. But let me return to what befell me in the siege.

On learning that my father had been brought wounded into Genoa, Colindo Trepano hastened to his bedside, and we met again there. He helped me in the most affectionate way to tend the sick man; and I was the more grateful to him since in the midst of our troubles my father had no one with him. All staff officers had received orders to place themselves at the service of the commander-in-chief. Very soon provisions were no longer allowed to our servants; and they were compelled to take a musket and enrol themselves among the combatants in order to claim the wretched ration which was given to the soldiers. The only exemptions were made in favour of a young valet named Oudin and a young groom who looked after our horses; but Oudin left us on learning that my father had been seized with typhus.

This terrible disorder, like the plague (with which it has much affinity), always attacks the wounded and those who are already ill. My father took it; and just when he needed most care, he had no one with him but myself, Colindo and the groom, Bastide. We carried out the doctor's prescriptions to the best of our power, and got no sleep day or night, being incessantly occupied in rubbing my father with camphorated oil, and in changing his bedclothes and bandages. He could eat nothing but broth, and to make this we had only horseflesh. My heart sank within me. Providence, however, sent us some aid. The great buildings of the public bakeries were close to the walls of the palace in which we lived; their terraces were almost in contact. That of the bakeries was very spacious; the crushing and mixing of the various grains which were added to the damaged flour to make bread for the garrison was carried on there. Bastide, the groom, had observed that when the workmen of the bakery had left the terrace, it was invaded by swarms of pigeons, which had their nests in the towers of the city, and came thither to pick up what few grains might have been let fall after sifting. Being a man of intelligence, he contrived to cross the short space which separated this from

41

our terrace, and on it set traps of various kinds wherewith he took the pigeons. Of these we made my father a broth which he found excellent in comparison with that made from horse.

To the horrors of famine and pestilence were added those of obstinate and incessant warfare. All day long the French troops were fighting on the land side against the Austrians; and when night put a stop to this, the English, Turkish and Neapolitan fleets, sheltered by the darkness from the fire of our harbour batteries, poured enormous quantities of shells into the town, doing terrible damage. Thus we had not an instant of repose. The noise of the cannonade and the cries of the dying reached my father's room and agitated him greatly. He regretted that he could not be at the head of his division; and his mental state made his bodily condition even worse. From day to day his illness grew more serious, and he became visibly weaker. Colindo and I never left him for an instant.

At last, one night, whilst I was kneeling beside him, bathing his wound, he spoke to me with his mind perfectly clear. Then, sensing his end approaching, he laid his hand on my head, stroked it caressingly, and said: 'Poor child! what is to become of you with no one to look after you, in the midst of the horrors of this terrible siege?' He murmured a few words, among which I made out my mother's name; then he dropped his hands and closed his eyes.

Young as I was, and short as had been my service, I had seen plenty of men die in the field, and still more in the streets of Genoa; but these had fallen in the open air and in their clothes. Very different is the sight of a man dying in bed; and I thought, therefore, that my father had dropped off to sleep. Colindo, who understood the truth, had not the heart to tell me, and I was only undeceived some hours later, when Monsieur Lachèze came in and I saw him draw the sheet over my father's face, saying, 'A terrible loss for his family and his friends.' Then, for the first time, I realised my full misfortune. My grief was so heartrending that it even touched the commander-in-chief, Masséna, who was not easily moved, especially in circumstances like the present where firmness was so much required. The critical position of affairs caused him to take a step which at that time I thought atrocious, though if I ever commanded in a besieged town I should do the same myself.

In order to avoid anything which might weaken the morale of the troops, Masséna had forbidden all funeral processions. He knew that I was unwilling to quit the mortal remains of my father, and suspected that my intention was to accompany them to the grave. Fearing the effect on the troops of seeing a young officer – little more than a child – sobbing behind the bier of his father, a general of division, Masséna came into the room where my father was lying and, taking me by the hand, led me under some pretext into a distant apartment. Meanwhile, at his orders, twelve grenadiers, accompanied only by Colonel Sacleux and another officer, took up the bier in silence and carried it off to the temporary grave on the ramparts facing the sea. Not until this ceremony was over did Masséna tell me what had been done, explaining the motives behind his decision. I cannot express the despair into which I was thrown. It seemed to me that by this removal of my father's body without the last cares from me, I had lost him a second time. It was no use complaining: there was nothing more for me to do but to go and pray at his grave. I did not know where it was, but my friend Colindo had followed the funeral at a little distance, and he took me there. This kind young fellow gave me at this time proofs of a touching sympathy at a moment when everyone was thinking of nothing but his personal position.

Almost all the officers on my father's staff had been killed or carried off by typhus; we were eleven before the campaign, and there remained only two of us: Major R—— and myself. But R—— thought only about himself and instead of being any help to his General's son, he continued to live by himself in the town; Monsieur Lachèze also left me to myself. Only the kind Colonel Sacleux showed any signs of interest in me, but as Masséna had given him the command of a brigade, he was constantly engaged in repelling the enemy outside the walls. I remained, therefore, alone in the vast Centurione Palace with Colindo, Bastide and the old porter.

Scarcely a week had passed since I had lost my father when General Masséna, who wanted a great many officers about him – for he got some killed or wounded almost every day – sent me orders to come and act as his aide-de-camp. R—— and all the officers of generals who were killed or disabled from riding were doing the like: I obeyed, and all day long attended the commander-in-chief during the fighting. When I was not kept at headquarters, I went home, and when night came Colindo and I, passing through the dead and dying who were lying about the streets, used to go and pray at my father's tomb.

Meanwhile the famine was increasing to an alarming extent. By order of the commander-in-chief each officer was allowed to retain only one horse; all the rest had to be sent to the butcher. My father had left several, and it would have been very painful to me to know that the poor beasts were going to be killed. I saved their lives by proposing to the staff officers to exchange them for their broken-down animals, and gave these over to the butcher. Later on, the state paid for these horses on presentation of the order to give them up. I preserved one of these orders as a curious relic: it bears the signature of General Oudinot, chief-of-staff to Masséna.

The cruel loss which I had undergone, the position in which I found myself, and the terrible scenes at which I was every day present, had in a short time developed my intelligence more than many years of happiness would have done. I understood that all those who a few months before had been surrounding my father with attentions were rendered selfish by the misery of the siege, and that I must find in myself courage and resource enough, not only for my own needs, but to support

Colindo and Bastide. The chief thing was to find the means of feeding them, since they got no provisions from the army stores. I had, indeed, as an officer double rations of horseflesh and bread; but all this together only made a pound of nourishment (and that very bad) and there were three of us. We very seldom now caught any pigeons, for their number had greatly diminished. As aide-de-camp to the commander-in-chief I had my place laid at his table, where once a day bread, roast horse and dried peas were served; but I was so angry with Masséna for having deprived me of the sad consolation of following my father to his grave that I could not make up my mind to take my place at his table. Ultimately, however, the desire of aiding my two unfortunate fellow lodgers decided me to take my meals with the General. After that Colindo and Bastide each got a quarter of a pound of bread and the same amount of horseflesh. I did not myself get enough to eat, for at the General's table the portions were extremely minute, and I was very hard-worked. I often found my strength failing, and more than once was obliged to lie down on the ground to save myself from fainting.

Once more Providence came to our aid. Bastide was a native of the Cantal, and in the previous winter had come across another Auvergnat of his acquaintance who was settled at Genoa as a small tradesman. He went to see him and was struck on entering the house by a smell like that of a grocer's shop. He remarked upon it to his friend, saying, 'You have got provisions!' The other admitted it, binding him to secrecy, for every kind of provisions found in private houses were carried off to the army stores. The sensible Bastide offered to find him a purchaser for any superfluous provisions who would pay in cash – and keep his secret – and came to let me know of his discovery. My father had left several thousand francs, so I had brought to the house at night a good store of cod, cheese, figs, sugar, chocolate, and so on. All this was horribly dear; the Auvergnat got nearly all my money, but I deemed myself only too happy in letting him do what he liked with me, for according to what I heard every day at headquarters, the siege was going to last a good deal longer and the famine to go on increasing, which, unhappily, came true. What doubled my joy in getting means of subsistence was the thought that I was saving the life of my friend Colindo, who but for this would literally have starved to death, for he knew no one in the army except me and Colonel Sacleux.

Before very long the Colonel met with a terrible disaster under the following circumstances: Masséna, attacked every day on every side, and seeing the troops mowed down by constant famine and fighting, and being obliged at the same time to keep in check an immense population driven by hunger to despair, found his position critical. Knowing that if he was to maintain any order in his army he must establish an iron discipline, he cashiered without pity every officer who did not execute his orders precisely. Many examples of this kind had already been made. One day, in a sortie which we pushed to a distance of six leagues from the town, the brigade commanded by Colonel Sacleux failed to be at the appointed hour in a valley where it was to have barred the Austrians' passage. Consequently, the enemy escaped and Masséna, furious at seeing his combination fail, cashiered poor Colonel Sacleux, and announced it in a general order. It was quite possible that Sacleux had not understood what was expected of him; but there was no doubt about his courage. He would, in his despair, have certainly blown out his brains if his heart had not been set on winning back his honour. He took a musket and placed himself in the ranks as a soldier.

One day he came to visit us; Colindo and I were touched to the heart at seeing this excellent man in a private's uniform. We bade farewell to Sacleux, who, after the surrender of the place, was restored by Bonaparte to the rank of colonel at Masséna's instance, Sacleux having by his courage compelled him to reconsider his decision. But in the following year, seeing that peace was made in Europe,[8] and wishing to free himself completely from the slur which had been so unjustly cast upon him, Sacleux asked to go and fight in San Domingo,[9] and there was killed just as he was about to be appointed brigadier-general. There are some men with whom, in spite of their merit, destiny deals very harshly.

The obstinate courage with which Masséna held Genoa had important consequences. Major Franceschi, sent by him to the First Consul, succeeded – both in going and returning – in passing through the enemy's fleet at night undetected. He was back at Genoa on 6 *Prairial* with the news that he had left Bonaparte descending from the Great St Bernard Pass at the head of his reserve force. Field Marshal Melas was so convinced of the impossibility of bringing such an army across the Alps, that while the force under General Ott was blockading us, he had gone with the rest of his army to attack General Suchet on the River Var fifty leagues away, with the intention of invading Provence: this allowed Bonaparte to enter Italy unopposed. Thus the resistance of Genoa had effected a powerful diversion in the aid of France. Once in Italy, Bonaparte's first desire would have been to succour the garrison of that town; but in order to do this he had to wait until his whole force was assembled, and the passage of the Alps offered great difficulties to the artillery and commissariat wagons. This delay allowed time for Melas to hasten up with the bulk of his forces from Nice, thus blocking Bonaparte's road to Genoa.

While Bonaparte and Melas were marching and counter-marching in Piedmont, the garrison of Genoa was at the last gasp. Typhus was doing frightful execution; the hospitals had become charnel-houses and the measure of misery was full. Nearly all the horses had been eaten, and the half-pound of wretched food, which was all that the troops had for some time received, was never secure for one day in advance. Absolutely nothing was left when, on 15 *Prairial*, Masséna summoned all the generals and announced that he had determined to take such sound men as remained and try to cut his way through and reach Leghorn. The officers declared with one voice that the troops were utterly unfit to fight or march. So Masséna, deeming that by facilitating Bonaparte's entry into Italy he had carried out his instructions, and that it was now his duty to save the remains of a garrison which had fought so valiantly, finally decided to offer terms for the evacuation of the place. He would not hear of capitulation.

For more than a month the English admiral and the Austrian General Ott had been proposing an interview, but Masséna had always refused. Now, however, he was constrained by the circumstances to send word that he was willing to talk. The meeting took place in a little chapel which stands on the bridge of Conegliano, and was situated between the sea and the French and Austrian outposts. The French, Austrian and English staffs took their stand at the ends of the bridge. I was present at this most interesting scene. The enemy's commander showed special marks of esteem and respect to Masséna. Although the conditions which he required were unfavourable to them, Lord Keith said repeatedly: 'General, your defence has been so heroic that we can refuse you nothing.' It was agreed, therefore, that the garrison should not be prisoners, but should retain their arms, and proceed to Nice. As soon as they had reached that town, they were free to take part again in hostilities.

Masséna well understood how important it was that the keen desire which Bonaparte must be feeling to come to the aid of Genoa should not lead him into a trap. He demanded, therefore, that the conditions should include a safe-conduct through the Austrian army for two officers who were to bear the news of the evacuation of Genoa by the French troops. General Ott objected, having in view a speedy departure to join Melas with 25,000 men of the blockading force, and he did not wish this to be brought to the attention of Bonaparte by Masséna's troops. But Lord Keith overruled this objection. The treaty was on the point of being signed when sounds as of distant cannon were heard far away among the mountains. Masséna put down his pen, exclaiming, 'Here comes Bonaparte with his army!' The enemy generals were amazed; but after waiting some time it became evident that the sound was merely thunder, and Masséna was obliged to sign.

The loss to the garrison and its commander of the full credit of holding Genoa until Bonaparte could come up was not the only source of regret; Masséna would have been glad to hold out for a few days longer, and by so much to delay the departure of General Ott's force. He clearly foresaw that this General would march to join Field Marshal Melas, and thereby afford him valuable help in meeting the First Consul. His fear, though well founded, was unnecessary, for Ott was not able to effect a junction with the main Austrian army until the day after Marengo. The result of the battle would have been very different if the Austrians, whom we had so much trouble to beat as it was, had had another 25,000 men to bring against us. Thus Masséna's defence of Genoa had not only kept the Alps open for Bonaparte (and given Milan into his hands) but had also kept 25,000 men out of his way on the day of Marengo. On 16 *Prairial* the Austrians took possession of Genoa, after a siege of just two months.

So important did Masséna deem it that the First Consul should have timely notice of the treaty just concluded, that he had asked for a safe-conduct for two aides-de-camp, in order that if one fell ill the other might take on the despatch. It was as well that the officer to whom the duty was entrusted should be able to speak Italian, so Masséna selected for it Major Graziani, a Piedmontese (or Roman) in the French service. With his wonted excess of suspicion, however, fearing that one who was not a Frenchman might be tampered with by the Austrians and induced to delay, he attached me to him, with special instructions to urge him forward until we fell in with the First

Consul. There was really no need for this, for Major Graziani was perfectly loyal and thoroughly understood the importance of his mission. We started on 16 *Prairial*, and came up with Bonaparte the next evening at Milan.

General Bonaparte spoke with much sympathy of my recent loss, and promised that if I behaved well he would act as a father to me: he kept his word. He never tired of asking Monsieur Graziani and me about what had happened at Genoa and the strength and direction of the Austrian forces which we had passed on our way to Milan. He kept us near him, and lent us horses from his own stable, as we had performed the journey on post-mules. We accompanied him to Montebello, and on to the battlefield of Marengo,[10] where we served as his orderly officers. I will not enter into the details of this memorable fight, in which no harm befell me. As is well known, we were on the verge of defeat, and should probably have been beaten if Ott's men had come up before the end of the battle. Bonaparte, fearing that they would appear every moment, was very anxious and only recovered his spirits when our infantry and the cavalry of Desaix (whose death he only learned later) had decided the victory by repulsing Zach's column of grenadiers. Just then, noticing that the horse I rode was slightly wounded in the leg, he took me by the ear and said, laughing, 'You expect me to lend you my horses for you to treat them in this way?' As Major Graziani died in 1812, I am thus the only French officer who was present both at the siege of Genoa and at the Battle of Marengo.

5 Brothers When the Fight Was Over

The Battle of Austerlitz, December 1805

Our gunners opened fire and balls and shells
rained on the ice, which gave way beneath this
mass of Russians. All the troops clapped their
hands, and our Napoleon wreaked vengeance on
his snuff-box: it was a total rout.

Captain Coignet[1]

After victory there are no enemies, but only men.

Napoleon[2]

*After Marengo, Marbot returned to Genoa to visit his
father's grave for the last time. A French brig took him
back to Nice and from there he started for home on foot: all
carriages having been requisitioned by senior officers. The
reunion with his widowed mother was melancholy enough:
'I will not attempt to recount my meeting with my mother
and brothers. Some scenes can be realised by everyone who
has a heart, but are too sad to describe.' After a period of
mourning, Marbot found temporary employment on the
staff of General Bernadotte,[3] an old friend of his father's.
This was followed by a transfer to the 25th Chasseurs –
tears being shed upon giving up the Bercheny uniform – and*

a spot of active service in Portugal before returning to France and a course at the regimental cavalry school. By October 1802 a bored and restless Marbot decided to apply for a position on the staff of General Augereau, another old friend of the family. His mother, anxious, no doubt, to further her son's career, delivered the letter of application in person: an appointment as the General's aide-de-camp duly followed. It turned out to be a fortunate move: on 2 December 1804 Bonaparte was crowned Napoleon I, Emperor of the French; the following May he made Augereau a Marshal of the Empire; and on 16 August 1805, on Augereau's recommendation, Marbot was made full lieutenant. Ten days later he was back on the march: 'There I was once again on campaign. It was 1805, a year which saw the opening of a long period of warfare for me, not to end till Waterloo, ten years later . . . Constantly sent from north to south, and from south to north, wherever there was fighting going on, I did not pass one of these ten years without coming under fire, or without shedding my blood on the soil of some part of Europe.'

The Second Coalition had collapsed after the French victories of Marengo and Hohenlinden,[4] only to replaced by a third in the summer of 1805. An invasion of France was planned by an Austro-Russian army, but before it got off the ground Napoleon took the initiative. Whilst pretending to prepare an invasion of England, he secretly set off for war in the east. On 17 October the Emperor bagged an Austrian army under General Mack, haplessly awaiting the arrival of his Russian allies in the fortress of Ulm. He then pushed on to Vienna, entering it on 14 November; and having secured the bridges over the Danube, chased the combined armies of Austria and Russia into Moravia (now the Czech Republic), seeking a decisive battle. Marbot and his comrade Massy, forwarded by Augereau with a clutch of captured enemy colours, arrived at Napoleon's headquarters at Brünn (now

Brno) on 22 November. Ten days later the Emperor got his battle.

THE GREAT DRAMA was approaching its final scene. Most military authors are apt to confuse the reader's mind by overcrowding their story with details. So much is this the case, that in the greater part of the works published on the wars of the Empire, I have been utterly unable to understand the history of many battles at which I was present, and of which all the phases were known to me. In order to preserve due clearness in relating a military action, I think one ought to be content with indicating the respective conditions of the two armies before the engagement, and reporting only such facts as affected the decision. That is what I shall try to do in order to give you an idea of the Battle of Austerlitz, as it is called, though it took place short of the village of that name. On the eve of battle, however, the Emperors of Austria and Russia had slept at the château of Austerlitz, and when Napoleon drove them from this, he wished to heighten his triumph by giving that name to the battle.

You may see on a map of the area that the Goldbach brook, which rises on the other side of the Olmütz road, falls into the small lake of Mönitz. This stream, flowing at the bottom of a little valley with steep sides, separated the two armies. The Austro-Russian right rested on a hanging wood in rear of the Posoritz post house beyond the Olmütz road; their centre occupied Pratzen and the wide plateau of that name; their left was on swampy ground near the pools of Satschan. The Emperor Napoleon rested his left on a hillock, which the Egyptian veterans named the 'Santon', because it had on the top a little chapel with a spire like a minaret. The French centre was near the marsh of Kobelnitz, the right was at Telnitz. At this point, Napoleon had placed few soldiers, in order to draw the Russians on to the marshy ground, where he had arranged to defeat them by concealing Davout's corps at Gross Raigern, on the Vienna road.

On 1 December 1805, the day before the battle, Napoleon left Brünn early in the morning; spent the whole day inspecting the positions; and in the evening fixed his headquarters in rear of the French centre, at a point where the view took in the bivouacs of both sides, as well as the ground which was to be their field of battle next day. There was no other building in the place but a poor barn. The Emperor's tables and maps were placed there and he established himself in person by an immense fire, surrounded by his staff. Fortunately there was no snow and, though it was very cold, I lay on the ground and went soundly to sleep. But we were soon obliged to remount and go the rounds with the Emperor. There was no moon, and the darkness of the night was increased by a thick fog which made progress difficult. The *chasseurs* of the escort had the idea of lighting torches made of pine branches and straw, which proved very useful.

The troops, seeing a group of horsemen thus lighted come toward them, had no difficulty in recognising the Imperial Staff, and in an instant, as if by enchantment, we could see along the whole line all our bivouac fires lighted up by thousands of torches in the hands of the soldiers. The cheers with which, in their enthusiasm, they saluted Napoleon, were all the more animated for the fact that the morrow was the anniversary of his coronation: the coincidence seemed of good omen. The enemy must have been a good deal surprised when, from the top of a neighbouring hill, they saw in the middle of the night 60,000 torches lighted, and heard a thousand times repeated the cry, *'Vive l'Empereur!'* accompanied by the sound of the many bands of the French regiments. In our camp all was joy, light and movement; while across the dark valley all was gloom and silence.

Next day, the sound of cannon was heard at daybreak. As we have seen, the Emperor had shown but few troops on his right; this was a trap for the enemy, with the view of allowing them to capture Telnitz easily, to cross the Goldbach there, then to go on to Gross Raigern and take possession of the road from Brünn to Vienna, and so to cut off our retreat. The Russians and Austrians fell into the snare perfectly, for, weakening the rest of their line, they clumsily crowded considerable forces into the bottom of Telnitz, and into the swampy valleys bordering on the pools of Satschan and Mönitz. But as they imagined, for some not very apparent reason, that Napoleon had the intention of retreating without delivering battle, they resolved, by way of completing their success, to attack us on our left towards the 'Santon', and also on our centre before Puntowitz. By this means our defeat would be complete when we had been forced back on these two points, and found the road to Vienna occupied in our rear by Russian troops. As it befell, however, on our left Marshal Lannes not only repulsed all the attacks of the enemy upon the 'Santon', but drove him back on the other side of the Olmütz road as far as Blasiowitz. There the ground became more level, and allowed Murat's cavalry to execute some brilliant charges, the results of which were of great importance, for the Russians were driven out of hand as far as the village of Austerlitz.

While this splendid success was being won by our left wing, the centre, consisting of the troops under Soult and Bernadotte, which the Emperor had posted at the bottom of the Goldbach ravine, where they were concealed by a thick fog, dashed forwards towards the hill on which stands the village of Pratzen. This was the moment when the brilliant sun of Austerlitz, the recollection of which Napoleon so delighted to recall, burst forth in all its splendour. Marshal Soult carried not only the village of Pratzen, but also the vast tableland of that name, which was the culminating point of the whole country, and consequently the key of the battlefield. There, under the Emperor's eyes, the sharpest of the fighting took place, and the Russians were beaten back. But one battalion, the 4th Regiment of the Line, of which Prince Joseph, Napoleon's brother, was the colonel, had allowed itself to be carried too far in the pursuit of the enemy. In consequence of this, it was charged and broken up by the cavalry of the Noble Guard and the Grand Duke Constantine's *cuirassiers*, losing its eagle. Several lines of Russian cavalry quickly advanced to support this momentary success, but Napoleon hurled against them the cavalry of his own Imperial Guard: the Mamelukes, the *chasseurs* and the mounted grenadiers, under Marshal Bessières and General Rapp. The mêlée was of the most sanguinary kind; the Russian squadrons were crushed and driven back beyond the village of Austerlitz with immense loss. Our troopers captured many colours and prisoners; among the latter was Prince Repnin, commander of the Noble Guard. This regiment, composed of the most brilliant of the young Russian nobility, suffered particularly heavy losses. The swagger in which they had indulged prior to the battle caused our men to attack them with fury, shouting as they gave point with the sabre, 'We will give the ladies of St Petersburg something to cry for!'

The painter Gérard, in his picture of the Battle of Austerlitz, took for his subject the moment when General Rapp, coming back wounded from the fight and covered with the blood of his enemies, is presenting to the Emperor the flags just captured and his prisoner, Prince Repnin. I was present at this imposing spectacle, which the artist has reproduced with wonderful accuracy. All the heads are portraits, even that of the brave *chasseur* who, making no complaint (though he had been shot through the body), had the courage to come up to Napoleon and fall stone dead as he presented the standard which he had just taken. The Emperor, wishing to honour his memory, ordered the painter to find a place for him in his composition. In the picture may also be seen a Mameluke, carrying in one hand an enemy's flag and in the other the bridle of his dying horse. This man, named Mustapha, was well known in the Guard for his courage and ferocity. During the charge he had pursued the Grand Duke Constantine, who could only get rid of him by a pistol-shot, which severely wounded the Mameluke's horse. Mustapha, grieved at having only a standard to show to the Emperor, said in his broken French: 'Ah, if me catch Prince Constantine, me cut him head off and bring it to Emperor!' Disgusted, Napoleon replied, 'Will you hold your tongue, you savage?'

While Marshals Lannes, Soult and Murat (with the Imperial Guard) were beating the right and centre of the Allied army, and driving them back beyond the village of Austerlitz, the enemy's left, falling into the trap laid by Napoleon, threw itself on the village of Telnitz. The place was duly captured; and the enemy crossed the Goldbach, intending to occupy the road to Vienna – our only line of retreat. But the enemy generals seriously underestimated Napoleon's genius when they supposed him capable of committing such a blunder as to leave this important road undefended. Concealed in rear of the little town of Gross Raigern, the divisions under Marshal Davout fell upon the Allies at the moment when their masses became entangled in the defiles between the lakes of Telnitz and Mönitz and the stream.

The Emperor, whom we left on the Pratzen plateau, having freed himself from the enemy's right and centre, which were in flight on the other side of Austerlitz, descended with a small force of all arms, including Soult's corps, and went with all speed towards Telnitz. There he took the enemy's columns in rear at the very moment when Davout was attacking in front. At once the heavy masses of Austrians and Russians, packed onto the narrow roads which run alongside the Goldbach, fell into an incredible confusion. All ranks were mixed up together, and each sought to save himself by flight. Some hurled themselves headlong into the marshes which border the pools, but our infantry followed them there. Others hoped to escape by the road that lies between the two pools; our cavalry charged them and the butchery was frightful.

Lastly, the greater part of the enemy, chiefly the Russians, sought to pass over the ice. It was very thick, and 5,000 or 6,000 men, keeping some kind of order, had reached the middle of the frozen Satschan lake, when Napoleon, calling up the artillery of the Guard, gave the order to fire on the ice. It broke at countless points, and a mighty cracking was heard. The water, oozing through the fissures, soon covered the floes, and we saw thousands of Russians, with their horses, guns and wagons, slowly settle down into the depths. It was a horribly majestic spectacle which I shall never forget. In an instant the surface of the lake was covered with everything that could swim. Men and horses struggled in the water amongst the floes. Some – a very small number – succeeded in saving themselves by the help of poles and ropes, which our soldiers reached to them from the shore, but the greater part were drowned.

The number of combatants at the Emperor's disposal in this battle was 68,000 men; that of the Allied army amounted to 82,000. Our loss in killed and wounded was about 8,000 men; our enemies admitted that theirs, in killed, wounded and drowned, reached 14,000. We had made 18,000 prisoners, captured 150 guns, and a great number of standards and colours. After giving the order to pursue the enemy in every direction, the Emperor took himself to his new headquarters at the post house of Posoritz on the Olmütz road. As may be imagined, he was radiant, but frequently expressed regret that the very eagle we had lost should have belonged to his brother Joseph's regiment, and should have been captured by the regiment of the Grand Duke Constantine, brother of the Emperor of Russia. The coincidence was, in truth, rather quaint, and made the loss more noticeable. But Napoleon soon received great consolation. Prince John of Lichtenstein came from the Emperor of Austria to request an interview, and

Napoleon, understanding that this would result in a peace and would deliver him from seeing the Prussians march on his rear before he was clear of his present enemy, granted it.

Of all the divisions of the Grand Army, it was the Emperor's beloved *chasseurs-à-cheval*[5] who suffered the heaviest loss in their great charge against the Russian Guard on the Pratzen plateau. My poor friend Captain Fournier was killed, and General Morland too. The Emperor, always on the lookout for anything that might kindle the spirit of emulation among the troops, decided that General Morland's body should be placed in the memorial building which he proposed to erect on the Esplanade des Invalides at Paris. The surgeons, having neither the time nor the materials necessary to embalm the General's body on the battlefield, put it into a barrel of rum, which was transported to Paris. Subsequent events delayed the construction of the monument destined for General Morland; and the barrel in which he had been placed was still standing in one of the rooms of the School of Medicine when Napoleon lost the Empire in 1814. Not long afterwards the barrel broke through decay and people were much surprised to find that the rum had made the General's moustaches grow to such an extraordinary extent that they fell below his waist. The corpse was in perfect preservation; but in order to get possession of the body, the family was obliged to bring an action against some scientific man, who had made a curiosity of it. Cultivate the love of glory and go and get killed – just to let some oaf of a naturalist set you up in his library between a rhinoceros horn and a stuffed crocodile!

As for myself, I did not receive any wound at the Battle of Austerlitz, though I was often in a very exposed position; notably at the time of the cavalry mêlée on the Pratzen plateau. The Emperor had sent me with orders to General Rapp, whom I succeeded with great difficulty in reaching in the middle of that terrible hurly-burly of slaughterers and slaughtered. My horse came in contact with that of one of the Emperor

Alexander's bodyguard, and our sabres were on the point of crossing when we were forced apart by the combatants, and I got off with a severe bruising. On the next day, however, I incurred a much greater danger of a very different kind from those which one ordinarily meets on the field of battle: it happened in this way.

On the morning of 3 December, the Emperor mounted and rode round the different positions where the fights of the day before had taken place. Having reached the shores of the Satschan lake, Napoleon dismounted and was chatting with several marshals around a camp fire, when he saw (floating a hundred yards from the embankment) a large ice floe, on which was stretched a wounded Russian sergeant. The poor fellow could not help himself, having got a bullet through his thigh, and his blood stained the ice bright red: a horrible sight. Seeing a numerous staff surrounded by guards, the man judged that Napoleon must be near and raising himself as well as he could, cried out that soldiers of all lands became brothers when the fight was over; and that he begged his life of the powerful Emperor of the French. Napoleon (his interpreter having translated this entreaty), was touched by it and ordered General Bertrand, his aide-de-camp, to do what he could to save the poor man. Straightaway several men of the escort (and even two staff officers), seeing two great tree stems on the bank, pushed them into the water and getting astride of them, they thought that by moving their legs simultaneously, they would drive these pieces of wood forward. Scarcely were they a fathom from the edge when they rolled over, throwing into the water the men who bestrode them. Their clothes were saturated in a moment; and as it was freezing very hard, the cloth of their sleeves and trousers became stiff as they swam and their limbs – shut up as it were in cases – could not move; so that several came near to being drowned.

I bethought me then of saying that the swimmers ought to have stripped: in the first place to preserve their freedom of movement, and secondly, to avoid having to pass the night in wet clothes. General Bertrand having heard this, repeated it to the Emperor, who declared that I was right and that the others had shown more zeal than discretion. I do not wish to make myself out better than I am, so I will admit that having just taken part in a battle where I had seen thousands of dead and dying, the edge had been taken off my sensibility and I did not feel philanthropic enough to run the risk of a bad cold by contesting the ice floes for the life of an enemy: I felt quite content with deploring his sad fate. But the Emperor's answer had piqued me, and it seemed to me that I should be open to ridicule if I gave advice and did not dare to carry it into execution: so I leapt from my horse, stripped myself naked, and dashed into the water. I had ridden hard in the course of the day, consequently becoming quite hot, so that the chill struck me keenly; but I was young and the Emperor's presence encouraged me so that I struck out towards the Russian sergeant. At the same time my example – and probably the praise given me by the Emperor – determined a lieutenant of artillery by the name of Roumestain to imitate me.

While he was undressing, I was advancing; but with a good deal more difficulty than I had foreseen. The older ice, which had been smashed to pieces the day before, had almost entirely disappeared; but a new skin had formed, the sharp edges of which scratched and cut my skin like a sabre. Roumestain gradually caught me up and at last we reached the ice floe on which the poor Russian was lying and thought that the most laborious part of our enterprise was over: but we were quite wrong. As soon as we began to push the floe forward, the layer of new ice which covered the surface of the water, being broken by contact with it, piled itself up in front so as to form a mass, which not only resisted our efforts, but began to break the edges of the larger floe. The bulk of this got smaller every moment and we began to fear that the poor man whom we were trying to save would be drowned before our eyes. The edges of the floe were remarkably sharp, so that we had to choose spots on which to rest our hands and our chests as we pushed. We were very soon at our last gasp. Finally, by way of a crowning stroke, as we got near the bank the ice split in several places, and the portion on which the Russian lay was reduced to a slab, a few feet in breadth, and quite insufficient to bear his weight. He was on the point of sinking, when my comrade and I, feeling bottom at length, slipped our shoulders under the ice slab and bore it to the shore: wearied, torn, bruised, bleeding and hardly able to stand.

My kind comrade, Massy, who had watched me with the greatest anxiety throughout, had been so thoughtful as to have his horse-cloth warmed before the camp fire and as soon as I was out of the water he wrapped me in it. After a good rub down I put on my clothes and wanted to stretch out by the fire but this Dr Larrey[6] forbad, and ordered me to walk about, aided by two *chasseurs*. The Emperor came and congratulated Roumestain and me on our courage in undertaking (and achieving) the rescue of the wounded Russian; and calling his Mameluke, Roustam, who always carried refreshments, he poured us out a glass of excellent rum and asked us, laughingly, how we had liked our bath.

As for the Russian sergeant, the Emperor directed Dr Larrey to attend to him and gave him several pieces of gold. He was fed and put into dry clothes; and after being wrapped in warm rugs, he was taken to a house in Telnitz which was used as an ambulance, and transferred the next day to the hospital at Brünn. The poor lad blessed the Emperor, as well as Lieutenant Roumestain and me, and would kiss our hands. He was a Lithuanian; a native, that is, of a province of the old Poland now joined to Russia. As soon as he was well he declared that he would serve none other than the Emperor Napoleon; and so he returned to France with our wounded and was enrolled in the Polish Legion. Ultimately he became a sergeant in the lancers of the Guard; and whenever I came across him, he testified his gratitude in broken but expressive language.

My icy bath and the really superhuman efforts which I had had to make to save the poor man might have cost me dearly if I had been less young and vigorous. Lieutenant Roumestain, who did not possess the latter advantage to the same extent as I, was seized that same evening with violent congestion of the lungs and had to be taken to the hospital, where he passed several months between life and death. He never, indeed, recovered completely; and had to leave the service invalided some years later. As for myself, though I was very weak, I got myself hoisted onto my horse when the Emperor left the lake to go to the château of Austerlitz, where his headquarters now were. Napoleon always went at a gallop and in my shaken state this pace did not suit me; still, I kept up because night was coming on and I was afraid of straying: besides which, if I had gone at a walk, the cold would have got hold of me. When I reached the château it took several men to help me dismount; a shivering fit seized me, my teeth were chattering and I was quite ill. Colonel Dahlman, lieutenant general of the *chasseurs-à-cheval* who had just been promoted to general in place of Morland, took me into one of the outbuildings where he and his officers were established. After giving me some hot tea, his surgeon rubbed me all over with warm oil and they swaddled me in many rugs and stuck me in a great heap of hay, leaving only my face outside. Gradually, a pleasant warmth penetrated my numbed limbs and I slept soundly. It was thanks to all this kind care, as well as to my twenty-three years, that I found myself next morning fresh and in good condition; and was able to mount my horse and witness an extremely interesting spectacle.

The defeat which the Russians had undergone had thrown their army into such disorder that all who escaped the disaster of Austerlitz (including the Emperor Alexander, who had been so sure of victory) made haste to reach Galicia,[7] out of

63

Napoleon's power: the rout was complete. We took many prisoners and found the roads glutted with guns and baggage. On the very evening of the battle the Emperor of Austria, to save his country from utter ruin, begged an interview of the French Emperor, and Napoleon, agreeing, halted in the village of Nasiedlowitz. The interview took place on the 4th, near the mill of Poleny, between the French and Austrian lines and I was present at this memorable meeting. Napoleon, starting very early from the château with his staff, was the first at the place of meeting. He dismounted and was strolling about, when, seeing the Emperor of Austria approaching, he went towards him and embraced him cordially. A strange sight for the philosopher to reflect on! An Emperor of Germany come to humble himself by suing for peace to the son of a small Corsican family, not long ago a sub-lieutenant of artillery, whom his talents, good fortune and the courage of the French soldier had raised to the summit of power and made the arbiter of the destinies of Europe.

Napoleon took no unfair advantage of the Austrian Emperor's position, so far as we could judge from the distance at which respect kept us; but was kind and courteous in the extreme. An armistice was concluded and it was arranged that plenipotentiaries should be sent by both parties to Brünn to negotiate a treaty of peace. The Emperors embraced again at parting and returned to their respective quarters. During the next two days, Napoleon admitted Major Massy and myself to a farewell audience, charging us to report to Marshal Augereau what we had seen. At the same time the Emperor returned to Münich and informed us that Augereau had left Bregenz and that we could find him at Ulm. We got back to Vienna and continued our journey, travelling night and day in spite of the snow, which had begun to fall thickly.

6 Masters of Nearly the Whole of Prussia

The Battles of Jena-Auerstädt, October 1806

There are in Europe many good generals, but they see too many things at once; as for me, I see only one thing, namely, the enemy's main body. I try to crush it, confident that secondary matters will then settle themselves.

Napoleon[1]

After Austerlitz, Marbot accompanied Marshal Augereau to his new headquarters at Frankfort. While he was there, an officer of chasseurs was taken ill with fever and Marbot – hoping for a chance to call on his mother at Saint-Céré – gladly agreed to escort the invalid back to France. The journey, however, proved to be a nightmare: cooped up in a coach, the weather oppressive and unbearably hot, the officer's condition worsened, until, in a fit of delirium, he attempted to bludgeon Marbot with a coach-wrench! Thankfully, Marbot reached Paris safely and reported to the Emperor with the Marshal's despatches. Expecting to be swiftly sent on his way, and looking forward to meeting his mother, Marbot was crestfallen when Napoleon announced that another errand awaited him: he was to deliver an urgent letter from the Emperor to King Frederick William III of Prussia at his court in Berlin.

Prussia, which had been 'living for twenty years on the fame of Frederick the Great',[2] *had stood aside during the War of the Third Coalition. Now her leaders were outraged by Napoleon's rearrangement of the map of Europe, his domination of western Germany as self-styled 'Protector' of the newly formed Confederation of the Rhine, and his offer to return Hanover – which he had given to Prussia in February 1806 in return for a Franco-Prussian alliance – to its ex-owner, King George III. Prussian concerns were compounded by Napoleon's habit of giving kingdoms to his brothers: Joseph Bonaparte having been installed as King of Naples; and Louis, King of Holland. It was clear that Napoleon saw himself not as a mere monarch, but as a warrior-emperor, a new Charlemagne, dictating to the princelings of Germany.*

Although King Frederick William was a peaceable and mild-mannered man,[3] *his beautiful wife Louise was a patriot with a will of iron. Surrounding herself with a coterie of army hotheads, she formed an anti-French war party; and it is said that she even denied the poor King his conjugal rights until he agreed to fight! Napoleon, contemptuous of King Frederick (he called Queen Louise 'The only real man in Prussia'), nevertheless needed to know whether he was a friend or foe: 'Napoleon decided to write to him with his own hand, regardless of ordinary diplomatic efforts, to ask "Are you for or against me?"' Such were the contents of the letter which Marbot was to deliver.*

Marbot set off for Berlin in July 1806. He was well received at the Prussian court and was invited to stay on as a guest until the King had decided upon his reply to Napoleon. He was detained in Berlin for several weeks: attending balls and parties; and being fêted by the Prussian top brass, anxious to question him about his recent battle experiences. The fact was, however, that the Prussians were simply delaying him in order to gain time for mobilization. By August, Queen Louise's war party having persuaded the King to join Britain and Russia in a Fourth Coalition, the atmosphere in Berlin soured: a wave of anti-French feeling broke out; Prussian soldiers, full of bravado, sharpened their sabres on the steps of the French embassy; and the polite officers, who had entertained Marbot so amicably, no longer spoke – or even saluted – him. Finally, Marbot was sent back to Paris with the Prussian reply. Within weeks the two nations were at war: 'We prepared for war by getting all the amusement we could, for we thought that, nothing being more uncertain than soldiers' lives, they had better make haste to enjoy them.'

THE MARSHAL had reckoned on sleeping at Kala, which is only three leagues from Jena, but as night was falling, VII Corps received orders to proceed at once to the latter town, which the Emperor had entered without opposition at the head of his Guard. The Prussians had abandoned the place in silence; but it had been set on fire and part of the unhappy city was a prey to the spreading flames when we entered about midnight. It was sad to see so many old men and women, half-clothed, carrying away their children and trying to escape destruction by flight; while our soldiers, whom their duty and the presence of the enemy did not allow to leave the ranks, remained impassive – arms shouldered – making light of the fire in comparison with the dangers to which they were shortly to be exposed.

As the fire had not reached that part of the town by which the French were arriving, the Marshal and his staff took up their quarters in a handsome-looking house. I was just returning from carrying an order when I heard piercing cries coming from a neighbouring building, the door of which was open. I hurried up, and guided by the shrieks and cries, made my way into a suite of rooms, where I beheld two charming ladies of eighteen to twenty years old, in nightdresses, struggling with five Hessian soldiers. These troops were our allies, and had been sent to join the ranks of Augereau's corps. The men were far gone in liquor and, though they did not understand a word of French and I very little German, the very sight of me and my threats produced an effect on them: being used to the stick from their own officers, they took without a word the kicks and blows which, in my indignation, I administered to them freely as I drove them down the stairs.

When I returned to the ladies' rooms (they had hurriedly put on some clothes) I received from them warm expressions of gratitude. They were the daughters of one of the university professors and he, having gone with his wife and servants into the quarter of the town that was on fire to help one of their sisters who had just been confined with child, had left them all alone, when the Hessian soldiers appeared. One of the girls said to me with much energy, 'You are marching to battle at the moment when you have just saved our honour. God will repay you; be sure that no harm will come to you.' The father and mother, who came back at that moment, bringing the young mother and her child, were at first greatly surprised to find me there; but as soon as they learned the reason of my presence they too heaped blessings upon me. I tore myself away from the thanks of this grateful family to report myself to Marshal Augereau, who was resting in the neighbouring house while awaiting orders from the Emperor.

Jena is commanded by a height called the Landgrafenberg, at the foot of which flows the Saale. This is very steep on the side towards the town, and the only road is that to Weimar through the Mühlthal – a long and difficult passage – the exit from which (covered by a little wood) was guarded by Saxon troops. A cannon-shot in rear of them part of the Prussian army was drawn up in line. The Emperor, being able to reach the enemy only by this passage, was prepared for heavy losses in attacking it, for it did not seem possible to turn the position. But Napoleon's lucky star, which still guided him, provided him with an unexpected means. So far as I am aware no historian has spoken of it, but I can vouch for the fact.

As we have seen, the King of Prussia had compelled the Elector of Saxony to join forces with him.[4] The Saxon people saw with regret that they were involved in a war which could bring them no advantage in the future, and which in the present was bringing ruin on their country. The Prussians were therefore detested in Saxony and the town of Jena shared the feeling. A priest of the town, excited by the sight of the conflagration which was devouring it, and regarding the Prussians as the enemies of his sovereign and country, thought he might give Napoleon the means of driving them from the land by pointing out to him a little path which infantry could use to climb the steep sides of the Landgrafenberg. He therefore guided a detachment of *voltigeurs* and some staff officers to the place which the Prussians, thinking the passage impracticable, had omitted to guard. Napoleon, however, took a different view, and on the strength of the report which the officers made went up there himself, accompanied by Marshal Lannes and guided by the Saxon priest. Having observed that between the highest point of the path and the plain which the enemy occupied there existed a rocky platform, the Emperor resolved to assemble there a portion of his troops, who might issue from it as from a citadel to attack the Prussians.

The difficulty of the task was such that no one but Napoleon (commanding Frenchmen) could have surmounted it. He sent at once for 4,000 pioneering tools from the engineers' wagons, and ordered that every battalion should work, in turn, for an hour at widening and levelling the path; and that as each finished its task it should go and form up silently on the Landgrafenberg, while another took its place. They were lighted at their work by torches, concealed from the eyes of the enemy by the blaze of Jena. The nights being long at this time of the year, we had time to make the climb accessible not only to the columns of infantry, but even to the wagons and artillery, so that before daylight the corps of Lannes and Soult, and Augereau's first division, together with the foot guards, were massed on the Landgrafenberg. The term 'massed' was never more correct, for the breasts of the men were almost touching the backs of those in front of them. But the troops were so well disciplined that, in spite of the darkness and the packing of more than 40,000 men on that narrow platform, there was not the least disorder; and although the enemy were only half a cannon-shot off, they perceived nothing.

On the morning of 14 October a thick fog covered the country and favoured our movements. Augereau's second division made a feigned attack, advancing from Jena through the Mühlthal by the Weimar road. Believing this to be the only point by which we could issue from Jena, the enemy had massed a considerable force there. But while he was preparing to defend this narrow passage with vigour, the Emperor Napoleon ordered the troops which he had assembled on the Landgrafenberg during the night to debouch into the plain, and drew them up in order of battle. The first cannon-shots, aided by a light breeze, dispersed the fog; the sun shone out brilliantly; and the Prussians were aghast at seeing the French army deployed in their front and advancing to the contest. They could not understand how we had arrived on the plateau while they believed us at the farther end of the Jena valley, with no other means of getting at them but the Weimar road, which they were carefully watching. We engaged without loss of time, and the first line of the Prussians and Saxons, under the Prince of Hohenloe, was forced to give way. Their reserve was advancing but we received a strong reinforcement on our side: Ney's corps and Murat's cavalry (which had been de-layed in the defile) emerging into the plain. A Prussian army corps commanded by General Ruchel checked our columns for a moment, but it was charged by our cavalry and almost annihilated, General Ruchel being killed.

Augereau's first division, on descending from the Landgrafenberg into the plain, joined the second arriving at the Mühlthal; and the corps following the road from Vienna to Weimar captured Cospoda and then the wood of Iserstädt; while Lannes took Vierzehnheiligen and Soult, Hermstädt. The Prussian infantry fought badly and the cavalry did not do much better. We often saw it coming on with loud shouts, but intimidated by the calm attitude of our battalions, it never dared to push the charge home. On getting within fifty paces of our line it would wheel about, pursued by a hail of bullets and the hoots of our soldiers. The Saxons fought with courage; they resisted Augereau's corps for a long time, and only after the retreat of the Prussian troops did they form in two great squares and begin to retire, firing. Augereau, admiring the courage of the Saxons and wishing to spare these brave fellows, sent a flag of truce inviting them to surrender, as they had no longer any hope of support. But just at that moment Prince Murat, coming up with the cavalry, launched his *cuirassiers* and dragoons on the Saxon squares and by this resolute charge broke them; compelling the dazed survivors to lay down their arms. The next day the Emperor set these Saxons free, sending them back to their sovereign, with whom he lost no time in making peace.

The whole Prussian force retired, completely routed, along the Weimar road. The fugitives, with their artillery and baggage, were crowded at the gates of the city when the French appeared. Panic-stricken at the sight of them, the whole mob fled in the greatest disorder, leaving a great number of prisoners, flags, guns and baggage in our hands. The town of Weimar, which has been called the 'modern Athens', was at this time inhabited by many distinguished artists and men of science and letters, assembled from all parts of Germany under the enlightened patronage of the reigning duke. The noise of the cannon, the passage of the fugitives, the entry of the conquerors, caused a lively emotion in this peaceable and studious population. Marshals Lannes and Soult

71

preserved perfect order, however, and beyond having to supply the necessary provisions for the troops, the town underwent no exactions.

The Prince of Weimar was serving in the Prussian army, nevertheless his palace, in which the Princess had remained, was respected, and none of the marshals took up his quarters there. Marshal Augereau established himself near the gate of the town, in the house of the Prince's chief gardener. All the servants having fled, the staff found nothing to eat except pineapples and hothouse plums – light food for men who had eaten nothing for twenty-four hours, had passed the previous night on their legs, and the whole day in fighting. But we had the victory, and that magic word makes privation easy to bear.

The Emperor returned to sleep at Jena, where he received news of a success no less than that which he had himself won. The peculiarity of the Battle of Jena was that it was, if one may say so, double, for neither the French nor the Prussian army was wholly before that town: both were divided into two parts and fought two separate battles. While Napoleon was beating the Prussians under Prince Hohenloe as described, the King of Prussia, at the head of his main army, and commanded by the famous Duke of Brunswick, had marched from Weimar towards Naumburg. The King had slept at the village of Auerstädt, not far from the French corps of Marshals Bernadotte and Davout,[5] who were in Naumberg and the neighbouring villages. In order to rejoin the Emperor on the level ground beyond Jena, Bernadotte and Davout had to pass the Saale in front of Naumburg, and traverse the narrow hilly defile of Kösen. Although Davout supposed the King of Prussia and the bulk of his army to be in front of the Emperor, and had no idea that they were so close to him as Auerstädt, the careful soldier took possession during the night of the defile of Kösen and the steep hills enclosing it. The King of Prussia and his marshals had omitted to occupy them, thus imitating the mistake which the Prince of Hohenloe had committed at Jena in not guarding the Landgrafenberg.

The united troops of Bernadotte and Davout amounted to only 44,000 men, while the King of Prussia had 80,000. At daybreak on the 14th the French marshals learned the superiority of the forces which they had to fight, so on all accounts it was their duty to act in concert. Davout, realising this, declared that he was quite willing to put himself under the orders of Bernadotte; but the latter, making light of laurels which he had to share with another, and unable to make a sacrifice in the interest of his country, thought fit to act independently. His pretext was that as the Emperor had ordered him to be at Dornburg by the 13th, he must proceed there on the 14th, leaving Davout to defend himself as best he could with only 25,000 men against 80,000 Prussians.

Issuing from the Kösen defile, the French had drawn up near the village of Hasenhausen, and it was really at this point that the battle took place: the Emperor was mistaken in thinking that he had in front of him at Jena the bulk of the Prussian army. The fight sustained by Davout's troops was one of the most terrible in our history. His divisions, after having triumphantly resisted all the attacks of the enemy's infantry, formed square, repelled numerous cavalry charges and, not content with that, advanced with such resolution that the Prussians gave way at all points; leaving the ground strewn with corpses: including that of the Duke of Brunswick. The King of Prussia and his troops executed a retreat on Weimar in pretty good order, expecting to rally in rear of the victorious corps – as they supposed – of Prince Hohenloe and General Ruchel. These, meanwhile, beaten by Napoleon, were from their side coming to seek support from the troops under the King. The two huge bodies of beaten and demoralised troops having come together on the Erfurt road, the appearance of some French regiments was sufficient to throw them into the greatest confusion: the rout was complete. Thus the bragging of the

73

Prussian officers was punished. The results of this victory were incalculable, and made us masters of nearly the whole of Prussia.

The Emperor expressed his great satisfaction with Marshal Davout and the divisions under him in a general order which was read out to all the companies, even to the wounded in the ambulances. In the following year Napoleon created Davout Duke of Auerstädt, although the battle was fought less in that village than in Hasenhausen; but the King of Prussia had made his headquarters at Auerstädt, and the enemy had given that name to the battle which the French call Jena. The army expected to see Bernadotte severely punished, but he got off with a smart reprimand. The Emperor feared that it would vex his brother Joseph, whose sister-in-law, Mademoiselle Clary, Bernadotte had married. Ironically, it was Bernadotte's behaviour on the day of that battle which, in some sense, was his first step towards the throne of Sweden.[6]

I was not wounded at Jena; but my pride was hurt in a way which, after forty years, still awakens my wrath to remember. It happened thus. The moment when Augereau's corps was attacking the Saxons, the Marshal sent me to General Durosnel, commanding a brigade of *chasseurs*, with orders to charge the enemy's cavalry. I was to guide the brigade by a road which I had already reconnoitred. I hastened to place myself at the head of our *chasseurs* who were dashing at the Saxon squadrons. These latter resisted bravely, but after a short mêlée were compelled to retire with loss. Towards the end of the fight, I found myself face to face with a hussar officer in the white uniform of Prince Albert of Saxony's Regiment. I summoned him to surrender at the sabre's point, which he did by handing me his weapon. The combat over, I was generous enough to give it back to him, as is the practice in such cases, and I added that although by the laws of war his horse now belonged to me, I did not wish to deprive him of it. He thanked me warmly and followed me as I made my way back to the Marshal, to whom I looked forward to presenting my prisoner.

We were 500 paces from the French *chasseurs* when the confounded barbarian drew the sword which I had been gallant enough to return to him, laid open my horse's shoulder, and was on the point of sabring me when I threw myself upon him, although I had no weapon in hand. Fortunately, our bodies were in close contact and he had no room to bring his blade to bear; but he caught me by my epaulette – for I was in full uniform that day – and pulled hard enough to make me lose my balance. My saddle spun round, and there I was with one leg in the air and my head pointing downwards, while my prisoner bolted back towards his comrades. I was furious: both at the position in which I found myself, and at the ingratitude with which the villain repaid my chivalrous treatment of him. As soon as the prisoners were rounded up, I went in search of my Saxon *sabreur* in order to teach him a lesson; but he had disappeared.

The Emperor richly rewarded the parson of Jena; and the Elector of Saxony, when, as the result of the victories of his new ally Napoleon, he had become King, also rewarded this priest, who lived very peaceably until 1814, at which time he took refuge in France to escape the vengeance of the Prussians. They carried him off and imprisoned him in a fortress for two or three years, then the King of Saxony interceded in his favour with Louis XVIII and he claimed the priest as having been arrested without authority. The Prussians agreed to release him and he came to live at Paris.

After the victory of Jena the Emperor gave orders to pursue the enemy in every direction, and our columns made a vast number of prisoners. The King of Prussia only reached Berlin by way of Magdeburg with great difficulty and it is even asserted that the Queen was on the point of falling into the hands of our advance guard. Augereau's corps crossed the Elbe near Dessau. It would take too long to recount the disasters of the Prussian army; it must be sufficient to say that of the troops which had marched against the French not one battalion escaped: they were all captured before the end of the month. The fortresses of Torgau, Erfurt, and Wittenberg opened their gates to the conquerors, who marched on Berlin. Napoleon halted at Potsdam and visited the tomb of Frederick the Great; then he went on to Berlin, where, contrary to his practice, Davout's corps marched at the head of the procession – an honour which it well deserved – for it had done the most fighting of all; Augereau's corps followed, and then the Guard.

My first feeling on returning to Berlin, which I had left not long before a brilliant capital, was one of sympathy with a patriotic population thus brought low by defeat, invasion and the loss of relations and friends. The entry of the Noble Guard however, disarmed and prisoners, aroused in me very different sentiments. The young officers who had sharpened their sabres on the steps of the French embassy were now humble enough. They had begged to be taken around, not through, Berlin; not caring to be paraded in view of the inhabitants who had been witnesses of their old swagger. For this very reason the Emperor gave directions to the troops guarding them to march them through the street in which the French embassy stood. This little bit of revenge was not disapproved by the Berliners, who had no love for the Noble Guard and charged them with having driven the King into war.

7 Lisette

The Battle of Eylau, February 1807

In short, no matter where one looked one saw
nothing but corpses; and beheld men dragging
themselves over the ground; one heard nothing
but heartrending cries. I went away horror-struck.

Jean-Baptiste Barrès[1]

*The French victories of 14 October 1806 were overwhelming.
Within a day Prussia's military capability had been smashed
and on the 27th Napoleon entered Berlin, 'at the head of
20,000 grenadiers and cuirassiers and all our splendid foot
and horse guards. The uniform was as magnificent as at the
Tuileries; the Emperor moved proudly along in his plain dress
with his small hat and his one-sou cockade. His staff was in
full uniform and it was a curious sight to see the worst dressed
man the master of such a splendid army.'[2] It was while in
Berlin, strolling with his comrades, 'Unter den Linden', that
Marbot was accosted by a familiar figure: 'Is it you my boy?
. . . Look at him! I made him what he is!' A delighted Sergeant
Pertelay, having spotted his former protégé, could not resist
embracing him, offering him comical advice, and showing him
off to his cronies: much to the bewilderment of Marbot's
brother officers.*

*Meanwhile the war dragged on. King Frederick William,
now a refugee seeking protection from the Tsar, refused to*

make peace; and a Russian army under General Bennigsen was marching to his aid from the east. Napoleon, determined to prevent Russian intervention in Prussia, pushed on into Poland: his advance guard encountering Bennigsen's Cossacks in the vicinity of Warsaw. The Russians withdrew; and after several inconclusive combats, the French army went into winter quarters. While the bulk of the army was billeted in squalid villages, Marbot lodged with Marshal Augereau in a country house at Christka; and on New Year's Day 1807, he was promoted captain. The French, however, were not to be left in peace. On 18 January Bennigsen launched an offensive against the corps of Marshals Ney and Bernadotte. He retired, however, upon the swift arrival of Napoleon, who pursued him 'at the sword's point' to the town of Eylau (now Bagrationovsk in the Russian enclave around Kaliningrad).

Having hounded the Russians through abominable winter weather, the French evicted them from Eylau on the evening of 7 February. Taking up positions outside the town, the Russians spent a bitter night (30° of frost) in the open. However, with an army of 67,000 men and 450 cannon, Bennigsen decided to offer battle at dawn. Napoleon, equally determined to stand his ground, but with an army of just 45,000, was counting on the arrival of Marshals Ney and Davout. Early next morning, in appalling conditions, the Russians attacked and the French were soon in trouble. Needing to gain the initiative, Napoleon ordered a sickly Marshal Augereau onto the offensive. Marching into a blizzard, VII Corps got hopelessly lost and wandered into the main Russian battery: Augereau was wounded and his corps massacred, sustaining 5,000 casualties in fifteen minutes. The Russians intensified their attacks on the French position; and desperate fighting broke out around the cemetery of Eylau: even the soldiers of Napoleon's bodyguard being drawn into the mêlée.

By 11.30 a.m. Napoleon decided to play his trump card, launching Marshal Murat and the 10,500 troopers of the

Cavalry Reserve against the Russian centre. Smashing through the enemy battalions, wheeling about, and crashing through once more, they executed one of the greatest charges in history: over 1,000 troopers were lost, but Napoleon had bought valuable time. With the arrival of Davout, Ney, and dusk, the fighting gradually died down. Overnight, Bennigsen withdrew, leaving Napoleon master of the field. He, of course, claimed this as a victory: Ney called it a 'massacre without a result'. Marbot, meanwhile, had suffered one of the most traumatic experiences of his career. His story begins, however, back in the autumn of 1805, with the search for a horse.

HAVING two good horses for the coming campaign, I was looking for a third even better specimen to be my charger. It was a difficult thing to find, for though horses were far less dear than now, I had very little money: but chance served me admirably. I met a learned German, Herr von Aister, whom I had known when he was a professor at Sorèze. He had become tutor to the children of a rich Swiss banker, Monsieur Scherer, established at Paris in partnership with Monsieur Finguerlin. He informed me that Monsieur Finguerlin – a wealthy man living in fine style – had a large stud, in the first rank of which figured a lovely mare called Lisette. She was reputedly easy in her paces, as light as a deer, and so well broken that a child could lead her. But this mare, in fact, had a terrible fault: she bit like a bulldog and furiously attacked people whom she disliked; and this had determined Monsieur Finguerlin to sell her. She was bought for Madame de Lauriston, whose husband (one of the Emperor's aides-de-camp), had written to her to get his campaigning outfit ready. When selling the mare, Monsieur Finguerlin had forgotten to mention her fault and that very evening a groom was found disembowelled at her feet. Madame de Lauriston, reasonably alarmed, brought an action to cancel the bargain and the police ordered that a written statement should be placed in Lisette's stall to inform prospective purchasers of her ferocity. Further, any bargain with regard to the mare should be void unless the purchaser declared in writing that his attention had been called to this notice. You may suppose that with such a character as this, the mare was not easy to dispose of, and Herr von Aister informed me that her owner had decided to let her go for what anyone would give. I offered 1,000 francs and, sure enough, Monsieur Finguerlin delivered Lisette to me, though she was worth 5,000. This animal gave me a good deal of trouble for some months. It took four or five men to saddle her and she could only be bridled by covering her eyes and binding all four legs. Once seated upon her back, however, she was a really incomparable mount.

Lisette proved to be a demon. She had already bitten several people while in my possession (not even sparing me) and I was thinking that perhaps I should part with her, when I engaged in my service one Francis Woirland, a man who was afraid of nothing. He had heard of Lisette's bad character and before approaching her, armed himself with a hot roast leg of mutton. When the animal flew at him he held out the mutton – which she seized in her teeth – and burning her gums, palate and tongue, gave out a scream of agony, letting the mutton drop. From that moment Lisette was perfectly submissive to Woirland and did not venture to attack him again. I employed the same method with a like result and Lisette became as docile as a dog. She even became a little more tolerant of the stablemen whom she saw every day; but woe to any strangers who passed her! I could quote twenty instances of her ferocity but I will confine myself to one. While Marshal Augereau was staying at the château of Bellevue near Berlin, the servants of the staff, having observed that when they went to dinner a thief was stealing the sacks of corn that were left in the stable, got Woirland to unfasten Lisette and leave her near the door. The thief duly arrived, slipped into the stable, and was in the act of carrying off a sack when the mare seized him by the neck, dragged him into the middle of the yard and trampled on him; breaking two of the poor fellow's ribs. She had become still more vicious since the Saxon hussar, of whom I have told you, treacherously laid open her shoulder with a sabre-cut on the battlefield of Jena.

Such was the mare I was riding at Eylau at the moment when the fragments of Augereau's army corps, shattered by a hail of musketry and cannon-balls, were trying to rally near the cemetery.[3] Now the 14th Regiment of the Line had remained on a hillock which it could not quit except by order of the Emperor. The snow had ceased for the moment, and we could see how the intrepid regiment, surrounded by the enemy, was waving its eagle in the air to show that it still held its ground and to ask for support. The Emperor, touched by the devotion of these brave men, resolved to save them and ordered Augereau to send an officer with orders to leave the hillock, form square, and make their way towards us; while a brigade of cavalry should be sent to their assistance (this was before Murat's great charge). It was, however, almost impossible to carry out the Emperor's wishes because a swarm of Cossacks was between us and the 14th and it was clear that any officer who was sent towards the unfortunate regiment would be killed or captured.

It was customary in the imperial army for the aides-de-camp to place themselves a few paces from their general and for the one who was in front to go on duty first; then, when he had performed his mission, to return and place himself last, so that each might carry out his orders in turn and dangers be shared equally. A brave captain of engineers named Froissard, who, though not an aide-de-camp, was on the Marshal's staff, happened to be nearest to him and was bidden to carry the Emperor's order to the 14th. Froissard galloped off and we lost sight of him in the midst of the Cossacks and never saw him again nor heard what became of him. The Marshal, seeing that the 14th had not moved, then sent an officer named David: he shared the same fate as Froissard. Probably both were killed and stripped, lying unrecognised among the piles of corpses which littered the ground. For the third time the Marshal called, 'The officer for duty!' It was my turn.

Seeing the son of his old friend (and I venture to say his favourite aide-de-camp) come up, the Marshal's face froze and his eyes filled with tears, for he could not hide the fact that he was sending me to almost certain death. But I was a soldier and the Emperor must be obeyed. It was impossible to make one of my comrades go in my place, nor would I have allowed it, for I would have been disgraced. So I dashed off, ready to sacrifice my life: but bound to take all necessary precautions to preserve it. I had observed that the two officers who went before me had gone with swords drawn, ready to defend themselves against any Cossacks who might attack them on the way. Such a defence I thought ill-considered, since it must have forced them to halt in order to fight a multitude of enemies who were sure to overwhelm them in the end. So I went otherwise to work, and leaving my sword in the scabbard, I regarded myself as a horseman who is trying to win a steeplechase and goes as quickly as possible, by the shortest route, to his appointed goal. Now, as my goal was the hillock occupied by the 14th, I resolved to get there without taking any notice of the Cossacks, whom I abolished in thought. This plan answered perfectly. Lisette, lighter than a swallow and flying rather than running, devoured the intervening space; leaping piles of dead men and horses, ditches, broken gun-carriages and half-extinguished bivouac fires. Thousands of Cossacks swarmed over the plain. The first who saw me acted like sportsmen, who, when beating, start a hare and announce its presence to each other by shouts of 'Your side! Your side!' but none of the other Cossacks tried to stop me. Their numbers being so great, each man thought that I could not avoid his comrades farther on; so that I escaped them all and reached the 14th without either myself or my excellent mare having received the slightest scratch.

I found the 14th formed in square on top of the hillock, but as the slope was very slight the enemy's cavalry had been able to deliver several charges. These had been vigorously repulsed and the regiment was encircled by a bloody rampart, composed of dead horses and dragoons, which I had great difficulty in passing over. Eventually, after much effort, I found my way into the square. Since Colonel Savary's death at the passage of the Wkra,[4] the 14th had been commanded by a major. While I imparted to this officer – under a hail of balls – the order to quit his position, he pointed out to me that the enemy's artillery had been firing on the 14th for an hour and had caused it such loss, that the handful of soldiers which remained would be slaughtered to a man if moved down into the plain. Then, directing my gaze towards a Russian column bearing down on his position and not more than a hundred paces away, the Major said, 'I see no means of saving the regiment. Return to the Emperor, bid him farewell from the 14th of the Line and bear to him the eagle which he gave us and which we can defend no longer: it would add too much to the pain of death to see it fall into the hands of the enemy.' He handed me the eagle, which the survivors saluted for the last time with cries of '*Vive l'Empereur!*' They were about to die for him. It was a cry uttered by heroes.

The infantry eagles were very heavy and their weight was increased by the stout oak pole upon which they were fixed. The length of the pole embarrassed me much and as the stick without the eagle could not constitute a trophy for the enemy, I resolved – with the Major's consent – to break it and carry off the eagle only. At the very moment when I was leaning forward in my saddle, in order to separate the eagle from its pole, one of the numerous cannon-balls which the Russians were sending at us went clean through my hat, less than an inch from my head. The shock was all the more terrible since my hat, being fastened on by a strong leather strap under my chin, offered more resistance to the blow. I seemed to be blotted out of existence; but I did not fall from my horse. Blood flowed from my nose, my ears, and even my eyes: nevertheless, I could still see and hear, and although my limbs were paralysed to such an extent that I could not move a single finger, still I kept my intellectual faculties.

Meanwhile the column of Russian infantry was mounting the hill: grenadiers wearing mitre-shaped caps, with metal ornaments. Soaked with spirits and in vastly superior numbers, these savages hurled themselves furiously on the feeble remains of the 14th, whose soldiers had for days been living on nothing but potatoes and melted snow. Still our brave Frenchmen made a valiant defence with their bayonets; and even when the square was broken, they held together in groups and sustained the unequal fight for a long time.

During this terrible struggle, several of our men, in order not to be struck from behind, set their backs against my mare's flanks; she, contrary to her practice, remaining perfectly quiet. If I had been able to move, I should have urged her forward to escape this field of slaughter, but it was impossible for me to make her understand my wish. My position was the more frightful since, as I have said, I retained the power of sight and thought. Not only were they fighting all around me, which exposed me to bayonet thrusts, but a Russian officer with a hideous countenance kept making efforts to run me through. As the crowd of combatants prevented him from reaching me, he pointed me out to the men around him and they, taking me for the regiment's commander (as I was the only mounted man), kept firing at me over their comrades' heads. Bullets whistled past my ear and one of them would certainly have taken away the small amount of life left in me had not a terrible incident led to my escape from this murderous mêlée.

Among the Frenchmen pressing against my mare's flanks

was a quartermaster-sergeant whom I recognised. This man, having been attacked and wounded by several of the enemy, fell under Lisette's belly and was seizing my leg to pull himself up, when a Russian grenadier, too drunk to stand steady, attempted to finish him with a thrust to the breast. The Russian, losing his balance, plunged his bayonet into my cloak, which at that moment was puffed out by the wind. Seeing that I did not fall, the grenadier left the sergeant and aimed a great number of blows at me, eventually piercing my left arm. I felt with a kind of horrible pleasure my blood flowing warmly. The Russian, with redoubled fury, made another thrust at me, but stumbling with the force which he had put into it, drove his bayonet straight into Lisette's thigh.

Her ferocity restored by the pain, she sprang at the Russian and at one mouthful tore off his nose and all the skin of his face, making of him a living death's head, dripping with blood. Then, hurling herself with fury among the combatants, kicking and biting, Lisette upset everything in her path. The officer who had made so many attempts on my life tried to hold her by the bridle: she seized him by his belly and carrying him off with ease, bore him out of the crush to the foot of the hillock, where, having torn out his entrails and mashed his body under her feet, she left him dying in the snow. Then, taking the road by which she had come, she made her way at full gallop towards the cemetery of Eylau. Thanks to my hussar's saddle I kept my seat; but now a new danger awaited me. The snow had begun to fall again and great flakes obscured the daylight when, having arrived close to Eylau, I found myself in front of a battalion of the Old Guard, who, unable to see clearly, took me for an enemy officer leading a charge of cavalry. The whole battalion at once opened fire on me. My cloak and saddle were riddled but I was not wounded, and nor was my mare. She continued her rapid course and went through the three ranks of the battalion as easily as a snake through a hedge. This last spurt exhausted Lisette's strength; she had lost much blood and the poor animal collapsed suddenly and fell on one side, rolling me over on the other.

Stretched on the snow among piles of dead and dying, unable to move in any way, I gradually and without pain, lost consciousness: gently rocked to sleep by the mighty clatter which Murat's ninety squadrons, advancing to the charge, made in passing close by me. I would guess that my swoon lasted four hours, and when I came to my senses I found myself in this horrible position: I was completely naked, having on nothing but my hat and my right boot. A man of the Transport Corps, thinking me dead, had stripped me in the usual fashion; and wishing to pull off the only boot that remained, was dragging me by one leg, with his foot against my body. I succeeded in sitting up and spitting out the clots of blood from my throat. The shock caused by the wind of the ball had produced such an extravasation of blood that my face, shoulders, and chest were black, while the rest of my body was stained red by blood from my wound. My hat and hair were full of blood-stained snow and as I rolled my haggard eyes I must have looked like some frightful spectre. Anyhow, the Transport man fled (with my property) without my being able to say a single word to him.

My thoughts turned to God and my mother. The setting sun cast some feeble rays through the clouds and I took what I believed to be a last farewell of it. 'If,' thought I, 'I had only not been stripped, someone would notice the gold lace on my *pelisse* and, recognising that I am a marshal's aide-de-camp, would perhaps have carried me to the ambulance. Seeing me naked, they do not distinguish me from the corpses with which I am surrounded; and indeed, there will soon be no difference between them and me.' So I made up my mind to die: for if I had been saved by a miracle in the midst of the terrible mêlée between the Russians and the 14th, could I reasonably expect a second miracle to extract me from my present horrible situation? But it did take place, that second miracle, in the following manner.

Marshal Augereau had a valet named Pierre Dannel, a very intelligent and very faithful fellow, though somewhat given to arguing. Now it happened that during our stay at La Houssaye,[5] Dannel, having answered his master, got dismissed. In despair, he begged me to plead for him. This I did so zealously that I succeeded in getting him taken back into favour. From that time the valet had been devotedly attached to me. The outfit having been left behind at Landsberg, he had started out on his own initiative on the day of the battle, to bring provisions to his master. These he had placed in a wagon, the driver of which being a comrade of the man who had just stripped me. This latter, with my property in his hands, passed near the wagon, which was standing at the side of the cemetery; and recognising the driver – his old comrade – he hailed him and showed off the splendid booty which he had just taken from a 'dead' man.

Now you must know that when we were in cantonments on the Vistula, the Marshal happened to send Dannel to Warsaw for provisions and I commissioned him to get the trimming of black astrakhan taken from my pelisse and have it replaced with grey: this having recently been adopted by Prince Berthier's aides-de-camp, who set the fashion in the army. Up to now, I was the only one of Augereau's officers who wore grey astrakhan. Dannel, who was present when the Transport man made his display, quickly recognised my *pelisse*, which made him look more closely at the other effects of this 'dead' man. Among these he found my watch, which had belonged to my father and was marked with his cypher. The valet no longer had any doubts that I had been killed and, while deploring my loss, he wished to see me for the last time. Guided by the Transport man, Dannel eventually reached me and found me living. Great was the joy of this worthy man, to whom I certainly owed my life. He made haste to fetch my servant and some orderlies, and had me carried to a barn where he rubbed my body with rum. Meanwhile, someone went to fetch Dr Raymond, who came at length, dressed the wound in my arm, and declared that the release of blood due to it would be the saving of me.

My brother and my comrades were soon round me. Something was given to the Transport soldier who had taken my clothes, which he returned very willingly; but as they were saturated with water and blood, Marshal Augereau had me wrapped in clothes belonging to himself. The Emperor had given the Marshal leave to go to Landsberg but as his wound forbad him to ride, his aides-de-camp had procured a sledge, on which the body of a carriage had been placed. The Marshal, who could not make up his mind to leave me, had me fastened up beside him, for I was too weak to sit upright.

Before I was removed from the field of battle I had seen my poor Lisette near me. The cold had caused the blood from her wound to clot and prevented the loss from being too great. The creature had hobbled on to her legs and was eating the straw which the soldiers had used the night before for their bivouacs. My servant, who was very fond of Lisette, had noticed her when he was helping to remove me, and cutting up the shirt of a dead soldier, he made bandages to bind her leg and she limped behind us to Landsberg. The officer in command of the small garrison there had had the forethought to prepare quarters for the wounded, so the staff found places in a good inn. In this way, instead of passing the night without help, stretched naked on the snow, I lay on a good bed surrounded by the attention of my brother, my comrades and the good Dr Raymond. He had been obliged to cut off the boot which the Transport man had not been able to pull off and which had become all the more difficult to remove owing to the swelling of my foot. You will see presently that this very nearly cost me my leg and perhaps my life.

We stayed thirty-six hours at Landsberg. This rest and the good care taken of me restored to me the use of speech and when, on the second day after the battle, Marshal Augereau started for Warsaw, I was able to be carried in the sledge. The journey lasted eight days. Gradually I recovered my strength but at the same time I began to be aware of an icy cold sensation in my right foot. The doctor knew not how to diagnose my inability to rise until, hearing me complaining of my leg, he examined it and found that my foot was gangrened. An accident of my youth was the cause of this new trouble. At Sorèze I had my right foot wounded by the unbuttoned foil of a schoolfellow with whom I was fencing.[6] It seemed that the muscles had become sensitive, and had suffered much from cold while I was lying unconscious on the field of Eylau: thence had resulted a swelling, which explained the difficulty experienced by the soldier in dragging off my right boot. The foot was frostbitten and as it had not been treated in time, gangrene had appeared in the site of the old wound. The place was covered with a scab as large as a five franc piece. The doctor turned pale when he saw the foot. Then, making four servants hold me, he took his knife, lifted the scab and dug the mortified flesh from my foot as one cuts the core of an apple. The pain was great but I did not complain. It was otherwise, however, when the knife reached the living flesh and laid bare the muscles and bones till one could see them moving. Then the doctor, standing on a chair, soaked a sponge in hot sweetened wine, and let it fall, drop by drop, into the hole which he had just dug out of my foot. The pain was unbearable. Still, for eight days I had to undergo this torture morning and evening: but my leg was saved.

Nowadays, when promotions and decorations are bestowed so lavishly, some reward would certainly be given to an officer who had braved danger as I had done in reaching the 14th Regiment; but under the Empire, a devoted act of that kind was thought so natural that I did not receive the cross, nor did it ever occur to me to ask for it.[7] A long rest having been ordered for the cure of Marshal Augereau's wound, the Emperor wrote to bid him return for treatment to France; and sent to Italy for Marshal Masséna, to whom Brô and several of my comrades were attached. Augereau took me with him, as well as Dr Raymond and his secretary. I had to be lifted in and out of the carriage, otherwise I found my health coming back as I got away from those icy regions towards a milder climate. Our road lay through Silesia.[8] So long as we were in that horrible Poland, it required twelve, sometimes sixteen horses to draw the carriage at a walk through the bogs and quagmires; but in Germany we found, at length, civilisation and real roads. Lisette, my mare, passed the winter in the stables of Monsieur de Launay, head of the forage department.

After a halt at Dresden and ten or twelve days' stay at Frankfort, we reached Paris about 15 March. I walked very lame, wore my arm in a sling and still felt the terrible shaking caused by the wind of the cannon-ball; but the joy of seeing my mother again and her kind care of me, together with the sweet influences of the spring, completed my cure. Before leaving Warsaw I had meant to throw away the hat which the ball had pierced, but the Marshal kept it as a curiosity and gave it to my mother. It still exists in my possession and should be kept as a family relic.

8 Furious Heroism

The Battle of Friedland, June 1807

This is no longer a fight, it is butchery.

General Count Bennigsen[1]

Marbot spent the next few months convalescing in Paris and becoming acquainted with a certain Mademoiselle Desbrières, his future wife. By the beginning of May, however, he was ready for duty. Marshal Augereau was still recovering from the wound he received at Eylau. Seeing that Marbot was eager for service, and not wanting to hold the young man back, he recommended him to Marshal Lannes, who received him 'very cordially on his staff'. Marbot joined Lannes on 25 May 1807, being also happily reunited with his mare, Lisette.

On 5 June hostilities recommenced. The Russians, leaving their winter quarters, launched an assault against Marshal Ney's corps. After some initial success, an anxious Bennigsen pulled back to prepared positions around Heilsberg, in the face of a counter-attack by Napoleon. On the 10th the French attacked the Russian line and although Bennigsen made a successful stand, he decided to withdraw during the following night, making for the safety of the River Alle and his base at Friedland (now the Russian town of Pravdinsk). Napoleon, concerned that Bennigsen might occupy the fortress of Kö-nigsberg, sent his army in pursuit. On 13 June, the advance guard of Lannes' V Corps reported a Russian concentration at

Friedland. Heavily outnumbered, Lannes managed to hold off the Russians for nine hours, after which reinforcements began to arrive. At noon the following day Napoleon appeared and realized that Bennigsen had made a fatal error: he had deployed his troops in a bend of the Alle with the river at their backs. The Russians were trapped. Launching a devastating attack, including a deadly short-range artillery bombardment, Napoleon inflicted a massive defeat on the Russians. Bennigsen, who, due to ill health, had collapsed several times during the battle, managed to extricate his army; but at the cost of a third of his men. The defeat at Friedland persuaded Tsar Alexander – unable to stomach further losses – to sue for peace. The Treaty of Tilsit followed: Napoleon was master of Europe.

THE EMPEROR was still at Eylau. The various army corps were marching on Friedland, from which they were several leagues distant, when Lannes, who had marched all night, arrived before the town. If the Marshal had only listened to his own eagerness he would have attacked the enemy on the spot; but they had already 30,000 men in position on the plain in front of Friedland, and their lines (the right of which was in front of Heinrichsdorf, the centre at Millstream, and the left on the village of Sortlack) were being continually strengthened. Lannes had only 10,000 men. These, however, he placed very skilfully in the village of Posthenen, and in the wood of Sortlack, whence he threatened the Russian left, while, with two divisions of cavalry, he tried to stop their march on Heinrichsdorf, a village on the road from Friedland to Königsberg.[2] A brisk fire was opened but Marshal Mortier's[3] corps appeared without delay, and in order to dispute the way to Königsberg with the Russians while he waited for reinforcements, he occupied Heinrichsdorf and the intervening space as far as Posthenen.

Still, it was not possible that Mortier and Lannes could, with 25,000 men, make headway against the 70,000 Russians who would shortly be facing them. The situation was becoming critical. Marshal Lannes was sending officers every instant to warn the Emperor to hurry up the army corps which he knew were on the march behind him. I was the first sent and, mounted on my swift Lisette, I met the Emperor leaving Eylau and found him beaming. He made me come to his side, and as we galloped I gave him a full account of all that had happened before I left the field of battle.

When I had finished my report the Emperor said (smiling), 'Have you a good memory?' 'Pretty fair, sir.' 'Well, what anniversary is it today, 14 June?' 'Marengo.' 'Yes,' replied the Emperor, 'that of Marengo; and I am going to beat the Russians as I beat the Austrians.' So convinced was Napoleon on this point that as he rode along the columns, and while the soldiers saluted him with frequent cheers, he repeatedly cried, 'Today is a lucky day, the anniversary of Marengo!'

It was past eleven when the Emperor arrived on the field of battle. Several army corps had already joined Lannes and Mortier; the rest, with the Guard, came up in due course. Napoleon at once rectified the lines: Ney[4] commanded the right wing, which was placed in the woods of Sortlack; Lannes and Mortier the centre, between Posthenen and Heinrichsdorf; the left extended beyond the latter village. Napoleon, first allowing the troops an hour's rest (for it had become oppressively hot), ordered that a cannonade should be the signal for a general attack.

Ney's corps had the toughest task. Concealed in the wood of Sortlack, it had to issue from it and make its way into Friedland, where the enemy's reserves were massed, capture the bridges, and thus cut off the Russians' retreat. It is difficult to understand how Bennigsen could have made up his mind to place his army in advance of the Friedland defile, where it had in rear the Alle, with its steep banks, and before it the French, who held the plain. To account for this action, the Russian General explained later that, being a day's march ahead of Napoleon, and not being able to conceive that the French could cover in twelve hours a distance equal to that which his troops had taken twenty-four to traverse, he had supposed that Lannes' corps at Friedland was the isolated advance guard of the French army, which he would have no difficulty in crushing.

About 1 p.m. the twenty-five cannon at Posthenen opened up at the Emperor's command and battle was joined all along the line. Our left and centre advanced at first very slowly, in order to give Ney time to carry the town. The Marshal, issuing from the wood at Sortlack, captured the village of that name and advanced very swiftly on Friedland, clearing everything in his path. But in passing from the wood and village of Sortlack to the first houses of Friedland, the troops had to march without cover, and found themselves exposed to a terrible fire from the Russian batteries, which, being placed in rear of the town on the high ground of the opposite bank, caused them immense loss. What made the fire more dangerous was that the enemy's gunners, having the river between us and them, could aim in security, since they saw that it was impossible for our infantry to attack them. This serious disadvantage might have prevented the capture of Friedland but Napoleon remedied it by sending fifty guns, which were placed by General Sénarmont, and fired across the river at the Russian batteries, pouring upon them such a hail of shot as must soon have dismounted them. As soon as the fire from the enemy's guns was silenced, Ney continued his bold march, rolling back the Russians in Friedland, and entering with them pell-mell into the streets of that unlucky town, which shells had already set on fire. There then began a terrible bayonet fight and the Russians, crowded one upon another and hardly able to move, lost very heavily. Ultimately they were obliged, in spite of their courage, to retire in disorder, and seek refuge on the opposite bank, crossing the bridges again. But here a new danger awaited them. General Sénarmont's artillery, having drawn nearer the town, took the bridges in flank, breaking them, and killing a great many Russians who were crossing in their hurried flight. All who remained in Friedland were captured, killed, or drowned in crossing the river.

Up to this time Napoleon had, so to say, made his centre and left wing mark time. Now he pushed them rapidly forward. The Russian general, Gortschakoff, who commanded the enemy's centre and right wing, obeying merely his own courage, decided to recapture the town. This would have been of no use to him, since the bridges were broken, but this he did not know; so he dashed forwards at the head of his troops into Friedland, blazing as it was. However, smartly evicted by Ney's troops, who occupied the town, and compelled to regain the open country, the enemy General soon found himself surrounded by our centre, which pushed him back on the Alle, in front of Kloschenen. The Russians defended themselves with furious heroism, and although driven in on all sides, refused to surrender. A large number fell under our bayonets, and the rest were rolled back from the top of the bank into the river, where most were drowned.

The enemy's extreme right, consisting chiefly of cavalry, had attempted to carry or turn the village of Heinrichsdorf; but repulsed briskly by our troops, it had regained the banks of the Alle, under the command of General Lambert. Seeing Friedland occupied by the French, and the Russian left and centre destroyed, he rallied as many regiments as he could of the right wing, and escaped from the field of battle by descending the Alle. Nightfall prevented the French from pursuing, so that of all the enemy's corps this one alone escaped utter rout. Our victory was most complete: all the Russian artillery fell into our hands. We had taken few prisoners during the action, but the numbers of enemy killed and wounded amounted to more than 26,000.[5] Our loss was only 3,000 killed and about 5,000 wounded. The remains of the enemy army marched in disorder all night, and retired behind the River Pregel, destroying the bridges. Marshals Soult, Davout and Murat had not been able to take part in the battle, but their appearance had decided the Prussians to abandon Königsberg, and our troops took possession of it, finding there immense stores of all kinds.

No accident befell me during the Battle of Friedland, although I was exposed to very great dangers. I had been sent by Marshal Lannes to warn the Emperor that the enemy was crossing the Alle at Friedland and that a battle appeared imminent. Napoleon was at Eylau and I had nearly six leagues to cover in order to meet him. This would have been a small matter for my excellent mare had the roads been clear, but encumbered as they were by troops hastening to the support of Marshal Lannes, I found it impossible to gallop; so I cut across country with the result that Lisette, having jumped fences, hedges and ditches, was well blown by the time I reached Napoleon, coming out of Eylau.

Without a moment's rest, I was obliged to turn tail and return with the Emperor to Friedland – this time everyone drew aside to let us pass – but my poor mare, who had galloped twelve leagues at a stretch on a very hot day, was completely beaten when I reached the field of battle and rejoined Marshal Lannes. Lisette, having done so much, could do no more and I took advantage of a moment's rest which the Emperor granted the troops, to try and find my servant and change horses. But in the midst of an army of that size, how was I to find my belongings? It was impossible and I returned to the staff, still mounted on the exhausted Lisette.

Marshal Lannes, seeing the fix I was in, advised me to dismount and let my mare rest for a few hours. At that moment I saw one of our hussars leading a horse which he had captured. I bought it there and then, and entrusting Lisette to a trooper of the Marshal's escort, resumed my place among the aides-de-camp and took my turns of duty. At first I was well satisfied with my new mount, until Lannes sent me off to Marshal Ney (who was by that time in Friedland) to warn him of a movement which the enemy was making. Hardly was I in the town when this devil of a horse, who had behaved so well in open country, finding himself in a little square with houses on fire all around, the pavements covered with burning timber and half-roasted corpses, was so terrified that he refused to budge. Putting his four feet together, he stood stock still and snorted violently, without taking the slightest notice of the spur, which I vigorously applied.

Meanwhile the Russians, having gained a momentary advantage in a street close by, were pushing our men back; pouring a hail of bullets from a church tower and plying the battalions, by whom I was surrounded, with grape from two guns which they had dragged up. Many fell around me and I was reminded of the position in which I had found myself at Eylau. As I had no curiosity whatever to see what another wound felt like, I got off my infernal horse and slipped along the houses to join Ney, who was in another square which some officers pointed out to me. I remained a quarter of an hour with him while the bullets dropped all around. Finally, a bayonet charge drove the Russians back and compelled them to retire on all sides towards the bridges. Ney bade me take this good news to Lannes. I returned by the same way which I had taken in coming and passed again the spot where I had left my horse: it had been the scene of a sanguinary fight – nothing was to be seen but dead and dying – and in the middle of them was the obstinate horse, his back broken by a cannon-ball and his body riddled with bullets.

I hurried on to the end of the suburbs, for burning houses were falling down on all sides and I feared to be buried in the ruins. At last I got out of the town and reached the edge of the lake. The heat of the day, combined with that of the fire in the streets which I had passed through had made me steam. I was

half-suffocated and dropping with fatigue; and did not, therefore, welcome the prospect of having to cross on foot (under a
burning sun and through tall corn) the immense plain which
lay between me and Posthenen, where I had left Marshal
Lannes: but fortune stood my friend. Grouchy's division of
dragoons, which had been briskly engaged with the enemy
close by, though victorious, had lost a certain number of men
and, as a result, the horses of the killed were being led by a
detachment some distance from the rest. I caught sight of this
picket, every man of which was leading four or five horses
towards the lake to water them. I spoke to the officer, who was
only too glad to let me take one, and I promised to send it back
to his regiment in the evening. He even selected for me an
excellent animal which had been ridden by a sergeant killed in
the charge. I mounted and returned quickly to Posthenen.
Hardly had I left the shore of the lake, when it became the
scene of a most bloody fight, owing to the desperate attack
made by General Gortschakoff in order to effect his retreat by
the Friedland road, of which Marshal Ney was in occupation.

I rejoined Lannes just as he was starting to attack Gortschakoff's force in the rear; while Ney, from the town, was
repulsing it in front. If the French army had made few prisoners on the battlefield of Friedland, it was not so on the morrow
and the following days, for the Russians, driven at the sword's
point in an utter rout, fell out from their ranks and slept in the
fields, where we captured a great number. We also gathered up
a good deal of artillery. All of Bennigsen's army that could
escape made haste to recross the Niemen, behind which the
Emperor of Russia had stayed. Remembering the dangers to
which he had been exposed at Austerlitz, he had not thought it
advisable to be present in person at the Battle of Friedland and
lost no time in asking – and obtaining – an armistice.

9 A Providential Rescue

Spain, November 1808

My mission . . . was most perilous; not merely in respect of the danger of death, but chiefly on account of the tortures that the Spaniards – with their natural ferocity exalted by religious and political passion – used to inflict on the French who fell into their hands. We had fresh proofs of it every day and the notion of being sawn asunder between two planks, and crucified after mutilation, was not pleasant.

Colonel de Gonneville[1]

By July 1807 Napoleon had defeated every army sent against him. Britain, however, remained his implacable enemy. The Emperor, therefore, decided to wage an economic war against the 'nation of shopkeepers' by closing all European ports to British goods. It was a drastic step, and one which threatened France and her allies with severe economic hardship – even ruin. Napoleon hoped, however, that the British economy would be hit harder and more quickly; and that 'perfidious Albion' would be forced to her knees. It was the inability of the corrupt and inefficient Spanish government to enforce this blockade; and the refusal of the pro-British Portuguese, which led Napoleon to meddle in the affairs of the Peninsula. In November 1807 General Junot was sent through Spain – a nominal ally of France – to attack the Portuguese: the royal family fled abroad (taking their treasure with them – much to Junot's chagrin) and Lisbon fell on 1 December. The ensuing occupation of Portugal provided Napoleon with a pretext for a military presence in Spain; and in March 1808 Murat was sent to Madrid at the head of a large army – supposedly reinforcements for Junot. At first the Spanish welcomed the French as allies; but Murat had secret orders to occupy the capital. Marbot calls what followed a 'scandalous affair . . . unworthy of so great a man', as Napoleon engineered the downfall of the Spanish monarchy, 'persuading' King Charles IV and his son Ferdinand[2] to abdicate (in return for personal fortunes and exile in France); and having his own brother Joseph 'elected' king.

Napoleon had seen a rotten and corrupt Spanish administration, assumed it to be unpopular, and removed it. What followed was a spontaneous rising of the whole population in a wave of indignation and anti-French feeling. A violent insurrection broke out and a 'war to the knife' declared against the invaders. Although a somewhat unwilling Joseph Bonaparte (he was quite happy as King of Naples) was proclaimed king on 24 July, within eight days he had fled his capital as the country erupted about him: Napoleon's 'Spanish ulcer' was only just beginning.

Marbot was not proud of the French subjugation of Spain: 'As a soldier I was bound to fight any who attacked the French army, but I could not help recognising in my inmost conscience that our cause was a bad one, and that the Spaniards were quite right in trying to drive out strangers, who, after coming among them in the guise of friends, were wishing to dethrone their sovereign and take forcible possession of the kingdom. This war, therefore, seemed to me wicked, but I was a soldier, and I must march or be charged with cowardice. The greater part of the army thought as I did, and, like me, obeyed orders all the same.'

Napoleon, however, was enraged to hear of his brother's flight and the French defeats which preceded it; especially General Dupont's capitulation at Bailén, where a French force of 23,000, laden with plunder, surrendered to General Castaños. Gathering together an army of veterans, he determined to march into Spain and take personal command of events.

BY NAPOLEON'S OWN ADVICE, Marshal Augereau declined to go on the Spanish campaign and he therefore asked Marshal Lannes to take me with him. So in November 1808 I set out for Bayonne, where I was to report to my new chief. Nearly all the officers who had been on Lannes' staff having got promotion at the Peace of Tilsit, the Marshal was obliged to form a new staff for Spain. He himself was a man of strong character; but from various causes he was obliged to select officers of little experience in war. They were all brave enough; but it was the least military staff on which I had ever served. The senior aide-de-camp was Colonel O'Meara, brother-in-law to Clarke, Duke of Feltre.[3] He ended his days as commandant of a small place on the Belgian frontier. Then came Major Guéhéneuc, brother-in-law to Lannes, who commanded the 26th Light Infantry at the Beresina. Major Saint-Mars was the third. After being taken prisoner in Russia, he became general secretary of the Legion of Honour. I was the fourth. The fifth was Marquis Serafino d'Albuquerque, a great Spanish noble, fond of good living, but as brave as a bull: he was killed by a cannon-ball at Essling. The sixth was Captain de Watteville, who also went on the Russian campaign as a major of lancers. In spite of my care, he succumbed to cold and fatigue at Wilna. The seventh was the famous Labédoyère. He was a tall and handsome man; brave, cultivated, witty, and a good talker, though with a slight stammer. He became aide-de-camp to Prince Eugène Beauharnais, and was a colonel in 1814. The story of how he brought his regiment over to the Emperor at his return from

Elba is, of course, well known. Under the Restoration he was tried and shot.[4] The eighth aide-de-camp was named de Viry; he belonged to an ancient Savoyard family. So far as I knew, he had no bad qualities, and I became very intimate with him. He was severely wounded at Essling and died in my arms at Vienna. Besides these, the Marshal had two supernumerary officers attached to his staff, Captain Dagusan and Sub-Lieutenant Le Couteulx de Cantelu.

On my joining the staff, Marshal Lannes warned me that he reckoned very much on my help, both on account of the report of me which he had received from Augereau, and from the manner in which I had served under himself in the Friedland campaign. 'If you don't get killed,' said he, 'I will see that your promotion comes quickly.' The Marshal never promised in vain, and he was in such high favour with the Emperor that everything was possible to him. I promised to do my duty with unswerving courage and zeal.

We left Bayonne and marched with the troops as far as the River Ebro, where we joined King Joseph and the army which had made the recent campaign. Camp life had given these young recruits a military air, which they had been far from having in the previous July. But what most raised their tone was finding themselves under the command of the Emperor in person, and hearing that the veterans of the Grand Army had arrived. The Spaniards on their side were astonished and alarmed at the sight of the old grenadiers of the Grand Army, and realised that a change in the aspect of affairs was going to take place. And indeed, hardly had the Emperor arrived on the Ebro, when he launched numerous columns across the river. All that tried to make head against them were crushed or saved themselves by a rapid flight. The Spaniards, however, astonished but not discouraged, rallied several army corps under the walls of Burgos, and made bold to accept battle. It took place on 9 November and did not last long: driven in at the first charge, the enemy fled in all directions, pursued by our cavalry, and with heavy loss.

During this battle, a remarkable incident occurred. Two young infantry sub-lieutenants quarrelled and fought a duel in front of their battalion, under a storm of cannon-balls hurled from the enemy lines. One of them had his cheek laid open by a sword-cut. The Colonel put them under arrest and brought them before the Marshal, who sent them to the citadel of Burgos, and reported them to the Emperor. He gave them a further punishment, forbidding them to go into action with their company for a month. At the end of this period, the regiment to which these two foolish fellows belonged was being reviewed by the Emperor at Madrid. He ordered the Colonel to present to him (as usual) those whom he proposed to promote in the place of officers killed. The sub-lieutenant who had been wounded in the cheek was an excellent soldier and his Colonel thought that he ought not to lose his promotion for a fault which, though serious, was not dishonourable. He therefore submitted his name to the Emperor, who, perceiving the scar on the young man's face, and remembering the duel at Burgos, asked him in a severe tone: 'Where did you get that wound?' Thereupon the sub-lieutenant, wishing neither to tell a lie nor to confess, turned the difficulty rather cleverly. Placing his finger on his cheek, he said, 'I got it *there* sir.' The Emperor understood, and as he liked men of a ready wit, far from being angry at this original repartee, he smiled and said to the officer, 'Your Colonel proposes you for the rank of lieutenant; I grant it to you, but in future behave better or I will cashier you.'

At Burgos I found my brother, who was on the staff of Marshal Berthier, Chief of the General Staff. Lannes' military talent increased every day and the Emperor, who had a very high opinion of him, no longer gave him any stated command, wishing to keep him about his person and send him wherever things had got into disorder, being sure that he would quickly set them to rights. Thus, considering that he had left the town of Zaragoza occupied by the insurgents of Aragon, and supported by the army of Castaños which had conquered Dupont, and that old General Moncey was only bungling, Napoleon ordered Lannes to go to Logroño, to take command of the army on the Ebro, and attack Castaños. Thus Moncey came under the orders of Lannes. It was the first case in which one marshal of the Empire had commanded another.

Lannes showed himself worthy of this mark of confidence and distinction. He started, accompanied by his staff alone, and we travelled by post. You must know that at this time there were no draught horses in Spain, but the post houses kept the best nags in Europe. We rode night and day, escorted from stage to stage by detachments of cavalry. In this way we went back as far as Miranda del Ebro, whence we reached Logroño, following the river. Marshal Moncey appeared much annoyed at finding himself, the senior marshal, placed under the orders of the junior, but he had no choice but to obey.

See what the presence of a single capable and energetic man can do! This army of recruits, which Moncey had not dared to lead against the enemy, were set in motion by Lannes on the day of his arrival, and marched against the enemy with ardour. We came up on the following day, the 23rd, in front of Tudela, and after three hours' fighting the conquerors of Bailén were driven in, beaten, and completely routed: fleeing headlong towards Zaragoza, leaving thousands of dead on the field. We captured a great many men, several colours, and all the artillery.

During this affair I had a lively quarrel with Labédoyère over the following matter. He had just bought a young and ill-broken horse, which at the sound of the cannon reared up and absolutely refused to go on. Labédoyère leaped off in a rage, drew his sword, and hamstrung the poor beast, who fell bleeding on the grass, dragging himself along by his forefeet.

I could not contain my indignation, and expressed it to him in strong terms; but Labédoyère took it very ill, and we should have come to blows had we not been in the presence of the enemy. The report of this incident got about in the staff and Marshal Lannes, very angry, declared that he would not have Labédoyère any more among his aides-de-camp. The latter, in despair, had seized his pistols to blow out his brains, when our friend de Viry suggested to him that it would be more honourable to seek death in the ranks of the enemy than to inflict it upon himself.

Just at that moment, de Viry, who was near the Marshal, was ordered to lead a cavalry regiment against the Spanish battery. Labédoyère joined the regiment as it was charging, and was one of the first to dash into the battery. It was carried, and we saw de Viry and Labédoyère bringing back a gun which they had taken together. Neither of them was wounded, but Labédoyère had got a grapeshot through his bearskin,[5] two inches from his head. The Marshal was much touched by this courageous act; all the more so that, after having handed over the gun to him, Labédoyère was getting ready to hurl himself a second time onto the enemy's bayonets. The Marshal held him back and, pardoning his fault, restored to him his place on the staff. That evening Labédoyère came in the most honourable way to shake hands with me, and we ever afterwards lived on the best of terms. He and de Viry were named in the despatches and promoted to captains a little time after the battle.

I have now reached one of the most terrible experiences of my military career. Marshal Lannes had just won a great victory and the next day, after having received the reports of the generals, he wrote his despatch for one of our officers to take to the Emperor. Napoleon's practice was to advance a step the officer who brought him news of an important success; and the marshals, on their side, entrusted such tasks to officers for whose speedy promotion they were anxious. It was a form of recommendation which Napoleon never failed to recognise. Marshal Lannes did me the honour of appointing me to carry the news of the victory at Tudela; and I could indulge the hope of being a major before long. But alas! I had yet much blood to lose before I reached that rank.

The high road from Bayonne to Madrid by Vittoria, Miranda del Ebro, Burgos and Aranda, forks off at Miranda from that leading to Zaragoza by Logroño. A road from Tudela to Aranda across the mountains forms the third side of this great triangle. While Lannes was reaching Tudela, the Emperor had advanced from Burgos to Aranda. It was, therefore, much shorter for me to go from Tudela to Aranda than by way of Miranda del Ebro. The latter road, however, had the advantage of being covered by the French armies; while the other, no doubt, would be full of Spanish fugitives, taking refuge in the mountains after the recent battle. The Emperor, however, had informed Lannes that he was sending Marshal Ney's corps direct from Aranda to Tudela; so, thinking Ney to be at no great distance, Lannes ordered me to take the shortest road. I may frankly admit that if I had had my choice, I should have preferred to make the round by Miranda and Burgos, but the Marshal's orders were positive; and how could I express my fear in the presence of a man who didn't even know the meaning of the word?

The duties of a marshal's aide-de-camp in Spain were terrible. During the Revolutionary Wars the generals had couriers paid by the state to carry their despatches; but Napoleon, finding that these gentlemen were not capable of giving any intelligible account of what they had seen, did away with them, and ordered that in future all despatches should be carried by aides-de-camp. This was all very well as long as we were at war among the Germans – to whom it never occurred to attack a French messenger – but the Spaniards waged a fierce war against them.[6] This was of great advantage to the insurgents, for the contents of our despatches informed them of the movements of our armies. I do not think I am exaggerating when I say that more than twenty staff officers were killed or captured during the Peninsular War. One may regret the death of an ordinary courier, but it is less serious – in a military sense – than the loss of a promising officer, who is also exposed to the risks of the battlefield in addition to those of a posting journey.

Just as I was starting from Tudela, Major Saint-Mars hazarded a remark intended to dissuade Lannes from sending me over the mountains. The Marshal, however, answered, 'Oh, he will meet Ney's advance guard tonight and find troops echeloned all the way to the Emperor's headquarters.' This was too decided for any opposition, so I left Tudela on 4 November[7] at nightfall, with a detachment of cavalry, and got as far as Taragona, at the foot of the mountains, without any trouble. In this little town I found Lannes' advance guard. The officer in command, hearing nothing of Ney, had pushed an infantry post six leagues ahead, in the direction of Agreda; but as this body was detached from its supports, it had been ordered to fall back on Taragona if the night passed without Ney's scouts appearing.

After Taragona there is no more high road. The way lies entirely over mountain paths covered with stones and rocks. The officer commanding our advance guard had, therefore, only infantry and a score of hussars of the 2nd (Chamborant) Regiment. He gave me two orderlies, and I went on my way in brilliant moonlight. When we had gone two or three leagues, we heard several musket shots. Bullets whistled past us close-by but we could not see the marksmen, who were hidden among the rocks. A little farther on we found the corpses of two French soldiers, recently murdered. They were entirely stripped, but their shakos were lying nearby, the numbers on which told me that they had belonged to one of the regiments in Ney's corps. A little farther, and we saw another, more horrible sight. A young officer of the 10th Chasseurs, still wearing his uniform, had been nailed, upside down, to a barn door. A small fire had been lighted beneath him. As his blood still flowed from his wounds, it was clear that his murderers were not far off. I drew my sword; my two hussars clutched their carbines.

It was just as well that we were on our guard, for a few moments later seven or eight Spaniards, two of them mounted, fired upon us from behind the bushes. My two hussars replied to the fire (we were none of us wounded) and each killed his man. Then, drawing their swords, they dashed at the rest. I should have been very glad to follow them, but my horse had lost a shoe among the stones and was limping so badly that I could not get him into a gallop. I was the more vexed because I feared that the hussars might let themselves be carried away in their pursuit and get killed in some ambush. I called them for five minutes; then I heard the voice of one of them crying, in a strong Alsatian accent, 'Ah! You thieves! You don't know the Chamborant Hussars yet. You shall see that they mean business!' My troopers had knocked over two more Spaniards: a Capuchin friar mounted on the horse of the poor murdered lieutenant (whose haversack he had put over his own neck), and a peasant on a mule, with the clothes of the slaughtered soldiers on his back. The Emperor had given strict orders that every Spanish civilian taken in arms should be shot on the spot; and, moreover, what could we do with these two brigands who were already badly wounded, and who had just killed three Frenchmen so barbarously? I moved on, therefore, so as not to witness the execution; and the hussars polished off the monk and the peasant, repeating, 'Ah, you don't know the Chamborant!' I could not understand how an officer and two privates of Ney's corps could be so near Taragona, when their regiments had not come that way. Most probably they had been captured elsewhere, and were being taken to Zaragoza, when their escort learned of the defeat of their countrymen at Tudela, and slaughtered the prisoners in revenge.

After this not very encouraging start I continued my journey. We had gone for some hours when we saw a bivouac fire
belonging to a detachment of the advance guard which I had
left at Taragona. The lieutenant in command, having no news
of Ney, was prepared to return to Taragona at daybreak, in
pursuance of his orders. He knew that he was barely two
leagues from Agreda, but did not know which side had
possession of the town. This was perplexing for me. The
infantry detachment would return in a few hours, and if I
went back with it (when it might be that in another league I
should fall in with Ney's column) I should be giving a poor
display of my courage, and laying myself open to reproach
from Marshal Lannes. On the other hand, if Ney was still a
day or two's march away, it was almost certain that I should
be murdered by the peasants of the mountains. What was
more, I had to travel alone, for my two hussars had orders to
travel to Taragona when we had found the infantry detachment. No matter: I determined to push on. But then came the
difficulty of finding a mount. There was no farm or village in
this deserted place where I could procure a horse. That which I
was riding was dead lame; and even if the hussars had been
able – without incurring severe punishment – to lend me one of
theirs, they were blown anyway and much fatigued. The horse
that had belonged to the officer of *chasseurs* had received a
bullet in the thigh during the fighting, so there was only the
peasant's mule left. This was a handsome beast, and according
to the laws of war, belonged to the two hussars who, no doubt,
reckoned on selling her when they got back to the army. Still,
the fellows made no demur about lending her to me, and put
my saddle on her back. But the infernal beast – more accustomed to the pack than the saddle – was so restive that she fell
to kicking; until I had to choose between being sent over a
precipice and dismounting: so I set out on foot.

After I had taken farewell of the infantry officer, this
excellent man, Tassin by name (he had been a friend of my

brother Felix at the military school), came running after me saying that he could not bear to see me go on alone; and that although he had no orders, and his men were all raw recruits, he must send one with me; so that I might at least have a musket and some cartridges in case of an attack. We agreed that I should send the man back with Ney's corps, whenever I should meet it; and so off I went, with the soldier accompanying me. He was a slow-speaking Norman, with plenty of slyness under an appearance of good nature. The Normans are brave, for the most part, as I learned when I commanded the 23rd Chasseurs, where I had five or six hundred of them. Still, in order to know how far I could rely on my follower, I chatted with him as we went along, and asked if he would stand his ground if we were attacked. He said neither yes or no, but answered, 'Well, zur, we shall zee.' Whence I inferred that when the moment of danger arrived, my new companion was not unlikely to go and see how things were getting along in the rear.

The moon had just set and it was pitch dark. At every step we stumbled over the great stones with which these mountain paths are covered. It was an unpleasant situation, but I hoped soon to come upon Ney's troops, and the fact of having seen the bodies of soldiers belonging to his corps increased that hope. So I went steadily on, listening to the Norman's stories by way of diversion. Dawn at last appeared, and I saw the first houses of a large village: it was Agreda. I was alarmed at finding no outposts, for it showed that not only did no troops occupy the place, but that Ney's corps must be at least half a day's march further on. The map showed no village within five or six leagues of Agreda, and it was impossible that the regiments could be quartered in the mountains, far from any inhabited place: so I kept on my guard and before going any farther reconnoitred the position.

Agreda stands in a broad valley. It is built at the foot of a lofty hill, deeply escarped on both sides. The southern slope, which reaches the village, is planted with large vineyards. The ridge is rough and rocky, and the northern slope covered with thick coppice: a torrent flowing at the foot. Beyond are seen high mountains, uncultivated and uninhabited. The principal street runs the whole length of the place, with narrow lanes leading to the vineyards beyond. As I entered the village, I had these lanes and vineyards on my right. This detail is important to the understanding of my story. All were asleep in Agreda: the moment was favourable for going through it. Besides, I had some hope – feeble, it is true – that when I reached the farther end I might perhaps see the fires of Marshal Ney's advance guard: so I went forward, sword in hand, bidding my soldier cock his musket. The main street was covered with a thick bed of damp leaves, which the people had placed there to make manure, and so our footsteps made no sound, of which I was glad. I walked in the middle of the street, with my companion on my right; but finding himself in a too conspicuous position, he gradually sheered off to the houses, keeping close to the walls, so that he might be less visible in case of attack, or better placed for reaching one of the lanes which open into the country. This showed me how little I could rely on the man; but I made no remark to him. Day was beginning to break.

We passed the whole of the main street without meeting anyone. Just as I was congratulating myself on reaching the last houses of the village, I found myself at twenty-five paces' distance, face to face with four Royal Spanish *carabiniers* on horseback: swords drawn. In any other circumstances I might have taken them for French *gendarmes*, their uniforms being similar, but the *gendarmes* never march with the advance guard. These men, therefore, could not belong to Ney's corps, and I at once perceived they were the enemy. In a moment I faced about; but just as I had turned around to the direction from which I had come, I saw a blade flash six inches from my face. I threw my head sharply back but nevertheless got a severe sabre-cut on the forehead; of which I still carry the scar over my left eyebrow to this day.

The man who had wounded me was the corporal of the *carabiniers*, who, having left his four troopers outside the village, had – according to military practice – gone forward to reconnoitre. That I had not met him was probably due to the fact that he had been in some side lane while I passed through the main street. Seeing me, he had come up noiselessly over the wet leaves, and was just going to cleave my head from behind, when, by turning round, I presented to him my face and received his blow on the forehead. At the same moment the four *carabiniers*, who, seeing that their corporal was ready for me, now trotted up to join him, and all five dashed upon me. I ran mechanically towards the houses on the right in order to get my back against a wall; but by good luck I found, two paces off, one of the steep and narrow lanes which went up to the vineyards. My soldier had already reached it. I flew up there too, with the five Spaniards after me; but they could not attack me all at once, for there was only room for one horse to pass at a time. The corporal went in front; the other four filed after him.

My position, although not as unfavourable as it would have been in the open street, still remained alarming; the blood flowing freely from my forehead had, in a moment, covered my left eye with which I could not see at all; and I could not staunch it, being obliged to defend myself against the corporal, who was cutting at me heavily. I parried as well as I could, going backwards all the time. After getting rid of my scabbard and my bearskin, the weight of which hampered me, and not daring to turn my head for fear of losing sight of my adversary, whose sword was crossed with mine, I told my infantryman (whom I believed to be behind me) to place his musket on my shoulder and fire at the Spanish corporal. Seeing no barrel, I leapt a pace back and turned my head quickly: lo and behold, there was my scoundrel of a Norman soldier, flying up the hill as fast as his legs could carry him. The corporal thereupon attacked with redoubled fury and, seeing that he could not reach me, made his horse rear, so that his feet struck me more than once on the breast. Luckily, as the ground went on rising, the horse had no good hold with his hind legs, and every time that he came down again, I landed a sword-cut on his nose with such effect that the animal presently refused to lunge at me any more.

The corporal, losing his temper, called out to the trooper behind him, 'Take your carbine: I will stoop down and you can aim at the Frenchman over my shoulders.' I saw that this order was my death-knell; but as the trooper had to sheathe his sword and unhook his carbine, and that all this time the corporal never ceased thrusting at me, leaning right over his horse's neck, I determined on a desperate action which would either be my salvation or my ruin. Keeping my eye fixed on the corporal and seeing in his that he was on the point of again stooping over his horse to reach me, I did not move until the very instant when he was lowering the upper part of his body towards me; then I took a pace to the right, and leaning quickly over to that side, I avoided my adversary's blow, and plunged half my sword-blade into his left flank. With a fearful yell the corporal fell back on the croup of his horse; he would probably have fallen to the ground if the trooper behind him had not caught him in his arms. My rapid movement in stooping had caused the despatch which I was carrying to fall out of the pocket of my *pelisse*. I picked it up quickly, and at once hastened to the end of the lane where the vines began. There I turned around and saw the *carabiniers* busy with their wounded corporal, and apparently much embarrassed with him and with their horses in the steep and narrow passage.

This fight took less time than I have taken to relate it. Finding myself rid, at least for the moment, of my enemies, I went through the vines and reached the edge of the hill. Then I considered that it would be impossible for me to accomplish my errand and reach the Emperor at Aranda. I resolved, therefore, to return to Marshal Lannes, regaining first the place where I had left Monsieur Tassin and his picket of infantry. I did not hope to find them still there; but at any rate the army which I had left the day before was in that direction. I looked for my soldier in vain, but I saw something that was of more use to me: a spring of clear water. I halted there a moment, and tearing off a corner of my shirt, I made a compress which I fastened over my wound with my hand-kerchief. The blood spurting from my forehead had stained the despatches which I held in my hand, but I was too much occupied with my awkward position to mind that.

The agitations of the past night, my long walk over the stony paths in boots and spurs, the fight in which I had just been engaged, the pain in my head, and the loss of blood had exhausted my strength. I had taken no food since leaving Tudela, and here I had nothing but water to refresh myself with. I drank long draughts, and should have rested longer by the spring, had I not perceived three of the Spanish *carabiniers* riding out of Agreda and coming towards me through the vines. If they had been sharp enough to dismount and take off their long boots, they would probably have succeeded in reaching me; but their horses, unable to pass between the vinestocks, ascended the steep and rocky paths with difficulty. Indeed, when they reached the upper end of the vineyards, they found themselves brought up by the great rocks, on the top of which I had taken refuge, and unable to climb any farther. Then the troopers, passing along the bottom of the rocks, marched parallel with me, a long musket-shot off. They called to me to surrender, saying that as soldiers they would treat me as a prisoner of war, while if the peasants caught me I should be murdered. This reasoning was sound, and I admit that if I had not been charged with despatches for the Emperor, I was so exhausted that I should perhaps have surrendered.

However, wishing to preserve to the best of my ability the

precious charge which had been entrusted to me, I marched on without answering. Then the three troopers, taking their carbines, opened fire upon me. Their bullets struck the rocks at my feet but none touched me, the distance being too great for a correct aim. I was alarmed, not at the fire, but at the notion that the reports would probably attract the peasants who would be going to their work in the morning, and quite expected to be attacked by these fierce mountaineers. My presentiment seemed to be verified, for I perceived some fifteen men less than half a league away in the valley, advancing towards me at a run. They held in their hands something that flashed in the sun. I made no doubt that they were peasants armed with their spades. I gave myself up for lost, and in my despair, I was on the point of letting myself slide down over the rocks on the north side of the hill to the torrent, crossing it as best I could, and hiding myself in some chasm of the great mountains, which arose on the farther side of the gorge. Then, if I was not discovered, and if I still had the strength, I should set out when night came in the direction of Taragona.

This plan, though offering many chances of failure, was my last hope. Just as I was about to put it into execution, I perceived that the three carabineers had given up firing on me, and gone forward to reconnoitre the group which I had taken for peasants. At their approach the iron instruments which I had taken for spades or mattocks were lowered, and I had the inexpressible joy of seeing a volley fired at the Spanish *carabiniers*. Instantly turning, they took flight towards Agreda with two of their number wounded. 'The newcomers are French!' I exclaimed. 'Here goes to meet them!' and, regaining a little strength from the joy of being delivered, I descended, leaning on my sword. The French had caught sight of me; they climbed the hill, and I found myself in the arms of the brave Lieutenant Tassin.

This providential rescue came about as follows. The soldier who had deserted me while I was engaged with the *carabiniers* in the streets of Agreda had quickly reached the vines; thence, leaping across the vinestocks, ditches, rocks and hedges, he had run the two leagues which lay between him and the place where we had left Monsieur Tassin's picket. The detachment was on the point of starting for Taragona, and was eating its soup, when my Norman came up all out of breath. Not wishing, however, to lose a mouthful, he seated himself by the cooking-pot and began to make a very tranquil breakfast, without saying a word about what had happened at Agreda. By great good luck he was noticed by Monsieur Tassin, who, surprised at seeing him returned, asked where he had quitted the officer whom he had been told to escort. 'Good Lord, sir,' replied the Norman, 'I left him in that big village with his head half split open, and fighting with Spanish troopers, and they were cutting away at him with their swords like anything.' At these words, Lieutenant Tassin ordered his men to arms, picked the fifteen most active, and went off at the double towards Agreda. The little troop had gone a league when they heard shots, and inferred from them that I was still alive but in urgent need of succour. Stimulated by the hope of saving me, the brave fellows doubled their pace, and finally perceived me on the ridge of the hill, serving as a mark for three Spanish troopers.

Monsieur Tassin and his men were tired, and I was at the end of my strength. We halted, therefore, for a little, and meanwhile you may imagine that I expressed my warmest gratitude to the lieutenant and his men, who were almost as glad as I was. We returned to the bivouac where Monsieur Tassin had left the rest of his people. The *cantinière* of the company was there with her mule, carrying two skins of wine, bread and ham. I bought the lot and gave them to the soldiers. Then we breakfasted – as I was very glad to do – and the two hussars whom I had left there the night before shared the meal. One of these mounted the monk's mule and lent me his horse, and so we set out for Taragona. I was in horrible pain because the blood had hardened over my wound. At Taragona I rejoined Lannes' advance guard; the general in command had my wound dressed, and gave me a horse and an escort of hussars. I reached Tudela at midnight, and was received by the Marshal, who, though ill himself, seemed much touched by my misfortune.

It was necessary, however, that the despatch about the Battle of Tudela should be promptly forwarded to the Emperor, who must be impatiently awaiting news from the army on the Ebro. Enlightened by what had happened to me in the mountains, the Marshal consented that the officer bearing it should go by Miranda and Burgos, where the presence of French troops on the roads made the way perfectly safe. I should have liked to have been the bearer, but I was in such pain and so tired that it would have been physically impossible for me to ride hard. The Marshal therefore entrusted the duty to his brother-in-law, Major Guéhéneuc. I handed him the despatches, stained with my blood. Major Saint-Mars, the secretary, wished to re-copy them and change the envelope. 'No, no,' cried the Marshal, 'the Emperor ought to see how valiantly Captain Marbot has defended them.' So he sent off the packet just as it was, adding a note to explain the reason for the delay, eulogising me, and asking for a reward to Lieutenant Tassin and his men.

The Emperor did, as a matter of fact, grant the Cross[8] both to Monsieur Tassin and to his sergeant, and a gratuity of 100 francs to each of the men who had accompanied them. As for the Norman soldier, he was tried by court martial for deserting his post in the presence of the enemy, and condemned to drag a shot for two years, and to finish his time of service in a pioneer company. I later met Major Guéhéneuc in Madrid, in the uniform of a colonel, having been promoted by the Emperor on delivering the despatch stained with my blood. He came up to me, saying, 'You had the danger and got the sword-cut, and I have got the step; but I do hope your promotion will not be slow in coming.' I hoped so too; but I will frankly admit that I was more than a little annoyed with Lannes for the obstinacy with which he had insisted on making me go by Agreda. However, one must submit to one's desiny.

10 That Which Is To Be Cannot Fail

Siege Of Zaragoza, January–February 1809

We were not called to fight against troops of the
line (everywhere nearly always the same) but
against a people insulated from all the other
continental nations by its manners, its prejudices,
and even the nature of its country. The
Spaniards were to oppose to us a resistance so
much more the obstinate, as they believed it to
be the object of the French government to make
the Peninsula a secondary state, irrevocably
subject to the dominion of France.

                    Albert Jean Michel de Rocca[1]

*On 4 December Napoleon entered Madrid. Marshal Lannes,
who had rejoined the Emperor, took the opportunity of
presenting the wounded Marbot (unable to wear a hat, he
had taken to wearing a turban made from a silk handkerchief!)
to the Emperor, who promised to reward him for his conduct
at Agreda. Having smashed the Spanish army – the right wing
of which had fled to Zaragoza – the French learned on the 21st
that they were about to be attacked by a new foe. The small
British army which had landed in Portugal the previous
August and evicted General Junot within a matter of weeks,[2]*

had advanced into Spain. Napoleon immediately set off to destroy it. The British commander, Sir John Moore, unaware of Napoleon's presence, had planned to surprise a scattered French force under Marshal Soult. However, learning on the 23rd of Napoleon's movements, he turned his army about and began a gruelling retreat to the north-western port of La Coruña.

Napoleon, determined to overtake the British, pushed his troops over the Guadarrama mountains in severe winter weather by forced marches. Despite the virtual collapse of his army, Moore managed to keep ahead of the pursuing French: inflicting upon their advance guard several bloody noses along the way.[3] On 1 January 1809 Napoleon received despatches from Paris which persuaded him to return immediately: Austria, encouraged by France's growing entanglement in the Peninsula, was preparing for war. Realizing the need to raise new armies, Napoleon quit Spain the following day; leaving Soult to follow the British[4] and Lannes to finish off the Spanish at Zaragoza.

WHILE SOULT was pursuing the enemy towards La Coruña, the Emperor, accompanied by Marshal Lannes, went back to Valladolid to get on the road to France. He stayed two days in that town, ordering Lannes to go and take command of the two corps that were besieging Zaragoza, and after taking that place, to rejoin him at Paris. But before leaving us, the Emperor, wishing to show his satisfaction with Lannes' staff, invited the Marshal to hand in a list of names to be recommended for promotion. I was entered for the rank of major and quite expected to get it, especially when I heard that the Marshal, on leaving the Emperor's study, had asked for me; but my hopes were cruelly overthrown. The Marshal said to me that when he was asking for my promotion, he thought he should also recommend his old friend Captain Dagusan, but that the

Emperor had begged him to choose between Dagusan and me. 'I cannot make up my mind,' said the Marshal to me, 'for the wound which you received at Agreda and your behaviour in that difficult business puts the right on your side; but Dagusan is old and is making his last campaign. Still, I would not commit an injustice for the world, and I leave it to you to settle which of the two names I shall enter on the commission which the Emperor is about to sign.' It was an embarrassing position for me and my heart was very full. However, I answered that he must put Monsieur Dagusan's name on the commission. The Marshal embraced me with tears in his eyes, promising that after the siege of Zaragoza I should certainly get my step. That evening the Marshal called his officers together to announce the promotions. Guéhéneuc had his colonelcy confirmed, Saint-Mars was appointed lieutenant colonel, Dagusan major, d'Albuquerque and de Watteville got the Legion of Honour, de Viry and Labédoyère were captains. I got nothing.

Before the great insurrection which followed the captivity of Ferdinand, the town of Zaragoza had been unfortified, but on learning what had happened at Bayonne, and the violence which Napoleon was doing in Spain in placing his brother Joseph on the throne, Zaragoza gave the signal for resistance. Its population rose as one man: monks, women and children all took up arms. The town was surrounded by immense and solidly built convents; these were fortified and guns placed in them. All the houses were loopholed and the streets barricaded; powder, cannon-balls, and bullets were manufactured, and great stores of food collected. All the inhabitants enrolled themselves, and took as their commander Count Palafox, one of the colonels of the bodyguard and a devoted friend of Ferdinand, whom he had followed to Bayonne, returning to Aragon after the King's arrest.[5]

It was during the summer of 1808 that the Emperor heard of the revolt, and the intention to defend Zaragoza, but being still under the delusion to which Murat's despatches had given

121

rise,[6] he regarded the insurrection as a fire of straw which the presence of a few French regiments would easily put out. Still, before employing force he thought to try persuasion. He applied to Prince Pignatelli, the greatest Aragonese noble who was then in Paris, begging him to use his influence in the province to calm the excitement. Prince Pignatelli accepted this pacific duty and went to Zaragoza. The people ran to meet him, not doubting that, like Palafox, he was come to fight the French. But no sooner had he spoken of submission than he was assailed by the mob, who would have hanged him if Palafox had not put him in a dungeon, where he remained for nine months.

Meanwhile, several French divisions under General Verdier appeared in June before Zaragoza. The fortifications were still incomplete, and an attempt was made to carry the place by assault. But no sooner were our columns in the streets than a murderous fire from windows, towers, roofs and cellars caused them such losses that they were obliged to retreat. Then our troops surrounded the place, and began a more methodical siege. This would probably have succeeded, had not King Joseph's retreat compelled the army before Zaragoza to retreat also, abandoning its guns.

The first siege thus failed, but when our troops had returned to Aragon victorious, Marshal Lannes came in 1809 to attack Zaragoza afresh. The town was by this time in a much better state of defence, for the fortifications were completed and all the warlike population of Aragon had thrown itself into the place. The garrison had been further strengthened by a large part of the army of Castaños, which we had beaten at Tudela, so that Zaragoza was defended by more than 80,000 men, while the Marshal had only 30,000 with which to besiege it. But our officers were excellent; order and discipline reigned in the ranks: while in the town all was inexperience and confusion. The besieged only agreed on one point: to defend themselves to the death.[7]

The peasants were the most determined; they had entered the town with their wives, their children, and even their herds. Each party of them had a quarter of the town, or a house, assigned to it for its dwelling place, which they were sworn to defend. The people lived mixed up with their beasts in the most disgusting state of filth, the entrails of slaughtered animals lay about the courtyards and in the rooms, and the besieged did not even take the trouble to remove the bodies of men who had died in consequence of the epidemic which this carelessness speedily developed. Religious fanaticism and the sacred love of country exalted their courage, and they blindly resigned themselves to the will of God. The Spaniards have preserved much of the Arab character: they are fatalists, constantly repeating, '*Lo que ha de no puede faltar*': 'That which is to be cannot fail.'

To attack such men by assault in a town where every house was a fortress would have been to repeat the mistake committed during the first siege. Accordingly, Marshal Lannes and General Lacoste, the commanding engineer, adopted a prudent method, which, though tedious, was the best way to bring about the surrender of the town. They began in the usual way by opening trenches, until the first houses were reached; then the houses were mined and blown up – defenders and all – then the next were mined, and so on. These works, however, involved considerable danger for the French, for as soon as one showed himself, he was a mark for musket-shots from the Spaniards in the neighbouring buildings. General Lacoste fell in this way, at the moment when he was taking his place in front of a window to examine the interior of the town.

Such was the determination of the Spaniards that while a house was being mined, and the dull sound of the rammer warned them that death was at hand, not one left the house which he had sworn to defend. We could hear them singing litanies, then at the moment when the walls flew into the air, and fell back with a crash, crushing the greater part of them, those who had escaped would collect about the ruins, and sheltering themselves behind the slightest cover, would recommence their sharpshooting. Our soldiers – warned of the moment when the mine was going off – held themselves in readiness, and no sooner had the explosion taken place than they dashed on to the ruins; and after killing all whom they found, established themselves behind bits of wall, threw up entrenchments with furniture and beams, and in the middle of the ruins, constructed passages for the sappers who were going to mine the next house. In this way a good third of the town was destroyed and the passages established among the ruins formed a labyrinth: through which one could only find one's way by the help of stakes, which the engineer officers placed. Besides the mines, the French used artillery freely, and threw 11,000 shells into the town.

In spite of all, Zaragoza held out. In vain did Lannes, touched by the heroism of the defence, send a flag of truce to propose a capitulation. It was refused, and the siege continued. The huge fortified convents could not be destroyed by mining: we therefore merely blew up a piece of their thick walls and, when the breach was made, sent forward a column to the assault. The besieged would flock to the defence and, in the terrible fighting which resulted from these attacks, we suffered our principal losses.

The best fortified convents were those of the Inquisition and of Santa Engracia. A mine had just been completed under the latter when the Marshal, sending for me in the middle of the night, told me that in order to hasten my promotion to the rank of major, he had designed for me a most important duty. 'At daybreak,' said he, 'the mine which is to breach the wall of Santa Engracia will be fired. Eight companies of grenadiers are to assault; I have given orders that the captains should be chosen from those junior to you: I give you command of the column. Carry the convent, and I am certain that the first messenger from Paris will bring your major's commission.' I accepted with gratitude, though suffering at the moment a good deal from my wound. No matter; there was no room for hesitation and I can admit that I was exceedingly proud of the command entrusted to me. Eight companies of grenadiers to a mere captain was magnificent!

I hastened to get ready, and as the day dawned I went to the trenches. There I found General Rasout, who, after having handed over the command of the grenadiers to me, observed that as the mine could not be fired for an hour, I should do well to use this time in examining the wall which was to be blown up; and in calculating the width of the resulting breach so as to arrange my attack. I started (with an adjutant of engineers to show me the way) through the ruins of a whole quarter which had already been blown down. Finally, I reached the foot of the convent wall where the territory conquered by us came to an end. I found myself in a little court. A light infantry picket, which occupied a sort of cellar hard by, had a sentry who was sheltered from musket-shots by a heap of planks and doors. The engineer officer, showing me a thick wall in front of us, said that was the one which was to be blown up. In one of the corners of the court, whence a pump had been torn away, some stones had fallen out and left a gap. The sentry showed me that by stooping down one could see through this opening the legs of the enemy, posted in the convent garden. In order to verify his statement and notice the lie of the land on which I was going to fight, I stooped down. At that moment, a Spaniard posted on the tower of Santa Engracia fired a shot at me, and I fell on the stones.

I felt no pain at first, and thought that the adjutant standing over me had inadvertently given me a push. Presently, however, the blood flowed copiously: I had got a bullet in the left side, very near the heart. The adjutant helped me to rise, and we went into the cellar where the soldiers were. I was losing so much blood that I was on the point of fainting. There were no stretchers, so the men passed a musket under my arms,

125

another under my knees, and thus carried me through the thousand-and-one passages which had been made through the débris to the place where I had left General Rasout. There I recovered my senses. The General wished to have me attended to, but I preferred to be under Dr Assalagny; so, pressing my handkerchief on the wound, I had myself taken to Marshal Lannes' headquarters, a cannon-shot from the town.

When they saw me arrive, all covered with blood, carried by soldiers, one of whom was supporting my head, the Marshal and my comrades thought I was dead. Dr Assalagny assured them to the contrary, and hastened to dress my wound. The difficulty was where to put me, for as all the furniture of the establishment had been burnt during the siege, there was not a bed in the place. We used to sleep on the bricks wherewith the rooms were paved. The Marshal and all my comrades at once gave their cloaks; these were piled up and I was laid upon them.

The doctor examined my wound and found that I had been struck by a projectile which must have been flat because it had passed between two ribs without breaking them, which an ordinary bullet would not have done. To find the object, Assalagny put a probe into the wound, but when he found nothing his face grew anxious. Finding that I complained of severe pain in the loins, he turned me on my face and examined my back. Hardly had he touched the spot where the ribs are connected with the spine, than I involuntarily gave a cry: the projectile was there. Dr Assalagny then took a knife, made a large incision, perceived the metallic object showing between the ribs and tried to extract it with the forceps. He did not succeed until he made one of my comrades sit on my shoulders and another on my legs. At length he succeeded in extracting a lead bullet of the largest calibre. The Spaniards had hammered it flat until it had the shape of a half-crown, a cross was etched on each face, and small notches all round gave it the appearance of the wheel of a watch. It was these teeth which had caught in the muscles and rendered the extraction so difficult. Flattened thus, the ball presented too large a surface to enter a musket, and must have been fired from a blunderbus. Striking edgewise, it had acted like a cutting instrument, passing between two ribs and travelling around the interior of my chest, to make its exit in the same way as its entry, fortunately preserving sufficient force to make its way through the muscles of the back. The Marshal, wishing to let the Emperor know with what fanatical determination the inhabitants of Zaragoza were defending themselves, sent him the bullet. Napoleon, after examining it, had it brought to my mother, at the same time announcing to her that I was about to be promoted to major.

Assalagny was one of the first surgeons of his day and thanks to him my wound – which might have been mortal – healed rapidly. Lannes had a folding bedstead which he took on campaign and this he lent me; my valise served for a pillow, and my cloak for a blanket. Still, I was not so well off, for my room had neither door nor window, and thus admitted both wind and rain; as well as the sounds and odours of the hospital, which had been set up on the ground floor of the building. The camp was close-by; so that there was eternal singing, shouting, drumming. The bass to this fiendish concert was supplied by the numerous cannon, booming both night and day: sleep was impossible!

At the end of a fortnight I was able to leave my bed. The climate being mild, I was allowed to take short walks, leaning on the arm of Dr Assalagny, or my friend, de Viry. One day, my servant came in to say that an old hussar, with tears streaming down his face, was asking to see me. As you will guess, it was my old tutor, Sergeant Pertelay. His regiment had just come to Spain and, hearing that I had been wounded, he came straight to me. I was glad to see the good man again, and gave him a cordial greeting. After this he often came to visit me, and divert me by his interminable yarns and the quaint advice which he still thought himself entitled to give me. My convalescence did not last long, and by 15 March I was nearly recovered.

Famine, fire, typhus and the sword had destroyed nearly a third of the inhabitants and garrison of Zaragoza,[8] and still no thought of surrender entered the minds of the survivors. The principal forts had been taken, and the mines had destroyed a very large portion of the town. The monks had persuaded the poor folk that the French would massacre them, and none dared come out: but good luck and Lannes' kindness at last put an end to this memorable siege. On 20 March the French carried a nunnery by assault. Besides the nuns, they found 300 women of all classes who had taken refuge in the church. They were treated with respect, and brought to the Marshal. The poor creatures, having been surrounded for several days, had received no food and were famishing. Lannes led them himself to the camp market, where he ordered food for the women, paying for it himself; then he had them escorted safely back to Zaragoza. On their return, the inhabitants, who had followed their movements from the rooftops and towers, rushed forward to hear their adventures. They all spoke well of the French Marshal and soldiers, and from that moment the excitement subsided and a surrender was decided upon. That evening, Zaragoza capitulated.

Lannes' first condition was that Prince Pignatelli should be given up to him alive. The poor man arrived, escorted by a savage-looking gaoler with pistols in his sash. Delivering his prisoner to the Marshal's room, he had the impudence to demand a receipt from the commander-in-chief. The Marshal had him turned out; but as the man would not go without his receipt, Labédoyère – never very patient – lost his temper and literally kicked him down the stairs and out of the building. As for Prince Pignatelli, he was indeed a painful sight, owing to his sufferings in prison. He was devoured by fever, and we had not a bed to offer him; for, as I have said, Lannes was lodging in an utterly unfurnished house, on the front line. General Junot, meanwhile, being less conscientious, had established himself in a rich convent, about a league away, where he lived very comfortably. He offered hospitality to the Prince, who, fatally for himself, accepted it. Junot gave him such a 'blow-out' that his stomach gave way, and Pignatelli died just as he was restored to freedom and happiness. He left an income of more than 900,000 francs to a relation who had hardly a farthing.

When a place capitulates, it is usual for the officers to retain their swords. This practice was followed at Zaragoza, except in the case of the governor, Palafox, concerning whom Lannes had received special instructions from the Emperor: he was to be treated not as a prisoner of war, but as a prisoner of the state, to be disarmed and sent to the gaol at Vincennes. Marshal Lannes, therefore, found himself under the necessity of sending an officer to arrest Palafox and demand his sword. He entrusted this duty to d'Albuquerque, who found it all the more painful as not only was he a fellow Spaniard, but also a relation and friend. I have never been able to fathom the Marshal's motive in selecting him for such a duty. D'Albuquerque, however, had to obey, and entered Zaragoza more dead than alive. He presented himself to Palafox, who handed him his sword, saying with a noble pride: 'If your ancestors, the famous d'Albuquerques, could return to life, there is not one of them who would not sooner be in the place of the prisoner who is surrendering this sword, covered with honour, than in that of the renegade who is receiving it on behalf of the enemies of his country.' Poor d'Albuquerque, terrified and almost fainting, had to lean on a piece of furniture to avoid falling. The scene was related to us by Captain Pasqual, who, having been ordered to take charge of Palafox after his arrest, was present at the interview. Count Palafox remained in France until 1814.

How strange are human affairs! Palafox, having been

proclaimed governor of Zaragoza when the insurrection broke out, has received both fame and glory from the heroic defence. In reality he contributed very little. He fell ill early in the siege, and handed over command to General Saint-Marc, a Belgian in the Spanish service, and it was he who sustained all our attacks with such remarkable courage and ability. But as he was a foreigner, Spanish pride assigned all the glory to Palafox, whose name will go down to posterity, while that of brave General Saint-Marc remains forgotten. The garrison of Zaragoza, 40,000 in number, were forwarded to France as prisoners of war; but most of them escaped and recommenced the slaughter of Frenchmen as members of guerrilla bands. The ruined streets of the city were a perfect charnel house, and the contagion spread to the French troops who formed the new garrison.

With the capture of Zaragoza, Marshal Lannes' work was done and he set off to rejoin the Emperor at Paris. We rode the distance from Aragon to the Bidassoa. The celebrated guerrilla, Mina, attacked our escort in the Pyrenees near Pampeluna, and a servant of the Marshal's who acted as outrider was killed. At Saint-Jean de Luz the Marshal found his carriage and offered places in it to Saint-Mars, Le Couteulx and myself. I sold my horses, and de Viry took my servant back. One of the Marshal's valets, having vainly tried to act as outrider, and there being no postilions, we three offered to do three stages apiece. I admit that this riding post cost me a good deal, hardly healed as I was of my wounds, but I reckoned on my youth and my strong constitution. I began my duties on the darkest of nights and under a violent storm, and as I was not preceded by a postilion – as the outrider who carries despatches usually is – I got into a few bad scrapes, and rode my horse into holes. The carriage was at my heels and I did not know the position of the post houses, which are hard to find at night and in such weather. To finish my misfortunes, I had to wait for some time for the ferry-boat across the Adour at Peyrehorade. I took cold and was shivering, and in a good deal of pain from my wound when I took my place in the carriage. You may see from these details that an aide-de-camp's life is not all rosewater.

11 The Chances of War

The Storming of Ratisbon, April 1809

A man does not have himself killed for a few
halfpence a day, or a paltry distinction; you
must speak to the soul in order to electrify the
man.

Napoleon[1]

*Ever since his humiliating defeat at Austerlitz, Emperor Fran-
cis of Austria had been waiting for a chance to strike back at
Napoleon. Although defeated many times by the French,
Francis and his advisors believed that a major victory on
the battlefield – perhaps even leading to an invasion of France
– was the only way to restore Austria's power and prestige in
Europe: once so great, and now, thanks to Napoleon, at an
embarrassing low.[2] French misfortunes in the Peninsula, particularly that of General Dupont, defeated at the hands of a
half-starved Spanish army at Bailén, had convinced Francis
that the time was ripe. Joining a fifth British-backed coalition,
he ordered the Archduke Charles, his younger brother and
Austria's ablest soldier, to prepare for war. No formal declaration of hostilities was made; but by March 1809 the
Austrians had mobilized and were ready to strike.*

*The wounded Marbot arrived in Paris on 2 April, after a
gruelling journey home: 'terribly tired and in much pain'. A
bittersweet reunion with his mother followed, she having just*

heard of Adolphe's capture by Spanish guerrilleros. Marbot found the capital 'much excited' at the prospect of war; and within a week of his homecoming the Austrians invaded Bavaria, a French ally. Three days later, accompanied by his servant Woirland ('a very bad rider, he often fell off, only saying, as he got up again, "How tough you are! Oh, yes; you are tough!"'), Marbot set off to join Marshal Lannes at the front. Once more, despite the discomfort of his wounds, he had to ride post, all the carriages having been reserved by 'the hundreds of generals and others'.

Marbot arrived at Lannes' headquarters in time to witness Napoleon's victory at Abensberg on 20 April. The Austrian army was now split in two: the right wing, under the Archduke Charles, headed east to Eckmühl; while the left wing, under General von Hiller, retreated south to Landshut, near Münich, on the River Isar. Napoleon had gained the initiative and proceeded to drive his soldiers hard in order to exploit it. Following Hiller with a force which included troops from Bavaria and Würtemberg, Napoleon defeated that General the following day. He then marched his army north to Eckmühl where Davout, with 20,000 men, was holding Charles's 75,000 at bay. Charles had delayed his main attack in order to await reinforcements, thus allowing time for Marshals Lannes and Masséna to arrive from Landshut, with Napoleon following up to deliver the final blow. The Austrians fled north to the fortress of Ratisbon (now Regensburg) in order to make good their escape across the Danube. Napoleon arrived on the 23rd and, ruling out a siege, ordered the city to be stormed. Meanwhile, leaving a strong rearguard to defend the town, Charles pulled his army across the river and out of Napoleon's clutches.

THE ARCHDUKE CHARLES had made use of the darkness to reach Ratisbon, where the bridge enabled him to transport his baggage and the greater part of his army to the left bank of the Danube. The Emperor could not march on Vienna until Ratisbon was taken; otherwise, as soon as he had moved forward, the Archduke would have crossed the Danube by the bridge, and bringing his army back to the right bank, would have attacked us in rear. We had then, at all costs, to take possession of the place. Marshal Lannes was charged with this difficult duty. The enemy had 6,000 men in Ratisbon, whom they could reinforce to any extent by help of the bridge. Many guns were in position on the ramparts and the parapet was garnished with infantry. The fortifications, however, were old and bad; the ditches dry, and used as kitchen gardens. Still, although the means of defence were not such as could have resisted a regular siege, the town was in a position – especially as the garrison could communicate with an army of more than 80,000 men – to repel an assault. To get into the place it was necessary to descend a deep ditch with the help of ladders, cross it under fire from the enemy, and scale the rampart, the angles of which were commanded by a flanking fire.

The Emperor, having dismounted, took up his position on a hillock a short cannon-shot from the town. Having noticed, near the Straubing gate, a house which had imprudently been built against the rampart, he sent forward some twelve-pounders and howitzers; and ordering them to concentrate their fire upon this house so that the ruins – falling into the ditch – might partially fill it and form at the foot of the wall an incline by which our troops might mount to the assault. While the artillery was executing this order, Lannes brought Morand's division up to the promenade which goes round the town; and in order to shelter his troops from the enemy's fire, up to the last moment he placed them in rear of a large stone storehouse which appeared to have been placed there on purpose to aid our undertaking. Carts laden with ladders taken from the neighbouring villages were brought up to this point where perfect protection was obtained against the Austrian projectiles.

While waiting until everything was ready, Marshal Lannes had gone back to the Emperor to receive his final orders. As they were chatting, a bullet – fired, in all probability, from one of the long-range Tyrolese[3] rifles – struck Napoleon on the right ankle. The pain was at first so sharp that the Emperor had to lean upon Lannes; but Dr Larrey, who quickly arrived, declared that the wound was trifling. If it had been severe enough to require an operation, the event would certainly have been considered a great misfortune for France: yet it might perhaps have spared her many calamities. However, the report that the Emperor had been wounded spread through the army. Officers and men ran up from all sides: in a moment Napoleon was surrounded by a throng of thousands, in spite of the fire which the enemy's guns concentrated on the vast group. The Emperor, wishing to withdraw his troops from this useless danger, and to calm the anxiety of the more distant corps, who were getting unsteady in their desire to come and see what was the matter, mounted his horse the instant his wound was dressed, and rode down the front of the whole line, amid loud cheers.

It was at this extempore review, held in the presence of the enemy, that Napoleon first granted gratuities to private soldiers; appointing them Knights of the Empire and members, at the same time, of the Legion of Honour. The regimental commanders recommended, but the Emperor also allowed soldiers who thought they had claims to come and represent them before him: then he decided upon them by himself. Now it befell that an old grenadier who had made the campaigns of Italy and Egypt, not hearing his name called, came up, and in a calm tone of voice asked for the Cross. 'But,' said Napoleon, 'what have you done to deserve it?' 'It was I, sir, who, in the desert of Joppa, when it was so terribly hot, gave you a watermelon.' 'I thank you for it again; but the gift of the fruit is hardly worth the Cross of the Legion of Honour.'

Then the grenadier, who up until then had been as cool as ice, working himself up into a frenzy, shouted, with the utmost volubility, 'Well, and you don't reckon seven wounds received at the bridge of Arcola, at Lodi and Castiglione, at the Pyramids, at Acre, Austerlitz, Friedland; eleven campaigns in Italy, Egypt, Austria, Prussia, Poland . . .' but the Emperor cut him short, laughing and mimicking his excited manner, cried: 'There there – how you work yourself up when you come to the essential point! That is where you ought to have begun; it is worth much more than your melon. I make you a Knight of the Empire, with a pension of 1,200 francs. Does that satisfy you?' 'But, your Majesty, I prefer the Cross.' 'You have both one and the other, since I make you a knight.' 'Well, I would rather have the Cross.' The worthy grenadier could not be moved from the point, and it took all manner of trouble to make him understand that the title of Knight of the Empire carried with it the Legion of Honour. He was not appeased on this point until the Emperor had fastened the decoration on his breast, and he seemed to think a great deal more of this than of his annuity of 1,200 francs. It was by familiarities of this kind that the Emperor made the soldiers adore him, but it was a means available only to a commander whom frequent victories had made illustrious: any other general would have injured his reputation by it.

As soon as Lannes gave notice that all was ready for the assault, we returned towards Ratisbon; the Emperor meanwhile going back to his hillock to witness operations. The various army corps around him awaited events in silence. Our artillery had completely destroyed the house by the rampart, and its fragments falling into the ditch had made a slope practicable enough, but not reaching higher than to ten or twelve feet from the top of the wall. To reach this, therefore, ladders had to be placed on the rubble no less than to descend into the ditch. On reaching the building, behind which Morand's division were taking shelter from the fire, Lannes called for fifty volunteers to go forward and plant the ladders. Many more than that number came forward, and the number had to be reduced. The brave fellows, led by picked officers, set out with admirable spirit; but they were hardly clear of the building when they met a hail of bullets and were nearly all laid low. A few only continued to descend into the ditch, where the guns soon disabled them, and the remains of this first column fell back, streaming with blood, to the place where the division was sheltered. Nevertheless, at the call of Lannes and Morand, fifty more volunteers appeared; and seizing the ladders, made for the ditch. No sooner, however, did they show themselves, than a still hotter fire nearly annihilated them.

Cooled by these two repulses, the troops made no response to the Marshal's third call for volunteers. If he had ordered one or more companies to march, they would no doubt have obeyed; but he knew well what a difference there is in point of effect between obedience on the soldiers' part and *dash*; and for the present danger volunteers were much better than troops obeying orders. Vainly, however, did Lannes renew his appeal to the bravest of a brave division; vainly did he call upon them to observe that the eyes of the Emperor and all the Grand Army were on them. A gloomy silence was the only reply, the men being convinced that to pass beyond the walls of the building into the enemy's fire was certain death.

At length Lannes, exclaiming, 'Well, I will let you see that I was a grenadier before I was a marshal, and still am one,' seized a ladder, lifted it, and would have carried it towards the breach. His aides-de-camp tried to stop him; he resisted, and got angry with us. I ventured to say, '*Monsieur le Maréchal*, you would not wish us to be disgraced, but that we should be if you were to receive the slightest wound in carrying that ladder to the ramparts, so long as one of your aides-de-camp was left alive!' Then, in spite of his efforts, I dragged one end of the ladder from him, and put it on my shoulder, while de Viry took the other end and our comrades, by pairs, took up the other ladders.

At the sight of the Marshal disputing with his aides-de-camp for the lead of the assault, a shout of enthusiasm went up from the whole division. Officers and soldiers wished to lead the column, and in their eagerness for this honour they pushed my comrades and me about, trying to get hold of the ladders. If, however, we had given them up, we should seem to have been playing a comedy to stimulate the troops: the wine had been drawn and we had to drink it, bitter as it might be. Understanding this, the Marshal let us have our way, though fully expecting to see the greater part of his staff exterminated as they marched at the head of this perilous attack.

I have said already that my comrades, although as brave as possible, lacked experience, and more especially what is called 'military tact'. I made, therefore, no demur about taking the command of the little column. The matter was important enough to warrant it and no one contested my right. Behind the building I organised the detachment which was to follow us. The destruction of the two former columns I ascribed to the imprudence with which their leaders had massed together the soldiers composing them. This arrangement was unsuitable in two ways. First, it gave the enemy the advantage of firing upon a mass instead of upon isolated men and, secondly, our grenadiers – who were laden with ladders – having formed a single group and getting in each other's way, had not been able to move fast enough to get quickly clear of the Austrian fire. I settled, therefore, that de Viry and I, carrying the first ladder, should start off at a run; that the second ladder should follow at twenty paces distant and the rest in due course; that when we reached the promenade, the ladders should be placed five feet apart to avoid confusion; that when we descended into the ditch we should leave every second ladder against the wall towards the promenade, so that the troops might follow without delay; that the others should be lifted and carried quickly to the breach, where we should place them only a foot apart, both on account of the want of space, and in order that we might reach the top of the rampart close together and push back the besieged when they tried to throw us down.

This plan having been expounded and comprehended, the Marshal, who approved it, cried, 'Off with you my boys, and Ratisbon is taken!' At the word, de Viry and I darted out, crossed the promenade at a run, and lowering our ladder, descended into the ditch. Our comrades followed with fifty grenadiers. In vain did the cannon thunder, the musketry rattle, grapeshot and bullets strike trees and walls. It is very difficult to take aim at isolated individuals moving very fast and twenty paces apart, and we got into the ditch without one man of our little column being wounded. The ladders already indicated were lifted, we carried them to the top of the rubble from the ruined house and, placing them against the parapet, we ran up them to the rampart. I was first up one of the first ladders. Labédoyère, who was climbing the one beside me, feeling that the lower end of it was not very steadily placed, asked me to give him my hand, and so we both reached the top of the rampart in full view of the Emperor and the whole army, who saluted us with a mighty cheer: it was one of the finest days of my life. De Viry and d'Albuquerque joined us in a moment with the other aides-de-camp and fifty grenadiers; and by this time a regiment of Morand's division was coming towards the ditch at the double.

The chances of war are often strange. The two first detachments had been massacred before reaching the foot of the breach, and yet the third suffered no loss whatever. Only my friend de Viry had a button of his *pelisse* carried away by a bullet; yet if the enemy on the parapet had had the presence of mind to charge with the bayonet on Labédoyère and me, it is possible that we should have been overwhelmed by their number and either killed or hurled back into the ditch. But Austrians lose their heads very quickly: the boldness and rapidity of our attack astonished them to such a point that when they saw us swarming over the breach they at first slackened their fire and soon ceased altogether. Not only did none of their companies march against us, but all went off in the opposite direction to the point which we had just carried.

As I said, the attack took place close to the Straubing gate. Marshal Lannes had ordered me to get it opened or break it down so that he could enter the town with Morand's division. Accordingly, as soon as I saw my fifty grenadiers on the ramparts and the head of the supporting regiment already arrived in the ditch, where their passage was secured by a further supply of ladders, I went down into the town without further delay, every moment being precious. We marched steadily towards the Straubing gate, only a hundred paces from the breach, and great was my surprise to find an Austrian battalion massed under the immense archway, all the men facing towards the gate, so as to be ready to defend it if the French broke it in. The Major in command, thinking only of the duty which was entrusted to him and taking no heed of the noise which he heard on the ramparts close by, was so confident that the French attack would fail, that he had not even placed a sentry outside the archway to let him know what was going on: so he was thunderstruck at seeing us come up in his rear.

He had taken up his position behind his men, so that having faced about on seeing us approach, he found himself fronting the little French column; the strength of which he was quite unable to judge, for I had formed it in two squads which rested on the sides of the arch and closed it completely. At their Major's cry of surprise, the battalion all faced around, and the

141

rear sections, which had become the front, presented their muskets at us. Our grenadiers also raised theirs, and as only one pace separated the two parties, you may imagine what a horrible massacre would have resulted if a shot had been fired. The situation was very dangerous for both sides but their greater numbers gave the Austrians an immense advantage: for if we had opened fire muzzle to muzzle, our little column would have been destroyed. It was lucky that our adversaries could not tell the weakness of our force and I hastened to tell the Major that as the town had been taken by assault and occupied by our troops, nothing remained for him but to lay down his arms under pain of being put to the sword.

The assured tone in which I spoke intimidated the officer; all the more so that he could hear the tumult produced by the successive arrival of our soldiers, who had followed us over the breach and hastened to form in front of the archway. He harangued his battalion; and after having explained the situation to them, ordered them to lay down their weapons. The companies who were close to our muzzles obeyed, but those who were at the other end of the archway, close to the gate and sheltered from our shot, fell to shouting, refused to surrender, and pushed forward the mass of their battalion until we were nearly overturned. The officers, however, succeeded in quieting them and everything seemed in a fair way to be settled, when the impetuous Labédoyère, impatient at the delay, lost his temper, and was on the point of ruining the whole thing: for, seizing the Austrian Major by the throat, he was about to run him through, if the rest had not turned his sword aside. The Austrians then resumed their arms and a bloody battle was about to take place: when the gate began to resound on the outside under the powerful blows which the axes of our pioneers – led by Lannes in person – were delivering upon it. Then the enemy, understanding that they would be between two fires, surrendered; and we made them march, disarmed, from under the archway towards the town. The gate thus cleared, we opened it to the Marshal, whose troops rushed into the place like a torrent.

After complimenting us, Lannes gave the order to march towards the bridge, in order to cut off such of the enemy's regiments as were in Ratisbon, and prevent the Archduke from sending reinforcements. Hardly, however, had we entered the main street when we were threatened by a new danger. Our shells had set several houses on fire and the flames were on the point of reaching some thirty wagons, which the enemy had abandoned. If these caught fire, the passage of our troops would certainly have been hindered, but we hoped to avoid the obstacle by slipping along close to the walls. Suddenly, however, the Austrian Major whom I had presented to the Marshal cried out in a tone of most profound despair, 'Conquerors and conquered, we are all lost; those wagons are full of powder!' We all turned pale, including the Marshal, but quickly recovering his calm in the presence of imminent death, he made the French column take open order and pile their muskets against the houses; he then ordered the soldiers to push the wagons along from hand to hand until they were under the arch and out of the town. He himself set the example and generals, officers and men all went to work. The Austrian prisoners worked with the French, for it was a question of life and death with them also. Many pieces of burning wood were already falling on the wagons, and if one of them had taken fire, we should have all been blown up and the town destroyed. But they worked with such energy that in a few minutes all the powder-wagons were pushed outside the town, whence the prisoners were made to draw them to our main park of artillery.

The wagons being safely out of the way and the danger over, the Marshal, with the infantry brigade, advanced to the centre of the town. Having reached this point, and wishing to make the quarters which he had already captured secure against any renewed attack, he followed the Spanish practice, and occupied all the windows in the principal streets. After this prudent arrangement, the Marshal ordered that the column should continue its route towards the bridge, and ordered me to march at the head and guide it. I obeyed, though it seemed a difficult task, for I had never been in Ratisbon before and naturally did not know the streets.

As the town belonged to our ally, the King of Bavaria, it might have been expected that the inhabitants would be sufficiently devoted to our cause to point out the way to the bridge; but they were too frightened to come out and we did not see one. All the doors and windows were shut and we were in too great a hurry to drive them in, for at every crossroad appeared groups of Austrians who retreated firing. The only retreat open to the enemy was across the bridge, and I thought that I might get there by following them; but there was so little concerted action among the Austrians that most of the squads of sharpshooters who were posted in front of us took flight at our approach.

As I was thus lost in the labyrinth of unknown streets, with no idea of the direction that the column should take, suddenly a door opened, and a young woman, pale and with wild eyes, came flying towards us, crying, 'I am French, save me!' The lady was a Parisian milliner in business at Ratisbon, who, fearing that – as a Frenchwoman – she might be ill-treated by the Austrians, had (as soon as she heard the sound of French voices) come to throw herself headlong into the arms of her compatriots. At the sight of her a bright idea flashed into my mind: 'Do you know where the bridge is?' said I. 'Certainly.' 'Show us the way then.' 'Great heavens! In the middle of all this shooting? I am frightened to death already and was going to ask you to let me have some soldiers to defend my house. I am going back this moment!' 'Very sorry, but you will show us the bridge before you go back. Two men take the lady's arms, and march her along at the head of the column.' This was done in spite of the tears and cries of our fair compatriot.

At every turning I asked her which direction we must take. The nearer we got to the Danube, the more skirmishers we met; the bullets whistled round the frightened woman's ears; but not being familiar with the sound, she was much less alarmed at the faint whistle than at the reports of the muskets. But suddenly one of the grenadiers who was supporting her got a bullet through his arm; the blood spurted on to her, her knees gave way, and we had to carry her. What had befallen her neighbour made me more cautious for her, so I put her in rear of the first section, so as to be in some measure sheltered from bullets by the men.

At last we reached a little square facing the bridge. The enemy, who held the further end of it, as well as the suburb on the right bank named Stadt-am-Hof, no sooner caught sight of the column than they opened artillery fire. I thought it was useless to expose the Parisian lady any longer, and let her go free. But as the poor woman (who was more dead than alive) knew not where to take shelter, I advised her to enter a little chapel of Our Lady at the further end of the square. She agreed; the grenadiers lifted her over the little grating which closed the entry, and she hastened to get out of reach of shot: crouching down behind a statue of the Virgin, where, I can assure you, she made herself pretty small.

On hearing that we had reached the bank of the river, Marshal Lannes came to the head of the column and recognised for himself the impossibility of crossing the bridge, the suburb on the left bank being on fire. While the assault was taking place, six Austrian battalions, posted on the ramparts at some distance from the point of attack, had remained tranquilly looking out to see if anyone was coming from the country. They were roused from their stolid inaction by the sound of firing in the direction of the bridge. Hastening thither, they found their retreat cut off both by us and by the burning suburb, and had to surrender.

The same day the Emperor entered Ratisbon, and ordered

the troops who had not fought to assist the inhabitants in fighting the fire; still, a great many houses were burned. After having visited and rewarded the glorious remains of the two first columns who had failed in their attempt, Napoleon wished also to see the third column, which had carried Ratisbon under his eyes. He testified his satisfaction and decorated several. On the Marshal reminding him of my old and new claims to the rank of major, Napoleon replied, 'You may consider the thing done.' Then, turning to Berthier, 'Make me sign his commission the first time you bring up any papers.' I could only congratulate myself, and could not reasonably expect the Emperor to suspend his important work that I might have my commission a few days earlier. Indeed, I was almost beside myself at the remarks of satisfaction which the Emperor and the Marshal had shown towards me, and at the praises which my comrades and I received on all hands. As you may suppose, before leaving the neighbourhood of the bridge, I had the Paris lady fetched from the chapel and taken to her house by an officer. The Marshal, seeing the soldiers helping her to recross the grating, asked me how she got there. I told him the story, which he passed on to the Emperor, who laughed a good deal and said that he should like to see the lady.

Ratisbon was taken on 23 April. The Emperor passed the next two days in the town, ordering all repairs to be done at his cost. As Napoleon, accompanied by Lannes, was going about the streets, I saw the milliner whom I had compelled to act as our guide to the bridge, and pointed her out to the Marshal. He showed her to the Emperor, who spoke to her with many jocose compliments on her courage; and subsequently sent her a handsome ring in memory of the assault. The crowd of soldiers and civilians who were about the Emperor, having made enquiries about the action of this little scene, the facts were somewhat distorted. The lady was represented as a heroine, who of her own accord had faced death to ensure the safety of her compatriots. In this form the tale was told, not only in the army, but throughout Germany. Even General Pelet was misled by the popular report. If the Parisian lady was for a time under fire from the enemy, love of glory had very little to do with it!

12 Sad Presentiments

The Battle of Aspern–Essling, May 1809

I don't feel right in regard to this business but whatever may be the result, it will be my last battle. Adieu, adieu, gentlemen!

Marshal Lannes[1]

With Ratisbon taken, the way lay open to Vienna. Napoleon's habitual strategy – so often successful in the past – was to seek the enemy's army, defeat it in detail, and then occupy his capital: bringing the war to a speedy close on terms favourable to himself. The French arrived at Vienna on 10 May 1809 and, after a brief bombardment, entered it on the 13th. But the Austrian field army was still at large: mauled in the recent clashes, it could hardly be said to have been decisively beaten. Napoleon, however, expected the Archduke Charles to withdraw into Moravia and decided, therefore, to cross the Danube and march in pursuit. The bridges over the river being broken at Vienna, a new crossing-site was found four miles downstream, opposite one of the many islands which at that time littered the Danube. Roughly two miles across, the island of Lobau was to be used as a stepping-stone, French engineers throwing across bridges linking it with both banks. On 20 May Masséna's corps crossed the river and occupied the nearby villages of Aspern and Essling. Cavalry patrols, sent out to reconnoitre the area, reported little enemy contact.

149

Archduke Charles however, was merely a few miles away with an army of 95,000 men and 200 guns. Having arrived on the broad plain of the Marchfeld on 16 May, he had decided not to dispute the passage of the Danube: instead, the French would be allowed to cross and then forced to fight with the river at their backs. By the 21st Napoleon had despatched more than 24,000 men across the Danube. That afternoon, having first broken the French bridges by sending flotsam downstream, the Austrians attacked. Desperately patching up the bridges time and again, the French poured in troops to bolster the bridgehead: their total eventually rising to 48,000 infantry and 7,000 cavalry. By nightfall a bloody and bitter battle had led to stalemate: the Austrians unable to drive the French into the Danube, the French unable to break out beyond the Aspern–Essling perimeter. The next day, having got the Guard across the river, Napoleon ordered an offensive to retake ground lost the day before. However, with the bridges destroyed yet again by Austrian fireboats, leaving Davout's corps stranded on the southern bank, and the beleaguered French running low on ammunition, Napoleon authorized a withdrawal onto Lobau around 2 p.m. On the morning of 23 May, the bridge linking Lobau with the northern bank was dismantled: the island was to become a fortress, an armed camp, from which a better planned French offensive would be launched in due course. Meanwhile, having taken around 21,000 casualties, the exhausted French soldiers settled down to a dinner of horseflesh, cooked in cuirasses and seasoned with gunpowder. Charles, appalled at the carnage – his army having sustained around 23,000 casualties – withdrew to await events: the dead remained unburied for ten days.

ON THE EVENING OF 20 MAY 1809, the Emperor and Marshal Lannes being lodged in the only house on Lobau Island, my comrades and I took up our quarters close by, in brilliant moonlight, on beautiful turf. It was a delicious night; and with the carelessness of soldiers, thinking nothing of the morrow's dangers, we chatted gaily and sang the last new airs – among others, two which were then very popular in the army, being attributed to Queen Hortense.[2] The words were very appropriate to our circumstances; there was:

You leave me, dear, to go where Glory awaits you;
My loving heart accompanies your steps.

And then again:

The gentle radiance of the evening star
Illumined with its beams the tents of France

Captain d'Albuquerque was the most joyous of us all and, after charming us with his fine voice, he sent us into fits of laughter by relating the most comical adventures of his most adventurous life. Poor fellow! He little thought that the next day's sun would be his last: as little as we guessed that the plain which lay over on the opposite bank was soon to be watered with the blood of our kind Marshal and with that of almost every one of us.

On the morning of the 21st the Austrian lines showed themselves and took up their position facing ours in front of Essling and Aspern. Marshal Masséna ought to have loopholed the houses of these villages and covered the approaches by fieldworks, but unluckily he had neglected to take these precautions. The Emperor found fault with him; but as the enemy was approaching and there was no time to repair the omission, Napoleon did his best to supply it by covering the last bridge with a bridgehead, which he traced himself. If Marshal Lannes' corps, the Imperial Guard, and the other expected troops had been present, Napoleon would certainly

151

not have given Archduke Charles time to deploy but would have attacked him on the spot. Having, however, only three divisions of infantry and four of cavalry to oppose the enemy's large force, he was constrained, for the moment, to act on the defensive. To this end he rested his left wing, consisting of three divisions of infantry under Masséna, on the village of Aspern. The right wing, formed by Boudet's division, rested on the Danube, near the great wood lying between the river and the village of Essling and occupied that village also. Lastly, the three cavalry divisions and part of the artillery, under the orders of Marshal Bessières,[3] formed the centre, spreading over the space which remained empty between Essling and Aspern. The Emperor compared his position to an entrenched camp, of which Aspern and Essling represented the bastions, united by a curtain formed by the cavalry and artillery. The two villages, though not entrenched, were capable of a good defence, being built of masonry surrounded by low banks, which protected them against the inundation of the Danube. The church and churchyard of Aspern could hold out for a long time. Essling had for its citadel a large enclosure and an immense house built of stone. We found these points very useful.

Although the troops composing the right and centre did not form any part of Lannes' corps, the Emperor wished in this difficulty to make use of the Marshal's talents and had entrusted the overall command to him. He was heard to say – to Marshal Bessières' annoyance – 'You are under the orders of Marshal Lannes.' I shall relate directly the serious quarrel to which this declaration gave rise and how, greatly against my will, I got mixed up in it.

About 2 p.m. the Austrian army advanced upon us, and we were very hotly engaged. The cannonade was terrible; the enemy's force was so much superior to ours that they might easily have hurled us into the Danube by piercing the cavalry line which formed our only centre; and if the Emperor had been in the Archduke's place he would certainly have taken that course. But the Austrian commander-in-chief was too methodical to act in this determined way; therefore, instead of boldly massing a strong force in the direction of our centre, he occupied the whole of the first day in attacking Aspern and Essling, which he carried and lost five or six times after murderous combats. As soon as one of these villages was occupied by the enemy, Napoleon sent up reserves to retake it; and if we were again driven from it, he took it again, though both places were on fire. During this alternation of successes and reverses, the Austrian cavalry several times threatened our centre, but ours repulsed it and returned to its place between the two villages, though terribly cut up by the enemy's artillery. Thus the action continued until ten in the evening, the French remaining masters of Essling and Aspern, while the Austrians, withdrawing their left and centre, did nothing but make some fruitless attacks on Aspern. They brought up, however, strong reinforcements for the morrow's action.

During this first day of the battle, though Marshal Lannes' staff, being always engaged in carrying orders to the most exposed points, had incurred great danger, we had yet no loss to deplore; and we were beginning to congratulate ourselves when, as the sun went down, the enemy, wishing to cover his retreat by a redoubled fire, sent a hail of shot at us. At that moment, d'Albuquerque, La Bourdonnaye and I, facing the Marshal, were reporting to him orders which we had been sent to convey, having our backs consequently towards the enemy's guns. A ball struck poor d'Albuquerque in the loins, flinging him over the head of his horse, and laying him stone dead at Lannes' feet. 'This,' he exclaimed, 'is the end of the poor lad's romance! But he has, at least, died nobly.' A second ball passed between La Bourdonnaye's saddle and the spine of his horse without touching either horse or rider: a really miraculous shot. But the front of the saddle-tree was so violently smashed between La Bourdonnaye's thighs, that the wood and the iron were forced into his flesh and he suffered for a long time with this extraordinary wound.

I had been between my two comrades, and saw them both fall at the same moment. I went towards the escort to order some troopers to come and carry La Bourdonnaye away, but I had hardly gone a few steps when an aide-de-camp of General Boudet, having come forward to speak to the Marshal, had his head taken off by a cannon-ball in the very spot which I had just left. Clearly this position was no longer tenable. We were right in front of one of the enemy's batteries, so the Marshal, for all his courage, thought it advisable to move a couple of hundred yards to the right.

The last order which Marshal Lannes had given me to carry was addressed to Marshal Bessières, and gave rise to a brisk altercation between the two Marshals, who hated each other cordially. In order to understand the scene which I am about to relate, it is necessary that you should know the reasons for this hatred.

General Bonaparte, when on his way to assume the command of the Army of Italy in 1796, took as his senior aide-de-camp Murat, whom he had just promoted colonel and for whom he had a great liking. Having, however, in the first actions noticed the military capacity, zeal and courage of Lannes, then commanding the 4th Regiment of the Line, he granted to that officer an equally large share of his esteem and friendship, thus exciting Murat's jealousy. When the two colonels had become generals of brigade, Bonaparte was accustomed, on critical occasions, to entrust to Murat the direction of the cavalry charges and put Lannes in command of the reserve of the grenadiers. Both did splendidly and the army had nothing but praise for either. But between these gallant officers there grew up a rivalry which, if the truth be known, was not at all displeasing to the commander-in-chief, tending, as it did, to stimulate their zeal and desire for distinction. He would extol before Murat the achievements of General Lannes, and enlarge in Lannes' presence on the merits of Murat. The rivalry soon led to altercations, in which Bessières, then merely a captain in Bonaparte's Guides and in high favour with the commander, always took the part of his compatriot Murat (they were both born in the department of the Lot); while taking every opportunity, as Lannes was well aware, of depreciating him.

After the Italian campaigns Lannes and Murat accompanied Bonaparte to Egypt. About this time both conceived a wish to marry Bonaparte's sister, Caroline; and Bessières found an opportunity to injure Lannes' suit irretrievably. As a member of the administrative council, charged with the distribution of the military fund, he became aware that Lannes had exceeded the allowance for the outfit of his regiment, the Consular Guard, by 300,000 francs. He revealed this to Murat, who brought it to the ears of Bonaparte, now First Consul. Lannes was dismissed from the command of the Guard, and allowed a month to make up the deficit, which, without the generous aid of Augereau,[4] he would have found it exceedingly hard to do. Napoleon afterwards received him back into favour; but meantime Murat had married Caroline. As may be supposed, Lannes never forgave Bessières and the antipathy was in full vigour when they came in contact at the Battle of Essling.

At the moment of the brisk cannonade which had just killed poor d'Albuquerque, Lannes, observing that the Austrians were making a retrograde movement, thought it a good opening for a cavalry charge. He called me to carry the order to Marshal Bessières, who, as I have said, had just been placed under his command by the Emperor. I was on duty; so the next aide-de-camp in course for service came up: it was de Viry. Marshal Lannes gave him the following order: 'Go and tell Marshal Bessières that I *order him to charge home.*' This expression, conveying that the charge must be pushed until the sabres are in the enemy's bodies, obviously is very like a reprimand; as implying that hitherto the cavalry had not acted with sufficient vigour. The expression 'I order', employed by one marshal to another, was also rather harsh. Lannes used these two phrases with deliberate emphasis.

Off went de Viry, fulfilled his instructions, and returned to Lannes, who asked, 'What did you say to Marshal Bessières?' 'I informed him that your Excellency begged him to order a general charge of the cavalry.' Lannes shrugged his shoulders and cried, 'You are a baby; send another officer!' This time it was Labédoyère. The Marshal knew he was of firmer character than de Viry, and gave him the same message, repeating the expressions 'I order' and 'charge home'. Labédoyère did not see Lannes' intention and did not like to repeat the words verbatim to Bessières; so he employed a circumlocution. Accordingly, when he came back and reported the words he had used, Lannes turned his back on him.

At that moment I galloped up to the staff. It was not my turn for duty, but the Marshal called me and said, 'Marbot, Marshal Augereau assured me that you were a man I could count on. So far I have found his words justified by your conduct; but I should like a further proof. Go and tell Marshal Bessières that I order him to charge home. You understand, sir? *Charge home!*' As he spoke he poked me in the ribs with his finger. I perfectly understood that Lannes wished to mortify Bessières, first by taking a harsh way of reminding him that the Emperor had put him in a subordinate post to himself, and further by finding fault with his management of the cavalry. I was perturbed at being obliged to transmit such offensive expressions to the other Marshal. It was easy to foresee that they might have awkward results; but my immediate chief must be obeyed.

So I galloped off to the centre, wishing that one of the shots which were dropping thickly might bowl over my horse, and give me a good excuse for not accomplishing my disagreeable mission! I approached Marshal Bessières with much respect and begged to speak with him in private. 'Speak up, sir!' he replied stiffly. So I had to say in presence of his staff and a crowd of superior officers, 'Marshal Lannes directs me to tell your Excellency that he orders you to charge home.' Bessières angrily exclaimed, 'Is this the way to speak to a marshal, sir? Orders! Charge home! You shall be severely punished for this impudence!' I answered, 'Marshal, the more offensive the terms I have used seem to your Excellency, the more sure you may be that in using them I only obeyed my orders.' I saluted and returned to Lannes. 'Well, what did you say to Marshal Bessières?' 'That your Excellency ordered him to charge home.' 'Right; here is one aide-de-camp at any rate who understands me.' In spite of this compliment, you may imagine that I was very sorry to have to deliver such a message. However, the cavalry charge came off: General d'Espagne was killed, but the result was very good. Where-upon Lannes said, 'You see that my stern injunction has produced an excellent effect; but for it *Monsieur le Maréchal* Bessières would have fiddled about all day.'

Night came on, and the battle ceased both in the centre and on our right, on which Lannes determined to join the Emperor, who was bivouacking within the works of the bridgehead. But hardly had we started, when the Marshal, hearing brisk firing in Aspern, where Masséna was in command, wished to go and see what was taking place in the village. He bade his staff go on to the Emperor's bivouac and, taking only myself and an orderly, bade me guide him to Aspern, where I had been several times in the course of the day. I went in that direction: with the moon and the blaze of Essling and Aspern we had plenty of light. Still, as the frequent paths were apt to be hidden by the tall corn and I was afraid of losing myself in it, I dismounted in order to better find the way. Soon the Marshal dismounted also, and walked by my side, chatting about the day's fighting and the chances of that which would take place on the morrow.

A quarter of an hour brought us close to Aspern, the

approaches to which were lined by the bivouac fires of Marshal Masséna's troops. Wishing to speak to him, Lannes bade me go forward to ascertain his quarters. Before we had gone many steps I perceived Masséna walking in front of the camp with Marshal Bessières. The wound in my forehead which I had received in Spain prevented me from wearing a bearskin, and I was the only one among the Marshal's aides-de-camp who had a cocked hat and Bessières, recognising me by this (but not yet noticing Marshal Lannes), came towards me saying, 'Ah! it is you, sir! If what you said to me earlier came from you alone, I will teach you to choose your words better when speaking to your superiors; if you were only obeying your Marshal then he shall give me satisfaction; and I bid you tell him so.'

Then Marshal Lannes, leaping forward like a lion, passed in front of me and seizing my arm, cried: 'Marbot, I owe you an apology; for though I believed I could be certain of your attachment I had some doubts remaining as to the manner in which you had transmitted my orders to this gentleman; but I see that I was unfair to you.' Then, addressing Bessières: 'I wonder how you dare to find fault with one of my aides! He was the first to scale the walls of Ratisbon, he crossed the Danube at the risk of almost certain death,[5] he has just been twice wounded in Spain, while there are some so-called soldiers who haven't had a scratch in their lives, and have got their promotion by playing the spy and informing on their comrades. What fault have you to find with this officer?'

'Sir,' replied Bessières, 'your aide-de-camp came and told me that you ordered me to charge home; it appears to me that such expressions are unseemly.' 'They are quite right, sir, and it was I who dictated them; did not the Emperor tell you that you were under my orders?' Bessières replied with some hesitation, 'The Emperor warned me that I must comply with your opinion.' 'Know, sir,' cried Lannes, 'that in military matters people do not comply, they obey! If the Emperor had thought fit to place me under your command, I should have offered him my resignation; but so long as you are under mine, I shall give you orders and you shall obey them; otherwise I shall withdraw the command of the troops from you. As for charging home, I gave you the order because you did not do it, and because all the morning you were parading before the enemy without approaching him boldly.' 'But that is an insult,' said Bessières angrily; 'you shall give me satisfaction!' 'This very moment if you like!' cried Lannes, laying his hand on his sword.

During this discussion old Masséna, interposing between the adversaries, sought to calm them, and not succeeding, he took the high tone in his turn: 'I am your senior, gentlemen; you are in my camp, and I shall not permit you to give my men the scandalous spectacle of seeing two Marshals draw on each other; and that in the presence of the enemy. I summon you, therefore, in the name of the Emperor, to separate at once.' Then, adopting a gentler manner, he took Marshal Lannes by the arm, and led him to the further end of the bivouac, while Bessières returned to his own. You may suppose how distressed I was by this deplorable scene. Finally, Lannes, remounting, set off for the Emperor's bivouac where my comrades were already established. On reaching it, he took Napoleon aside, and related what had happened. The Emperor at once sent for Marshal Bessières, whom he received sternly; then they went some distance away, and walked rapidly, Napoleon appearing to be reprimanding him severely. Bessières looked confused and must have felt still more so when the Emperor sat down to dinner without inviting him, while he made Lannes take a seat at his right hand. My comrades and I were as sad this evening as we had been cheerful the night before. We had seen poor d'Albuquerque killed; we had close beside us La Bourdonnaye horribly wounded and groaning so as to break our hearts; and we were, besides, agitated with sad presentiments with regard to the result of the battle, of which we had seen but the first part . . .

Everything foretold a complete victory for us. Masséna and General Boudet were making ready to issue from Aspern and Essling, and to fall back upon the Austrians, when, to our surprise, an aide-de-camp from the Emperor came up with orders for Marshal Lannes to suspend his attacking movement. Trees and other objects floating in the Danube had caused a new breach in the bridge and the arrival of Davout's troops was delayed. After an hour's waiting the passage was repaired and although the enemy had profited by the delay to reinforce his centre, we renewed our attack. Again the Austrians were giving ground, when we heard that an immense piece of the great bridge had been carried away and would take forty-eight hours to replace. The Emperor accordingly ordered Lannes to halt on the ground which he had taken.

This mishap, which prevented us from gaining a brilliant victory, came about as follows. An Austrian officer, posted on lookout duty with some companies of *jägers* in the islands above Aspern, had embarked in a small boat and gone out to the middle of the river to get a distant view of our troops crossing the bridges. Thus he witnessed the first breach caused by the floating trees, and the idea struck him that the same accident might be repeated as fast as we repaired the damages. He therefore had a number of beams and fireboats launched down the river which destroyed our pontoons, just as he had calculated. However, seeing that our engineers quickly replaced the damaged bridges, this industrious officer caused a large floating mill to be set on fire and towed out midstream. Borne down upon our principal bridge, it broke away a large part of it. Abandoning any hope of restoring the bridge that day and with Davout's corps still unable to reach the field of battle, Napoleon ordered Lannes to withdraw his troops by degrees to their former position, between Aspern and Essling, where they might hold their ground against the enemy.

The movement was being carried out in perfect order, when the Archduke, who had at first been puzzled by our retreat, heard that the bridge was broken and saw a chance of driving the French into the Danube. With this view, he sent his cavalry against the most advanced of our divisions, that of Saint-Hilaire. Our battalions repulsed the charge and the enemy then opened upon them with a heavy artillery fire. Just then I was bearing an order from Lannes to General Saint-Hilaire, and I had hardly reached him when a storm of grapeshot struck his staff, killing several officers and smashing the General's leg. He died under amputation. I was myself struck in the thigh by a grapeshot, which tore out a piece of flesh as large as an egg: but the wound was not dangerous and I was able to return and report to the Marshal. I found him with the Emperor, who, seeing me covered with blood, remarked, 'Your turn comes round pretty often!'

Seeing the division attacked at all points, the Marshal went to take command of it. He withdrew it slowly, often facing towards the enemy, until our right rested on Essling, which was still held by Boudet's division. Although my wound was still not yet dressed, I thought I ought to go with the Marshal. In the course of the retreat, my friend de Viry had his shoulder smashed by a bullet, and I had some difficulty in getting him brought to the entrenchments.

The position was critical. Compelled to act on the defensive, the Emperor posted his army in an arc, our right resting on the river in rear of Essling, our left in rear of Aspern. Under pain of being driven into the river we had to keep up the fight for the rest of the day; it was now 9 a.m. and not until nightfall should we be able to retire to the island of Lobau. The Archduke, recognising the weakness of our position, repeatedly attacked the two villages and the centre; but fortunately for us, did not think of forcing our weakest point – between Essling and the Danube – by which a strong column, pushed vigorously forward, might have reached the bridgehead and destroyed

161

us. All along our lines the slaughter was terrible, but absolutely necessary to save the honour of France and the portion
of the army which had crossed the Danube.

To check the energy of the enemy's attacks, Marshal Lannes
frequently resumed the offensive against their centre, and
forced it back; but they soon returned with reinforcements.
On one of these occasions, Labédoyère got a grapeshot in his
foot and de Watteville a dislocated shoulder, his horse being
killed under him by a cannon-ball. Thus of all the staff, Sub-
Lieutenant Le Couteulx and I remained, and I could not leave
the Marshal alone with that young officer, who, though brave
enough, had no experience. Wishing to retain me, he said, 'Go
and get your wound dressed; and if you can still sit on your
horse, come back to me.' I went to the first field hospital: the
crowd of wounded was enormous and lint had run short. A
doctor put into my wound some of the coarse tow which is
used as wadding for cannon and the rough fibres gave me a
good deal of pain.

In other circumstances I should have gone to the rear but
now every man had to display all his energy and I went back to
Lannes. I found him very anxious, having just heard that the
Austrians had taken half of Aspern from Masséna. That
village was taken and retaken many times.[6] Essling was being
vigorously attacked at that very instant and bravely defended
by Boudet's division. So fierce were both sides that they were
fighting in the midst of burning houses and barricading
themselves with the hacked corpses which blocked the streets.
Five times the Hungarian[7] grenadiers were driven back but
their sixth attack succeeded. They got possession of that
village, all but the great granary, into which General Boudet
withdrew, as into a citadel. While this fighting was going on,
the Marshal sent me several times into Essling. The danger was
considerable but in the excitement I forgot the pain of my
wound.

At length, perceiving that he was wasting his forces against our two bastions, Essling and Aspern, and neglecting our centre – where a well-sustained attack with his reserve would bring him to our bridge and thus secure the destruction of the French army – the Archduke launched large masses of cavalry, supported by heavy columns of infantry, on this point. Marshal Lannes, not surprised by this display of force, gave orders that the Austrians should be allowed to approach within gunshot range; and received them with such a furious fire of musketry and grape that they halted: nor could the stimulating presence of the Archduke himself induce them to come a pace nearer. They could perceive behind our line the bearskin caps of the Old Guard, which was advancing in a stately column with shouldered arms.

Cleverly profiting from the enemy's hesitation, Marshal Lannes ordered Bessières to charge them at the head of two divisions of cavalry. Part of the Austrian battalions and squadrons were overthrown, and the Archduke, finding his attack on our centre unsuccessful, thought to profit at least by the advantage which the capture of Essling offered. At that moment, however, the Emperor ordered his aide-de-camp, General Mouton, to retake the village. Hurling himself upon the Hungarian grenadiers, he drove them out, and remained master of Essling, a feat which covered himself and the Young Guard with glory and later earned him the title of Count of Lobau. These successes on our part having slackened the enemy's ardour, the Archduke, whose losses were enormous, abandoned hope of forcing our position; and for the rest of the day only kept up an ineffectual combat. This terrible thirty hours' battle was drawing to its close; and it was high time, for our ammunition was nearly exhausted.

While the two armies faced each other, watching but not moving, and the commanders (clustered in groups in rear of the battalions) were discussing the events of the day, Marshal Lannes, weary with riding, had dismounted and was walking with Major General Pouzet. Just then a spent ball struck the

General on the head, laying him dead at the Marshal's feet. He had been formerly a sergeant in the Champagne Regiment and at the beginning of the Revolution was at the camp of Le Miral when my father commanded there. At the same time the Battalion of Volunteers from Gers, in which Lannes was sub-lieutenant, formed part of the division. The sergeants of the old line regiments having the task of instructing the volunteers, that of Gers fell to the share of Pouzet. Quickly perceiving the young sub-lieutenant's talents, he did not confine himself to teaching him the manual of exercise, but gave him such instruction in manoeuvres that he became an excellent tactician. Attributing his first promotion to Pouzet's instruction, Lannes was much attached to him and in proportion as he got on himself, he used his interest to advance his friend. His grief, then, at seeing him fall was very great.

At that moment we were a little in advance of the tile works near Essling. In his emotion, wishing to get away from the corpse, Lannes went a hundred paces in the direction of Enzersdorf and seated himself, deep in thought, on the further side of a ditch. A quarter of an hour later, four soldiers laboriously carrying in a cloak a dead officer whose face could not be seen, stopped to rest in front of the Marshal. The cloak fell open, and Lannes recognised Pouzet: 'Oh!' he cried, 'is this terrible sight going to follow me everywhere?' Getting up, he went and sat down at the edge of another ditch, his hand over his eyes and his legs crossed. As he sat there, plunged in gloomy meditation, a small three-pound shot, fired from a gun at Enzersdorf, ricochetted, and struck him just where his legs crossed. The knee-pan of one leg was smashed and the sinews of the other torn.

Instantly I rushed towards the Marshal, who said, 'I am wounded; it's nothing much. Give me your hand to help me up.' He tried to rise but could not. The infantry regiments in front of us sent some men at once to carry the Marshal to an ambulance; but having neither stretcher nor cloak, we had to take him in our arms: an attitude which caused him horrible pain. Then a sergeant, seeing in the distance the soldiers who were carrying General Pouzet's body, ran and fetched the cloak in which the corpse was wrapped. We were about to lay the Marshal on it, so as to carry him with less discomfort; but he recognised the cloak and said to me, 'This is my poor friend's; it is covered with his blood: I will not use it. Drag me along how you can.' Not far off I saw a clump of trees; I sent young Le Couteulx and some grenadiers there and they presently returned with a makeshift stretcher covered with boughs.

We carried the Marshal to the bridgehead, where the chief surgeons proceeded to dress his wound; first holding a private consultation, in which they could not agree what should be done. Dr Larrey was in favour of amputating the leg of which the knee was broken; another (whose name I forget) wanted to cut off both; while Dr Yvan, from whom I heard these details, was against any amputation. This surgeon, who had long known the Marshal, asserted that his firmness of character gave some chance of a cure, while an operation performed in such hot weather would inevitably bring him to the grave. Larrey was the senior surgeon of the army, however, and his opinion prevailed: the leg with the shattered knee was amputated. Lannes bore the operation with great courage; it was hardly over when the Emperor came up. The interview was most touching: Napoleon kneeling beside the stretcher, wept as he embraced the Marshal, whose blood soon stained his white kerseymere waistcoat. 'You will live, my friend,' said the Emperor, 'you will live.'

The Emperor profited cleverly by the time which the Austrian Archduke left him, and never was his prodigious activity better employed. Aided by Davout and his divisions, he did on the 23rd alone more than any other general could have done in a week. A well-organised service of boats brought provisions and ammunition to the island of Lobau; the wounded were all got away to Vienna; hospitals were established; materials in great quantity collected to repair the bridges, build fresh ones, and protect them by a stockade; a hundred guns of the largest calibre, captured in Vienna, were taken to Ebersdorf. By the 24th communication with the island was re-established and the Emperor marched Lannes' division, the Guard, and all the cavalry on to the right bank; leaving only Masséna's corps to fortify the island and put in battery the big guns which had been brought up. This point being secured, the Emperor ordered Bernadotte's army corps and the various divisions of the Germanic Confederation to come on to Vienna, which would enable him to repulse the Archduke in the event of his venturing across the river to attack us. A few days later we received a powerful reinforcement: a French army under Eugène de Beauharnais,[8] coming from Italy, took up its position on our right.

As soon as the troops had effected their retreat onto the island of Lobau and onto the right bank of the Danube, the Emperor took up his quarters at Ebersdorf, in order to survey the arrangements for a fresh crossing. Not one bridge but three were to be constructed, all having a strong stockade of piles upstream from them in order to withstand any floating objects which the enemy might launch at them. The care which the Emperor bestowed on these important works did not prevent him from coming twice a day to visit Marshal Lannes.

For the first four days after his wound the Marshal went on as well as possible; he preserved perfect equanimity, and conversed very calmly. So far was he from renouncing the service of his country, as some writers have stated, that he made plans for the future. Learning that Mesler, the celebrated Viennese mechanician, had made for the Austrian general, Count Palfy, an artificial leg with which he could walk and ride as well as ever, Lannes asked me to write to that artist, bidding him come and measure him for a leg. But the oppressive heat which we had experienced for some time became more intense, with disastrous results to the wounded man. He was attacked by high fever, accompanied with terrible delirium. The critical situation in which he had left the army was always on his mind and he fancied himself still on the battlefield. He would call his aides-de-camp in a loud voice, bidding one tell the *cuirassiers* to charge, another to bring the artillery to such-and-such a point, and so on. In vain did Dr Yvan and I try to soothe him: he did not understand us. His excitement kept increasing; he no longer recognised even the Emperor.

This condition lasted several days without his getting a moment's sleep or resting from his imaginary combats. At length, in the night between the 29th and 30th, he left off giving his orders and a great weakness succeeded the delirium. He recovered all his mental faculties: recognised me, pressed my hand; spoke of his wife, his five children, his father; and as I was very near his pillow, he rested his head on my shoulder and appeared to be falling asleep, when he passed away with a sigh. It was daybreak on 30 May.

A few moments later the Emperor arrived for his morning visit. I thought it my duty to meet him and let him know of the sad event, cautioning him not to enter the infected atmosphere of the room. But Napoleon, putting me aside, advanced to the Marshal's body, which he embraced, bathing it with tears, and saying repeatedly, 'What a loss for France and for me!' Berthier tried in vain to draw him away from the sad sight; he remained for more than an hour, and only yielded when Berthier pointed out that General Bertrand and the engineer officers were waiting to execute an important piece of work, for which he had himself fixed the time. As he went away he expressed his satisfaction with the unremitting care which I had taken of the Marshal and bade me have the body embalmed and everything got ready for its journey to France.

13 The Point of Honour

The Battle of Wagram, July 1809

A man of war must be a man of honour.
Archduke Charles[1]

After the death of Lannes, Marbot went to Vienna, seeking treatment for the grapeshot wound in his thigh. While there, 'Deep in sad meditations', he received the gratifying news of his commission into the chasseurs-à-cheval of the Imperial Guard with the rank of major. This was an honour indeed and represented a significant step in his career. However, by joining the cavalry of the Guard, Marbot realized with dismay that he would come under the direct command of Marshal Bessières, whose wrath he had incurred at Aspern–Essling: 'No doubt it would be a great advantage to you to enter the Guard,' pointed out a sympathetic Marshal Masséna, 'but you would expose yourself to Marshal Bessières' vengeance. Come and be my aide-de-camp, and you shall be received like a child of my family . . . and I will take care of your promotion.' Persuaded by these words, Marbot declined his place in the Guard 'with a sore heart' and joined Masséna's staff instead; receiving at the same time his promotion to major. Ironically, an hour after this appointment, a gracious Marshal Bessières arrived in person to assure Marbot that he bore him no grudge, 'as he knew that in bearing the order to him on the field of Essling I was only obeying the instructions of Marshal

169

Lannes.' By his own rashness, Marbot had deprived himself of a place in Napoleon's 'Immortals'. He did, however, receive a special mark of the Emperor's esteem: being made a Knight of the Empire with an accompanying annuity of 2,000 francs.

Archduke Charles did not follow up his success at Aspern–Essling; electing instead to withdraw to the village of Wagram, about ten miles north of the river. Napoleon, profiting by the time allowed him, assembled an army of 190,000 men and 500 guns on the south bank of the Danube. On the night of 3–4 July the French massed on Lobau Island; and on the following night, in the middle of a thunderstorm, they crossed the Danube from the eastern side of the island, opposite the village of Enzersdorf. The Austrians, patiently watching the old crossing-point at Aspern, several miles upstream, were caught napping: the Battle of Wagram was about to begin. The two days of fighting which followed were among the bloodiest of the period and the concentration of artillery was unprecedented: nearly 1,000 guns being brought to bear on a front of approximately five miles. Casualties, therefore, were horrendous: 75,000 in total, including many top brass from both sides. Although the Austrians succeeded in breaking Bernadotte's Saxon contingent, and smashing the French left wing – sending Boudet's troops flying in disorder over the old battlefield of Aspern – these crises were contained. Meanwhile, the Austrian left wing having been pulverized by Davout, Napoleon sent in MacDonald to break their centre. By 1 p.m. on 6 July Charles had had enough and began an orderly withdrawal. His brother, the Archduke John, arrived too late with his promised reinforcements to avoid another Austrian defeat.

On the day after the battle, Masséna was sent in pursuit of Charles's army. By 11 July he had reached the town of Znaim (now Znojmo in the Slovak Republic), with orders to take it at all costs. During the fighting, however, Masséna received word of a ceasefire and Marbot was ordered into the mêlée

*to break the news: 'As I was shouting "Peace! peace!" and
with my left hand giving the sign for a halt, suddenly a bullet
from the outskirts of the town struck me on the wrist.'
Eventually, an Austrian aide-de-camp joined Marbot (receiving a bullet in the shoulder for his trouble) and the two,
embracing, signified that peace had broken out. The fighting
came to an end and Austria surrendered on 12 July. Once
again, Napoleon had triumphed; but Wagram represented the
zenith of his power: from now on his lucky star was on the
wane.*

AMONG the multitudes of episodes to which the Battle of
Wagram gave rise, the most important – and one which
produced very strong feeling in the army – has not been
related by any author. I mean the disgrace of Marshal Bernadotte, who was ordered off the field by the Emperor. Between
these two eminent persons no love was ever lost; and since the
conspiracy of Rennes,[2] got up by Bernadotte against the
consular government, they had been on very bad terms. This
notwithstanding, Napoleon had included Bernadotte in the
first creation of marshals, and made him Prince of Ponte
Corvo at the request of Joseph Bonaparte, whose sister-in-
law Bernadotte had married.[3] Nothing could appease, however, Bernadotte's hatred and envy of Napoleon. He flattered
him to his face and afterwards, as the Emperor well knew,
criticised and found fault.

The ability and courage which he had shown at Austerlitz
would have induced the Emperor to overlook his misdeeds,
had he not aggravated them by his conduct at Jena. In spite of
the urgent requests of his generals, he let his three divisions
remain wholly inactive, refusing to support Davout, who, a
league away at Auerstädt, was withstanding half the Prussian
army. The army and all France was indignant with Bernadotte; but the Emperor did no more than reprimand him

severely. Stimulated by this, the Marshal did well at Hall and Lübeck but soon fell back into his customary laziness and ill will; and in spite of orders, was two days late for the Battle of Eylau.

This lukewarm conduct roused afresh the Emperor's dissatisfaction, which grew more and more during the campaign in Austria. Bernadotte, in command of a corps of Saxons, always came up late, acted without energy, and criticised not only the Emperor's tactics, but the way in which the other marshals handled their troops. The Emperor, however, restrained his irritation until, on the first day of the Battle of Wagram, Bernadotte's lack of vigour and false tactics allowed the Austrians to retake the important position of Deutsch-Wagram. It seems that after this repulse Bernadotte said to some officers that the crossing of the Danube and subsequent action had been mismanaged and that if he had been in command he could, by a scientific manoeuvre, have compelled the Archduke to surrender almost without a blow. This remark was reported the same evening to the Emperor, who was naturally angry. Such were the terms on which Napoleon and Bernadotte stood when the undecided action resumed on the 6th.

When the battle was its height, the Saxons, badly handled by Bernadotte,[4] were repulsed and charged by the enemy's cavalry: being flung into disorder upon Masséna's corps, which they nearly carried with them. The Saxons are brave but the best of troops are sometimes routed; and in such cases it is of no use for the officers to try to rally the men who are within reach of the enemy's sabres and bayonets. Generals and colonels should get as quickly as possible to the head of the flying mass, then face about, and by their presence and their words arrest the movement of retreat and re-form the battalions. In conformity with this rule, Bernadotte, whose personal bravery was unquestioned, galloped off into the plain at the head of his staff, to get in front of the fugitives and stop them.

Hardly was he clear of the throng, when he found himself face to face with the Emperor, who observed ironically, 'Is that the scientific manoeuvre by which you were going to make the Archduke lay down his arms?' Bernadotte's vexation at the rout of his army was heightened by learning that the Emperor knew of his inconsiderate remark of the previous day and he remained speechless. Presently recovering himself, he tried to mutter some words of explanation; but the Emperor, in a severe and haughty tone, said: 'I remove you, sir, from the command of the army corps which you handle so badly. Withdraw at once and leave the Grand Army within twenty-four hours; a bungler like you is no good to me.' Therewith he turned his back on the Marshal and taking command of the Saxons, restored order to their ranks and led them again to meet the enemy.

In any circumstances Bernadotte would have been in despair at such an outburst; but as he had been ordered to leave the field at the moment when he was galloping ahead of the fugitives, which might give an opening for slanderous tongues to reflect on his courage – though the object of his retreat was to check that of his soldiers – he understood how much worse it made his position; and it is asserted that in his despair he wished to throw himself on the enemy's bayonets. His aides-de-camp, however, held him back and took him away from the Saxon troops. All day long he strayed about the battlefield and stayed towards evening behind our left wing at the village of Leopoldau, where his officers persuaded him to pass the night in the pretty little château belonging to that place. Hardly, however, was he established when Masséna, who had ordered his headquarters to be fixed at Leopoldau, came to take possession of the same house.

As it is customary for generals to be quartered in the midst of their troops, and not to lodge in villages where their colleagues' regiments are, Bernadotte wished to give way to Masséna; the latter, however, not yet knowing of his

173

colleague's mishap, begged him to stay and share the quarters with him, to which Bernadotte agreed. While arrangements were being made for their lodging, an officer who had witnessed the scene between the Emperor and Bernadotte came and told Masséna of it, whereupon he changed his mind and discovered that the house was not roomy enough for two marshals and their staffs. Wishing, however, to keep up the appearance of generosity, he said to his aides-de-camp, 'This lodging was mine by rights but as poor Bernadotte is in trouble I must give it up to him; find me another place – a barn, or anywhere.' Then he got into his carriage and went off without a word to Bernadotte, who felt this desertion deeply.

In his exasperation he committed another and very serious mistake; for although no longer in command of the Saxon troops, he addressed them in a general order, in which he made the most of their exploits – and consequently of his own – without waiting for the usual assignment of credit on the part of the commander-in-chief. This infringement of regulations increased the Emperor's anger and Bernadotte was obliged to withdraw from the army and return to France.

Among the remarkable incidents of the Battle of Wagram, I may mention the combat between two cavalry regiments, which, though serving in hostile armies, belonged to the same proprietary colonel, Prince Albert of Sachs-Teschen. He had married the celebrated Archduchess Christina of Austria, governor of the Low Countries, and having the title of prince in both states, he possessed a regiment of hussars in Saxony, and one of *cuirassiers* in Austria. Both one and the other bore his name and he appointed all the officers in each. Austria and Saxony having been at peace for many years, whenever he had an officer to place he would put him indifferently in whichever regiment had a vacancy, so that out of one family there could be found some members in the Saxon hussars and others in the Austrian *cuirassiers*. Now, by an accident at once deplorable and extraordinary, these two regiments met on the battlefield of Wagram; and impelled by duty and by the point of honour, they charged each other. Strange to say, the *cuirassiers* were broken by the hussars, who, in their desire to retrieve under the eyes of Napoleon the repulse of the Saxon infantry, fought with the greatest vigour. Indeed the Saxon infantry, though it has often shown its courage, is far from being either as solidly organised or as well trained as the cavalry, which is rightly held to be one of the best in Europe.

You will probably now like to hear my own adventures in this terrible battle. Though frequently much exposed, especially on the second day, when the enemy's artillery converged its fire on Marshal Masséna's carriage,[5] and we were literally under a hail of cannon-balls, which struck down a good many around me, I was lucky enough not to be wounded. I was also in considerable danger when the Austrian cavalry had broken and routed Boudet's division, and the Marshal sent me to that General in the middle of 10,000 flying soldiers, who were being hewn down by the cavalry. Again I was once more in danger when, by carrying orders, I had to pass near some spots where the corn was blazing. By frequent detours, I managed to escape the flames, but it was impossible to avoid crossing the fields where the ashes of the burnt straw were still hot enough to scorch the horses' feet. Two of mine were rendered useless for some time by the injuries they thus received, and a third was in such pain that he was within an ace of rolling me over in the half-extinguished straw. However, I got through without any serious accident; but though I escaped personal damage, a disagreeable thing befell me, which had very injurious results.

On the second day of the battle I got into almost hopeless trouble with Masséna: the way of it was this. The Marshal sent me with a message to the Emperor; I had the very greatest difficulty in reaching him, and was coming back after having galloped more than three leagues over the yet burning ashes of the corn. My horse, dead beat, and with his legs half-burnt, could go no further when I got back to Masséna and found him in a great difficulty. His corps was retreating before the enemy's right, along the Danube; and the infantry of Boudet's division, broken by the Austrian cavalry (which was sabring them mercilessly), were flying pell-mell across the plain: it was the most critical moment of the battle.

From his carriage the Marshal could see the imminent danger, and was calmly making his dispositions to maintain order in the three infantry divisions which, as yet, were unbroken. For this purpose he had been obliged to send so many aides-de-camp to his generals that he had none with him except his son, Prosper Masséna, a young lieutenant. At that moment he saw that the fugitives from Boudet's division were making for the three divisions which were still fighting, and were on the point of flinging themselves upon their ranks, and drawing them along in a general rout. To stop this catastrophe, the Marshal wished to tell the generals and officers to direct the torrent of fleeing troops towards the island of Lobau, where they would find a secure shelter behind our artillery. It was a dangerous mission, as there was every probability that the aide-de-camp who went into that disorderly rabble would not come out alive. Masséna could not make up his mind to expose his son to this danger, but he had no other officer near him and it was clear that the order must be carried.

I came up just at the right moment to extricate Masséna from this cruel dilemma; so, without giving me time to take my breath, he ordered me to throw myself into the danger which he dreaded for his son; but observing that my horse could hardly stand, he lent me one of his, which an orderly was leading. I was too well acquainted with military duty not to be aware that a general cannot bind himself to follow the arrangements which his aides-de-camp have made amongst themselves for taking their turn of duty, however great the peril may be; the chief must be free in a given case to employ whichever officer he thinks best suited to get his orders executed. Thus, although Prosper had not carried a single order all day and it was his turn to go, I made no remark. I will even say that my self-esteem hindered me from divining the Marshal's real motive in sending me on a duty both difficult and dangerous when it ought to have fallen to another, and I was proud of his confidence in me.

But Masséna soon destroyed my illusion by saying, in a wheedling tone, 'You understand, my friend, why I do not send my son. Although it's his turn I am afraid of getting him killed. You understand? You understand?' I should have held my tongue; but disgusted with such ill-disguised selfishness, I could not refrain from answering (and that in the presence of several generals): 'Marshal, I was going under the impression that I was about to fulfil a duty; I am sorry that you have corrected my mistake, for now I understand perfectly that, being obliged to send one of your aides-de-camp to almost certain death, you would rather it should be I rather than your son; but I think you might have spared me this cruel plain speaking.' And without waiting for a reply, I went off at full gallop towards Boudet's division, which the enemy's troopers were pitilessly slaughtering.

As I left Masséna's carriage I heard a discussion begin between the Marshal and his son, but the uproar of the battle and the speed at which I was going prevented me from catching their words. Their sense, however, was shortly explained, for hardly had I reached Boudet's division and begun doing my utmost to direct the terrified crowd towards the island of Lobau, when I beheld Prosper Masséna at my side. The brave lad, indignant at the way in which his father had sent me into danger, thus making of him a mere spectator, had escaped unawares to follow me. 'I wish,' said he, 'at least to share the danger from which I ought to have saved you.' The young man's straightforwardness pleased me; in his place I should have wished to do the same. Still, I had rather he had been further off at this critical moment, for no one who has not seen it can form an idea of a mass of infantry which has been broken and is being actively pursued by cavalry. Sabres and lances were working terrible execution among this rabble of terrified men, who were flying in disorder instead of taking the equally easy and much safer course of forming themselves into groups and defending themselves with the bayonet.

Prosper Masséna was very brave, and in no way dazed by the danger, although we found ourselves every moment in this chaos face to face with the enemy's troopers. My position then became very critical, since I had a threefold task to fulfil: first, to parry the blows aimed at the young Masséna, who had never learned the sword exercise and used his weapon clumsily; secondly, to defend myself; and lastly, to speak to our demoralised soldiers to make them understand that they were to go towards Lobau and not towards the divisions which were still in line. Neither of us received any wound, for when the Austrian troopers perceived that we were determined to defend ourselves vigorously, they left us, and turned their attention to the unresisting foot soldiers.

When troops are in disorder, the soldiers fling themselves like sheep in the direction where they see their comrades running, and thus, as soon as I had imparted the Marshal's orders to a certain number of officers, and they had shouted to their people to run towards the island, the stream of fugitives made in that direction. I found General Boudet at last, and he succeeded under the fire of our guns in rallying his troops. My task was thus at an end and I returned with Prosper towards the Marshal. But in my desire to take the shortest road, I imprudently passed near a clump of trees, behind which some hundred Austrian *uhlans* were posted. They charged upon us unawares, we meanwhile making at full speed for a line of French cavalry which was coming our way.

We were none too soon, for the enemy's squadron was on the point of reaching us, and was pressing us so close that I thought for a moment that we were going to be killed or taken prisoners. But at the approach of our men the *uhlans* wheeled about – all but one officer – who, being admirably mounted, would not leave us without having a shot at us. One bullet pierced the neck of Prosper's horse, and the animal, throwing up his head violently, covered young Masséna's face with blood. I thought he was wounded, and was getting ready to defend him against the *uhlan* officer, when we were met by the advanced files of the French regiment. These, firing their carbines at the Austrian, laid him dead on the spot, just as he was turning to gallop off.

Prosper and I then returned to the Marshal, who uttered a cry of grief on seeing his son covered with blood. But on finding that he was not wounded, he gave free vent to his anger, and in the presence of several generals, his own aide-de-camp, and two orderly officers of the Emperor's, he scolded his son roundly, and ended his lecture with the words, 'Who ordered you to go and stick your head into that row, you young idiot?'

Prosper's answer was really sublime: 'Who ordered me? My honour! This is my first campaign. I am already lieutenant and member of the Legion of Honour; I have received several foreign decorations, and so far I have done nothing for them. I wished to show my comrades, the army, and France that if I am not destined to have the military talent of my illustrious father, I am at least worthy by my courage to bear the name of Masséna.' Seeing that his son's noble statements met with the approbation of all bystanders, the Marshal made no answer; but his anger fell chiefly on me, whom he accused of having carried his son away, when, on the contrary, his presence was a great hindrance to me.

The two orderly officers having reported at headquarters the scene between the Marshal and his son, Napoleon heard of it, and happening to come that evening to Leopoldau, sent for Prosper, and said to him (taking him in a friendly way by the ear): 'Good, very good, my dear boy; that is how young people like you ought to start on their career.' Then turning to the Marshal, he said in a low tone, but loud enough to be heard by General Bertrand, from whom I have the story, 'I love my brother Louis no less than you your son; but when he was my aide-de-camp in Italy he did his turn of duty like the others, and I should have been afraid of bringing him into discredit if I had sent one of his comrades into danger instead of him.' This reproof from the Emperor, in addition to the answer which I had been foolish enough to make to Masséna, naturally set him still more against me. From that day forward, he never addressed me with *tu*[6] and although outwardly he treated me well, I knew that the grudge would remain.

14 Stop, Mr Frenchman!

Masséna's Retreat From Portugal, March 1811

> One battle is just like another, inasmuch as they
> always conclude with one or both sides running
> away.
>
> Captain Sir John Kincaid[1]

*In October 1809 Napoleon made Masséna Prince of Essling,
in recognition of his services during the recent fighting on the
Danube. In the following spring he was appointed commander-in-chief of the Army of Portugal, with orders to invade
that country and dislodge the small British army which, with
only 20,000 men, had been waging a successful war in support
of their ally. Masséna, it was hoped, would succeed where
Marshals Soult and Victor had failed. The old warrior, however, was past his prime: aged fifty-two, a thin, stooping
figure, and – thanks to Napoleon, who had put his eye out
in a hunting accident – partially blind.*

*French operations in the Peninsula were doomed from the
start. Napoleon's system of warfare was based on his army's
ability to march quickly, concentrate rapidly, and feed itself at
the expense of the enemy by living off the land. In order for
this system to work effectively, two things were needed: good
roads and good farmland. Spain and Portugal, however, were
two of the poorest nations in Europe: roads were either non-
existent, or little better than dirt tracks; high mountain ranges*

*and swift rivers formed natural barriers, difficult for large
armies to negotiate; and the land was so impoverished that it
was barely able to support the local peasantry, never mind an
invading force of thousands of men and horses. Added to these
difficulties, the French were faced with a local population
fanatically opposed to their presence, and a highly motivated
British army under one of the ablest generals of the day: Sir
Arthur Wellesley, Duke of Wellington. To make matters even
worse, the French top brass, in Napoleon's absence, seemed
incapable of acting in accord: jealousies, rivalries, and the
desire for independent glory kept the Peninsula marshals at
each others' throats, instead of the enemy's.*

*On 10 May 1810 Masséna arrived in Spain to take over his
new command. Marbot, his senior aide-de-camp, accompanied
him: 'Although the Minister of War had assured the Marshal
that everything was ready for the campaign in the Peninsula, it
was nothing of the kind, and the commander-in-chief had to
stay a fortnight at Valladolid, looking after the departure of the
troops and the transport of stores and ammunition. At last the
headquarters were removed to Salamanca, where my brother
and I were quartered with the Count of Montezuma, a lineal
descendant of the last Emperor of Mexico.' Masséna was not
only preoccupied with troops, stores and ammunition. Having
taken a fancy to a certain Henriette Leberton, the sister of one
of his aides-de-camp, Masséna had brought the lady along as
his mistress, dressing her up as an officer of dragoons (Marbot,
far too chivalrous to name the lady, refers to her in his memoirs
as Madame N——). Masséna's colleagues, Ney, Reynier,
Montbrun and Junot, disapproved strongly of the Marshal's
conduct and quickly were 'on the worst of terms with Masséna,
who, on his side, bore them no goodwill'. The campaign had
not started well.*

*After further setbacks and delays, Masséna's invasion of
Portugal finally began and on 9 July the French captured the
border fortress of Ciudad Rodrigo. It was here that Marbot,*

having slept in a damp, filthy sheepstall (he had given up his original billet, which was both comfortable and dry, to Mas-séna), took fever: 'It was the only time that I have been seriously ill without being wounded, and this time my life was despaired of, and I was left at Ciudad Rodrigo while the army crossed the Coa and marched on Almeida.' The fortress of Almeida fell to the French on 27 August and shortly afterwards Marbot was fit enough to rejoin Masséna, who 'never said a word to me about my illness'. The French pushed deeper into Portugal; and after various halts, delays and squabbles – usually caused by Masséna's concern for the comfort of his lady-dragoon – they were stopped by Wellington at Busaco, north of Lisbon, on 27 September. According to Marbot, Masséna hardly bothered to reconnoitre the Allied position; but influenced by Marshal Ney, boldly ordered a frontal attack. The ridge of Busaco, however, afforded the British and Portuguese an excellent defensive feature; and although heavily outnumbered, they beat off the French, inflicting over 4,000 casualties. Nevertheless, afraid of being outflanked, Wellington ordered a retreat on Lisbon: Masséna followed, hard on his heels.

On 11 October 1810 Masséna was stopped in his tracks. Completely unbeknown to the French, Wellington had sealed off Lisbon by a series of forts, stretching from the sea in the west, to the estuary of the Tagus in the east: the so-called Lines of Torres Vedras. Built by British engineers with the paid labour of 7,000 Portuguese peasants, work on this vast defensive network had been started the previous year. For miles about the land had been laid waste: rivers were blocked, villages burned, and trees felled. At a bitter cost to the local peasantry, many of whom were to die of starvation, Wellington had created a wasteland upon which – it was hoped – the French would not be able to survive. Safe behind the Lines and supplied by the Royal Navy, the British simply waited for Masséna to pack up and go home. Masséna, realizing that

Wellington's position was unassailable, lingered for a month, hoping that the British would make a move. When this did not happen, he headed north to Santarem and settled down to a winter of waiting. By March, having been let down by Marshal Soult (he went off to capture the fortress of Badajoz instead of reinforcing Masséna, as ordered), Masséna had had enough. On the night of the 5th, leaving scarecrow-sentries stuffed with straw to fool the British, the French slipped away.

Their retreat was a sordid affair: massacre, torture and arson being the order of the day, committed by soldiers brutalized by five months of famine and a guerrilla war of atrocity and counter-atrocity. Ney, commanding the rear-guard, fought a series of skirmishes as Wellington, now in pursuit, kept up the pressure: Pombal, Redinha, and on 14 March, Miranda de Corvo, where Marbot takes up the story.

DURING THIS long and toilsome march, Masséna's attention was much occupied with the danger to which Madame N—— was exposed. Several times her horse fell over fragments of rock invisible in the darkness; but although cruelly bruised, the brave woman picked herself up. After several of these falls, however, she could neither remount her horse nor walk on foot and had to be carried by grenadiers. What would have happened to her if we had been attacked, I do not know. The Marshal, imploring us all the time not to abandon her, said repeatedly, 'What a mistake I made in bringing a woman to the war!'

On the following day, 14 March 1811, after beating back a smart attack upon his rearguard, Masséna posted the mass of his troops in a strong position in front of Miranda de Corvo, in order to give the artillery and baggage wagons time to pass the defile beyond the town. Seeing the French army halted, Lord Wellington brought up a strong force and everything promised a serious engagement. When Masséna summoned his lieutenants to receive his instructions, all but Marshal Ney came at once; and as he did not arrive, the commander-in-chief ordered Major Pelet and me to go and ask him to come quickly. This errand, which seemed an easy one to discharge, nearly cost me my life.

The French army was drawn up on ground descending gently in the form of an amphitheatre towards a large brook, lying between two broad hills, over the summits of which passed country roads leading to Miranda. At the moment when Pelet and I galloped off to execute the Marshal's order, the English skirmishers appeared in the distance, coming up to attack the two hills. In order to be more certain of finding Marshal Ney, my companion and I separated. Pelet took the road on the left, I that on the right, passing through a wide clearing in which were our outposts. Hearing that Marshal Ney had passed by less than a quarter of an hour before, I felt bound to hasten to meet him; and just as I hoped to come up with him, I heard several shots and bullets whistled past my ears: I was no great distance from the enemy's skirmishers, posted in the woods surrounding the clearing. Although I knew that Marshal Ney had a strong escort, I was uneasy on his account, fearing that the English might have cut him off, until I saw him on the other side of the brook. Pelet was with him and both were going in the direction of Masséna.

So, being sure that the orders had been conveyed, I was about to return, when a young English light infantry officer trotted up on his pony, crying: 'Stop, Mr Frenchman; I should like to have a little fight with you!' I saw no need to reply to this bluster and made my way towards our outposts: the Englishman following, heaping insults upon me. At first I took no notice, but presently he called out: 'I can see by your uniform that you are on the staff of a marshal; and I will put in the London papers that the sight of me was enough to frighten away one of Masséna's or Ney's cowardly aides-de-camp!'

I admit that it was a serious error on my part, but I could no longer endure this impudent challenge coolly; so drawing my sabre, I dashed furiously at my adversary. But just as I was about to meet him, I heard a rustling in the wood and out came two English hussars, galloping to cut off my retreat. I was caught in a trap and understood that only a most energetic defence could save me from the disgrace of being taken prisoner – through my own fault – in sight of the whole French army, which was witness to this unequal combat. So I flew upon the English officer: we met; he gave me a slash across the face; I ran my sword into his throat. His blood spurted over me and the wretch fell from his horse to the ground, which he bit in his rage. Meanwhile, the two hussars were hitting me all over, chiefly on the head. In a few seconds my shako, my wallet,[2] and my *pelisse* were in strips, though I was not myself wounded by any of their blows. At length, however, the elder of the two hussars – a grizzled old soldier – let me have more than an inch of his blade in my side. I replied with a vigorous backhander; my blade struck his teeth and passed between his jaws as he was in the act of shouting, slitting his mouth to the ears. He made off promptly – to my satisfaction – for he was the braver and more energetic of the two. When the younger man found himself left alone with me, he hesitated for a moment because, as our horses' heads were touching, he saw that to turn his back to me was to expose himself to be hit. However, on seeing several soldiers coming to my aid, he made up his mind; but he did not escape the dreaded wound, for in my anger I pursued him for some paces and gave him a thrust in the shoulder, which quickened his speed.

During this fight, which lasted less time than it has taken to tell it, our scouts had come up quickly to set me free; and on the other side the English soldiers had marched towards the place where their officer had fallen. The two groups were firing at each other and I was very near getting in the way of the bullets from both sides. But my brother and Ligniville, who had seen me engaged with the English officer and his two men, had hastened up to me and I was badly in want of their help: for I was losing so much blood from the wound in my side that I was growing faint and I could not have stayed on my horse if they had not held me up.

As soon as I rejoined the staff, Masséna said, taking my hand, 'Well done; rather too well done! A field officer has no business to expose himself in fighting at the outposts.' He was quite right; but when I told him the motives which had led me on, he blamed me less and the more fiery Marshal Ney – remembering his own hussar days – cried, 'Upon my word, in Marbot's place I should have done the same!' All the generals and my comrades came to express their concern while Dr Brisset was attending me. The wound in my cheek was not important: in a month's time it had healed over and you can scarcely see the mark of it along my left whisker. But the thrust in my right side was dangerous, especially in the middle of a long retreat, in which I was compelled to travel on horseback, without being able to get the rest which a wounded man needs. Such, my children, was the result of my fight at Miranda de Corvo. You have still got the shako which I wore, and the numerous notches with which the English sabres have adorned it prove that the two hussars did not let me off. I brought away my wallet, too, the sling of which was cut in three places, but it has been mislaid.

As I said, at the moment when I was sent in search of Ney, the French army was drawn up in its position commanding Miranda de Corvo, expecting an attack. Wellington, however, deterred no doubt by the losses on the previous days,[3] checked the march of his troops and Masséna, seeing this, determined under cover of the approaching night to pass through the town and long defile of Miranda. I was in a painful position, having been on the march for two days and a night, and now severely wounded and weakened by loss of blood, being obliged to pass another night on horseback. The roads were fearfully

187

crowded with baggage and artillery wagons and numerous columns of troops, against which I was always running in the pitchy darkness. To crown our disasters, we came in for a heavy storm. I was soon wet through, and sat shivering on my horse, for I knew that if I got off to warm myself, I should not have strength to mount again. Meanwhile my wound caused me acute pain, so you may judge how I suffered during this cruel night.

On the morning of the 15th the army reached the banks of the Ceira, opposite Foz de Arunce,[4] a small town on a hill commanding the river and the level ground on the left bank. Crossing the bridge, I settled myself for a moment in a house, hoping to get a little rest; but the terrible scene which was passing before my eyes prevented this. Reynier's and Junot's corps were already in Foz de Arunce, Ney's still on the other side of the river; but the commander-in-chief, knowing that the enemy was close upon us, and not wishing his rearguard to fight with the river at its back, ordered Ney to bring all his troops across, cut the bridge, and strongly guard the neighbouring ford, so that the men might rest undisturbed. Ney, however, supposing that the enemy, tired by the labours of the last two days, were still at a distance – and deeming it cowardly to abandon the left bank wholly – left on that side two divisions of infantry, Lamotte's brigade of cavalry, and several guns, and did not cut the bridge: a fresh piece of disobedience which cost us dear.

As it happened, while Masséna was gone off to Ponte Murcelha to superintend the restoration of another bridge, which was to secure the passage of the River Alva on the next day, and Ney, full of confidence, had just given General Lamotte leave to cross the Ceira by the ford, in order to forage on the right bank, Lord Wellington suddenly appeared and instantly attacked the divisions left so imprudently on the hither bank. Ney himself, at the head of the 39th, bravely repulsed with the bayonet a charge of English dragoons, but their colonel, Lamour, having been killed by a bullet, the 39th, losing their heads, flung themselves back on the 59th and carried them away.

At the same moment, one of our batteries inadvertently sent a shot in their direction, and our men, thinking that they were surrounded, fled in a panic to the bridge. Lamotte, who could see all this from the other bank, tried to bring his cavalry across in support; but instead of coming by the difficult ford where he had gone over, he took the shortest way and so blocked the bridge with his brigade just as the fugitives came up from the opposite direction. No one could pass, and a good many men, seeing the bridge thus blocked, made for the ford and threw themselves in. Most got over, but several missed their footing and were drowned. Meanwhile Ney, exhausting every effort to repair his mistake, succeeded at length in collecting a battalion of the 27th and making his way to the divisions of Mermet and Ferey, who were holding their ground manfully, put himself at their head and, attacking on his side, drove the English back to their camp.

Astounded at this vigorous attack and hearing the shouts of our men who were struggling across the Ceira, they imagined that the whole French army was upon them. Panic-stricken in their turn, they flung down their arms, left their guns, and took to headlong flight. We on the right bank then witnessed a sight unusual in war: two sides flying each from the other in complete disorder! Finally the panic on both sides was checked and English and French returned to the abandoned ground to pick up their muskets; but both sides were so much ashamed of themselves that, though they were quite close to each other, not a shot was fired nor any challenges exchanged, and they returned to their positions in silence. Wellington did not venture to oppose Ney's retreat; and he recrossed the river and cut the bridge. In this queer engagement the English had some 200 men disabled and killed fifty of ours; but we lost a 100 by drowning and unhappily the 39th lost its eagle.[5] The best divers failed to recover it at the time; but it was found by Portuguese peasants in the following summer, when part of the river bed was dry.

Ney visited on General Lamotte his wrath for the check he had received, and withdrew from him the command of his brigade. Lamotte was, however, a good and brave officer, and later the Emperor did him justice. Next, eager to have his revenge, Ney waited on the banks of the Ceira throughout part of the 16th, in the hope of attacking Wellington when his turn came to cross. Masséna had to send four or five aides-de-camp before Ney could be induced to follow the retreat. On 17 March we crossed the Alva at Ponte Murcelha, and marched for five days, reaching Celorico unmolested.

The valley between the Mondego and the Estrella is exceedingly fertile and we lived in comfort. Thus, on finding ourselves again at Celorico, whence Masséna had had the unlucky idea of turning aside from this bountiful region on our outward march, and taking to the mountain district of Busaco, the army blamed him afresh, feeling that his mistake had cost many thousands of lives and brought the campaign to failure. The Marshal now – unable to make up his mind to re-enter Spain – resolved to hold his ground at any cost in Portugal. His plan was to regain the Tagus by way of Guarda and Alfayates, and having rebuilt the bridge of Alcantara, to join the French troops under Soult before Badajos; then, with them, to enter the Alemtejo and at once march upon Lisbon. He hoped to force Wellington to double back for the defence of the capital, which, being unfortified on the left bank of the Tagus, would have very little means of resistance.

To relieve the march, the Marshal sent all sick and wounded into Spain; but I declined to go with them, preferring to remain with my brother and my comrades. Masséna having communicated his plans to his lieutenants, Marshal Ney – who was burning with desire to recover his independence – opposed the idea of a new campaign, declaring that he was going to take his troops back to Spain because they could no longer find any bread in Portugal. This was true, but the army had been accustomed to live without bread for the last six months, each soldier receiving several pounds of meat and plenty of wine.

This fresh disobedience on Ney's part roused Masséna's wrath and he replied by a general order, removing Marshal Ney from command of VI Corps. This act of vigour, just and necessary as it was, had been too long delayed; he should have done it at the first sign of insubordination. Ney at first refused to go away, saying that as the Emperor had given him command of VI Corps he should not resign it but by his direction; but on the order being repeated, he returned to Spain, and thence to Paris.[6] The command of VI Corps fell by right of seniority to General Loison. Ney's dismissal produced an impression upon the army which was all the stronger that the principal cause of it was known, and that, insisting on a return to Spain, he had expressed the general wish of the troops.

On the 24th the army began to move back upon the Tagus and occupied Guarda. Of all the towns in the Peninsula, this is in the highest situation. Several men died from the cold, and my wound became very painful. Here Masséna received several despatches from Berthier, nearly all two months old; which shows what a mistake Napoleon had made in thinking that from Paris he could direct the movements of an army in Portugal. These despatches reached the commander-in-chief in a manner which, up to then, had been unknown in the French army. Prince Berthier had entrusted them to his aide-de-camp, Monsieur de Canouville, but that young officer – who was one of the beaux of the army – seeing the difficulty of reaching Masséna's army, was satisfied with depositing them at Ciudad Rodrigo and returned to Paris.

Now Paris was the very place from which, on account of a notorious caprice on his part, he was desired to keep away.

The story is as follows: it carries us back to the time when General Bonaparte was commanding the Army of Italy, and several ladies of his family joined him at Milan. One of them[7] married one of his most attached generals, and as – in the fashion of the time – she used, when riding, to wear a hussar *pelisse* over her habit, Bonaparte gave her one, handsomely furred and with diamond buttons. Some years afterwards, this lady, having lost her first husband, married a foreign prince. In the spring of 1811 the Emperor, when reviewing the Guard in the Place du Carrousel, noticed among Berthier's staff Canouville, wearing the *pelisse* which he had formerly given to his sister and Napoleon displayed much annoyance. The lady, it was said, was severely reprimanded; and one hour later the imprudent captain received an order to carry despatches to Masséna, who was enjoined in them to keep that officer with him for an unstated time.

Canouville had his suspicions and, as I have just related, took advantage of the chance which prevented him from entering Portugal. But hardly had he got back to Paris, when he was packed off again to the Peninsula, where he arrived very much ashamed at his discomfiture. The conversation of this modern Lauzun[8] amused us, as he gave us the latest news of what had been taking place in the Paris drawing rooms during our absence; and we laughed much at the contrast between his elegant costume and the dilapidations of our uniforms after a year's campaigning. Canouville, who at first was much astonished by his rapid transition from Parisian boudoirs to a bivouac among the rocks of Portugal, soon resigned himself to the change. He was a man of good wit, and of courage, and in the following year fell bravely in the Battle of the Moskowa.[9]

15 My Lord Marshal!

The Battle of Polotsk, August 1812

The expected war with Russia, the most gigantic
enterprise, perhaps, that the mind of man ever
conceived since the conquest of India by
Alexander the Great, now absorbed universal
attention . . . nothing was thought of but the
Niemen, already so celebrated by the raft of
Tilsit. Thither, as towards a common centre,
were moving men and horses, carriages and
provisions, and baggage of every description.

Louis Antoine Fauvelet de Bourrienne[1]

By April 1811 Masséna had been pushed out of Portugal by the
British. Determined to save the garrison of Almeida – not to
mention his own reputation – he launched a final sortie against
Wellington from Ciudad Rodrigo on 2 May. He was stopped
eight miles from his objective at the village of Fuentes de Oñoro.
There, between the 3rd–5th, the French were fought to a
standstill by Wellington's army and Masséna was forced to
quit: within days he was recalled to France in disgrace. Marbot,
in consequence of his wound, was invalided home: 'The campaign had nearly been my last, but I was in France and should see
my mother and another who had become very dear to me. So,
forgetting past troubles, I hastened on to Paris, arriving in July,
after an absence of fifteen toilsome months.'

193

Marbot spent the summer and autumn of 1811 in Paris, dividing his time between his mother and Mademoiselle Desbrières, who, on 11 November, became his bride (the recently remarried Emperor signing the marriage contract).[2] *He had left Masséna's staff and was confidently expecting to be promoted colonel and given a regiment of his own. Napoleon, however, put him into the 23rd Chasseurs-à-Cheval to assist the regiment's elderly Colonel, Monsieur Nougarède, who was too gouty to ride. Marbot, still a major, was to lick the regiment into shape: being, in effect, colonel in all but name. Napoleon promised him that in due course the regiment would be his, as Nougarède was likely to be put into the gendarmerie (or, if his health improved, promoted general). No longer the young, carefree hussar, Marbot was now in his thirtieth year, married, and responsible for the lives and well-being of the men and horses of his new regiment. As the summer of 1812 approached, he was on the eve of perhaps his sternest test.*

At the Peace of Tilsit in July 1807, Napoleon had charmed the young and impressionable Alexander, Emperor of Russia, who abandoned his friends of the Fourth Coalition, and became an ally and willing partner in the economic war against Britain. Napoleon was delighted with Alexander's friendship and loyalty; and the two Emperors parted on the best of terms. Once out of Napoleon's personal orbit, however, Alexander became prey to the opinions of his family and advisors – his mother referred to the agreement of Tilsit as a 'pact with the devil'[3] *– and over the next few years their relationship soured. Napoleon, who regarded Alexander as more of a disciple than a partner, began to ride roughshod over Russian interests: he was determined to thwart Alexander's attempts to gain influence in the Mediterranean; he meddled in the affairs of Poland – a sensitive issue – by creating the Grand Duchy of Warsaw, a pro-French puppet state packed with troops right on Russia's doorstep; and he insisted on Alexander's strict adherence to the economic* *blockade of Britain, even though the Russian economy was plunging towards ruination as a result.*

Eventually, Alexander came to see that Napoleon's friendship was a dangerous thing; and he began to backslide on the terms of the Tilsit agreement: leading to an atmosphere of mistrust and tension between the two leaders. When Alexander issued an ultimatum, stating that if Napoleon quit Prussia, he would be prepared to open negotiations in order to settle their accumulating grievances, Napoleon responded characteristically: he invaded. On 23 June 1812, Napoleon led his Grand Army across the River Niemen and into Russian territory. There was no formal declaration of war.

The army which Napoleon led into Russia in 1812 was, by the standards of the time, immense. He had successfully bullied most European states into providing troops for the venture (even dragging along Spanish and Portuguese prisoners of war) and of the half million men who crossed the Niemen, less than half were French. The remaining foreign contingents, although often highly professional, were loyal only to their own sovereigns, who, in their turn, were loyal to Napoleon – but only so long as fortune smiled upon him: his power and authority were founded solely on his ability to win battles.

As in previous campaigns, Napoleon depended on a quick, decisive action to settle the issue. The Russian army, however, simply melted before his advance and refused to be brought to battle. Their commanders, Bagration, Barclay de Tolly, Tormassov and, later, Kutusov, willingly gave ground as Napoleon lumbered forward, seeking a fight. On 17–18 August, the first major engagement occurred at Smolensk. Napoleon stormed the place and after fierce fighting, entered the smouldering city on the 19th, having lost 10,000 men. But the Russians had withdrawn during the night and Napoleon, disdaining the idea of going into winter quarters, continued the advance. This decision probably cost him the campaign.

My Lord Marshal!

    Marbot had crossed the Niemen with his regiment, the 23rd Chasseurs-à-Cheval, which was attached to II Corps, led by Marshal Oudinot. The Marshal's corps was part of a force posted to the north of Napoleon's main column (the area of operations being in modern-day Belarussia and Latvia), in order to protect its left flank from the Russian I Corps, commanded by General Count Wittgenstein. Marbot quickly realized that Oudinot was out of his depth: he dismissed Marbot's sighting of Wittgenstein's army at the town of Wilkomir as a 'fable'; he ordered Marbot's regiment into a costly and useless charge at Dünaborg (now Dugavpils); on the banks of the River Swolna, he kept his men under the Russian guns, guarding a ford which the enemy had no intention of crossing; and after the slightest setback he ordered a retreat. By the beginning of August, Napoleon was furious with his performance and ordered him to take the offensive, sending a sulky General Saint-Cyr and the Bavarian troops of VI Corps to his aid.

    Marbot, meanwhile, at the head of his regiment, had been in the thick of the fighting: leading ambushes against the Russian advance guard under General Kulniev ('a man of much enterprise, but having, like most of the Russian officers of that time, the bad habit of drinking too much brandy'); receiving a bullet in the shoulder during a skirmish with enemy grenadiers; and even capturing fourteen guns in a daring night attack on a Russian force, imprudently posted on the French bank of the River Drissa. On 11 August, during the fighting on the Swolna, news arrived that Napoleon was to reward the cavalry of II Corps with four crosses of the Legion of Honour for each regiment. The 23rd Chasseurs, however, were to receive an extra fourteen – one for each of the captured Russian guns. Marbot, beside himself with joy, 'assembled all the captains and guiding myself by their advice, I drew up my list and went to present it to Marshal Oudinot, begging him to let me announce it on the spot to the regiment. "What?

196

Here among the cannon-balls?" "Yes, Marshal, among the cannon-balls; it would be more chivalrous."'

Marbot's euphoria at the honours showered upon his regiment soon turned to dismay at the conduct of Marshal Oudinot who, while posted far away from Napoleon's guiding hand, was obviously floundering: 'our chief seemed to act with neither method nor plan. After a success he would pursue Wittgenstein without heeding any obstacle, and spoke of driving him to St Petersburg. But at the least check he would quickly retreat, and see an enemy everywhere. It was under this latter impression that he brought his troops back under the walls of Polotsk.'

ON 15 AUGUST, the Emperor's fête day, II Corps arrived, in very low spirits, at Polotsk; where we found VI Corps, formed by two fine Bavarian divisions, under General Wrede, and commanded-in-chief by a French general, Gouvion Saint-Cyr.[4] The Emperor had sent this reinforcement of 8,000–10,000 men to Marshal Oudinot, who would have received it with more satisfaction if he had not dreaded the influence of its leader. Saint-Cyr was, indeed, one of the most able soldiers in Europe. A contemporary and rival of Moreau, Hoche, Kléber and Desaix,[5] he had commanded successfully a wing of the Army of the Rhine at a time when Oudinot was a colonel or, at most, a major general. I never knew anyone handle troops in battle better than Saint-Cyr.

He was the son of a small landowner at Toul and had studied for a civil engineer; but disliking this profession, he became an actor in Paris, and it was he who created the famous part of Robert the Brigand Chief, at the Théâtre de la Cité. The Revolution of 1789 found him in this position; he entered a volunteer battalion, showed talent and much courage, and very quickly rose to the rank of lieutenant general. He was of tall stature, but looked more like a professor than a soldier, which may perhaps be ascribed to the habit which, like the other generals of the Army of the Rhine, he had acquired of wearing neither uniform nor epaulettes, but a plain blue overcoat. It was impossible to find a calmer man; the greatest danger, disappointments, successes, defeats, were alike unable to move him. In the presence of every sort of contingency he was like ice. It may be easily understood of what advantage such a character, backed by a taste for study and meditation, was to a general officer.

But Saint-Cyr had serious faults as well: he was jealous of his colleagues and was often seen to keep his troops inactive when other divisions were being shattered close to him. Then he would advance and, profiting by the enemy's weariness, would beat them, seeming thus to have the sole credit of the victory. Further, if he was among the commanders who were best able to handle their troops in the field, he was undoubtedly the one who took least thought for their welfare. He never enquired if his soldiers had food, clothing, or boots, or if their weapons were in good condition. He never held a review, never visited the hospitals, did not even ask if there were any. His view was that the colonels ought to see to all that. In a word, he expected that his regiments should be brought into the field all ready to fight, without troubling himself about the means to keep them in good condition.

This method of procedure had done Saint-Cyr much harm; and wherever he had served, his troops, while doing justice to his military talents, had disliked him. His colleagues all dreaded having to act with him and the different successive governments of France had only employed him from necessity. It was the same with the Emperor; and such was his antipathy for Saint-Cyr that he did not include him in his first creation of marshals:[6] although he had a better record and much greater talent than the majority of those to whom Napoleon gave the bâton. Such was the man who had just been placed under Oudinot's command, much to his regret, for he knew that he would be put in the shade by Saint-Cyr's superior ability.

On 16 August, the day on which my eldest son Alfred was born, the Russian army – more than 60,000 strong – attacked Oudinot who, with Saint-Cyr's Bavarians, had 52,000 men at his disposal.[7] In an ordinary war an engagement in which 112,000 men took part would have been called a battle, and its decision would have had important results; but in 1812, amid belligerent forces amounting to 600,000 or 700,000 men, the meeting reckoned only as a combat. At any rate, this is the name given to the affair between Oudinot and the Russians under the walls of Polotsk.

This town, which stands on the left bank of the Dwina, is surrounded with ancient earthworks. Before the principal front of the place the fields, in which vegetables are grown, are cut up by an infinite number of little water-courses: obstacles which, though not exactly impassable for guns and cavalry, hamper their march a good deal. These market gardens extended to some half a league before the town; but to their left, along the bank of the Dwina, is a vast stretch of meadow, level as a carpet. That was the side by which the Russian general should have attacked Polotsk. He would thus have become master of the single weak bridge of boats affording us our only communication with the left bank, whence we drew our supplies of ammunition and provisions. But Wittgenstein preferred to take the bull by the horns and directed his main body towards the gardens, hoping to be able from thence to carry the place by escalade: the ramparts being, in fact, nothing but slopes, easy to ascend. The attack was smartly delivered; but our infantry defended the gardens bravely, while from the top of the ramparts our artillery, including the fourteen guns captured at Sivoshina, did terrible execution in the enemy's ranks. The Russians retired in disorder to re-form in the plain; and Oudinot, instead of maintaining his good position, pursued them, only to be repulsed in his turn. Thus a great part of the day passed; the Russians returning incessantly to the attack and the French always driving them back beyond the gardens. While the slaughter thus swayed to and fro, Saint-Cyr followed Oudinot in silence; and whenever his opinion was asked he merely bowed and said: 'My lord Marshal!' as though he would say, 'As they have made you a marshal, you must know more about the matter than a mere general like me; get out of it as best you can.'

Meanwhile Wittgenstein was losing enormously; and despairing of success by continuing to attack the side of the gardens, he ended where he should have begun, and marched the bulk of his troops towards the meadows on the banks of the Dwina. So far, Oudinot had kept his twelve-pounders and all his cavalry at this point and they had taken no part in the fighting; but now General Dulauloy of the artillery, fearing for his guns, came and proposed to the Marshal to retire across the river not only the heavier pieces, but also the cavalry, under the plea that they would be in the way of the infantry movements. Oudinot asked Saint-Cyr what he thought; but instead of giving the good advice to employ the artillery and cavalry on ground where they could easily manoeuvre in support of the infantry, he replied with his eternal 'My lord Marshal!' Finally, in defiance of the remarks of General Laurencez, his chief-of-staff, Oudinot ordered both arms to withdraw across the river.

This deplorable movement, which seemed to herald the total abandonment of Polotsk and the right bank, was infinitely displeasing to the troops who were removed and affected the tone of the infantry, who would have to defend the side of the town towards the meadows; while on the other hand, the sight of ten cavalry regiments and several batteries leaving the field was a great stimulus to the Russians. Then, to carry disorder into this huge retreating mass, they promptly brought up their *unicorns*,[8] the projectiles of which, being hollow, acted like

round-shot and then burst like shells. The regiment near mine
had several men killed and wounded. I was fortunate enough
to have none of my troopers touched and only lost a few
horses. The one which I was riding had his head smashed and
in the fall my wounded shoulder came heavily on the ground,
causing me frightful pain. A trifle less slew in laying the
Russian gun, the shot would have struck me full in the body
and my son would have been orphaned a few hours before his
birth.

The enemy had now renewed the combat and when we had
crossed the bridge and turned our heads to see what was
taking place on the bank we had left, we witnessed a most
affecting sight. The French infantry, with the Bavarians and
the Croats, were fighting bravely and having the best of it; but
the Portuguese Legion and the Swiss were flying before the
Russians and did not halt until they were knee-deep in the
river. There, compelled to face the enemy or be drowned, they
fought at last, and by a well-sustained fire forced the Russians
to give ground somewhat. The French artillery commander,
who had just crossed the Dwina, cleverly seized the moment to
be of service. Bringing his guns to the bank and firing over the
river, he smote the enemy's battalions on the other side. This
powerful diversion stopped Wittgenstein in this quarter; and
as the French, Bavarians and Croats were elsewhere repulsing
him, the fighting slackened and for the last hour of the day
degenerated into sharpshooting.

But Marshal Oudinot could not hide from himself that he
would have to begin again next day. Full of thought over a
state of things of which he could not see the issue, and brought
up at every turn by Saint-Cyr's refusal to speak, he was riding
along at a walk among his infantry skirmishers, when the
enemy marksmen, noticing the horseman with white plumes,
made him their target and sent a bullet into his arm. The
Marshal at once sent word to Saint-Cyr that he was wounded
and handed the command over to him. Then he quitted the

field; and leaving the army, retired to Lithuania, to get his wound tended. It was two months before we saw him again.

Saint-Cyr seized the reins of command with a firm and capable hand and in a few hours the aspect of things changed entirely; so great is the influence of an able man who knows how to inspire confidence. Marshal Oudinot had left the army in a most alarming situation: part of the troops with the river at their backs, others scattered about beyond the gardens and keeping up a disorderly fire; the ramparts badly furnished with guns; the streets of the town blocked with caissons, baggage wagons and wounded, heaped together pell-mell; lastly, the troops had – in case of defeat – no other way of retreat than by the bridge of boats, which was very narrow and six inches deep in water. Night was coming on; and the regiments of the different nations were so out of hand that it was quite possible their sharpshooting would bring on a general action, which might be fatal to us.

General Saint-Cyr's first act was to call in the skirmishers. He was certain that the tired enemy would follow his example as soon as they were no longer attacked; and in fact the fire soon ceased on both sides. The troops could now concentrate and take some rest; and business seemed to be put off until the next day. So that he might be in a position to engage with the best chances of success, Saint-Cyr took advantage of the night to make his arrangements for repulsing the enemy, or securing his retreat in the event of a reverse. To this end he assembled the regimental commanders and after having explained the dangers of the situation – the most serious of which was the crowded state of the town and of the approaches to the bridge – he gave orders that the colonels, with other officers and patrols, should go through the streets directing all the uninjured soldiers of their regiments to the bivouacs, and sending the sick and wounded and all led horses and wagons across the bridge. He added that at daybreak he would go round the town and suspend any colonel who had not carried out his orders: no excuse would be accepted.

The orders were quickly carried out and all that was not required for the fight – all the impedimenta of the army, in short – was collected on the left bank. Soon the ramparts and the streets, as well as the bridge, were completely clear. The bridge was strengthened, the cavalry and artillery brought back to the right bank and established in the suburb furthest from the enemy. Finally, to facilitate his means of retreat, the prudent commander-in-chief had a second bridge, to be used only by infantry, constructed out of empty barrels and planks. All these preparations were finished before daylight and the army awaited the enemy with confidence. But he remained inert in his bivouacs on the plain along the edge of the vast forest which surrounds Polotsk on the side away from the river. General Saint-Cyr, who had expected to be attacked in the early morning, ascribed the tranquillity in the Russian camp to their enormous losses on the previous day. This might have had something to do with it, but the principal cause of Wittgenstein's inaction arose from the fact that he was expecting a strong division of infantry and several squadrons from St Petersburg by the next night; and had put off his attack until this reinforcement arrived, so that he might vanquish us with more ease on the morrow.

Although the great Polish landowners in the neighbourhood of Polotsk did not venture, for fear of compromising themselves with the Russians, to take sides openly with the French, they helped us in secret and made no difficulty about finding us spies. General Saint-Cyr, in his anxiety as to the enemy's preparations, had asked one of these nobles to send him one of his most intelligent serfs. He sent several wagons of forage to the Russian bivouac and among the wagoners placed his bailiff, dressed as a peasant. This person, a man of intelligence, chatted with Wittgenstein's soldiers and learned that a large body of troops was expected. He even witnessed the arrival of the Cossacks of the Guard, and a squadron of Gentlemen Guards,[9] and was told that several battalions would reach the camp towards midnight. Having got this information, the bailiff reported it to his master, who lost no time in imparting it to the French commander-in-chief.

On receiving this news, Saint-Cyr resolved to beat Wittgenstein before the reinforcements came up; but as he did not wish to enter upon too long an engagement, he warned the generals and colonels that he should not attack until six in the evening, so that night should set a term to the fighting; and that, in case the Russians were successful, they should not have time to follow it up. It is true that in the event of our getting the best of the fight we should be unable to pursue the enemy in the darkness, but this was not Saint-Cyr's purpose. He desired for the moment to give them a good lesson and make them move further away from Polotsk. Wishing to act by way of surprise, he gave orders that the most perfect quiet should be maintained in the town and along the whole line of outposts.

We found the day very long. Everyone, even the commander-in-chief (for all his coolness) had his watch constantly in his hand. Having noticed the day before that the retirement of the French cavalry had allowed the Russians to push our left wing back into the Dwina, General Saint-Cyr brought all his squadrons quietly, a moment before the attack, behind some large stone houses, beyond which the meadows began. On this level ground the cavalry were to act, charging the enemy's right and covering the left of our infantry, the two first divisions of which were to attack the Russian camp, while the third supported the cavalry, and the two last formed the reserve and guarded the town. All was ready when, at six in the evening, the general signal for the attack was given by a cannon-shot. This was followed by the thunder of all the French artillery, the projectiles of which fell upon the outposts and even upon the camp of the enemy. Instantly our two leading divisions, with the 26th Light Infantry in front, dashed upon the Russian regiments posted in the gardens, killed and captured all whom they could reach and, putting the others to flight, pursued them to the camp, where they made many prisoners and captured several guns.

The surprise, although in broad daylight, was so complete that General Wittgenstein was quietly dining in a small country house near his camp when he was warned that the French *voltigeurs* were in the courtyard. Leaping out of the window, he found a Cossack pony at hand, jumped on its back, and fled with all speed to his main body. Our men took possession of the Russian General's horses, his papers, his wagons and his wine; as well as his plate and the dinner on the table. Immense booty was also taken in the camp by other companies.

At the uproar of this unexpected attack panic seized the enemy. They fled in most cases without thinking of taking their arms. The disorder was complete; and meanwhile the approach of our infantry divisions was announced by a brisk fire and the drums beating the charge. Everything pointed to success for the French troops, at whose head was marching Saint-Cyr, calm as usual. But in war an unforeseen and often unimportant incident changes the aspect of affairs. A great number of the enemy's soldiers had reached the rear of the camp in their flight, where was bivouacking the squadron of the Gentlemen Guards, which had arrived only a few hours back. This force, composed of young men selected from the nobler families, was commanded by a major of tried courage, whose ardour, it was said, had recently been increased by copious libations.

As soon as he learned what was going on, this officer mounted his horse and, followed by 120 cavaliers, dashed upon the French. The first of our battalions whom he attacked belonged to the 26th. It offered a vigorous resistance and the Guards, repulsed with loss, were trying to rally to charge a second time, when their major – impatient at the time which it takes horsemen in disorder to recover their ranks – left the

French battalion (which he could not break) and, ordering his men to follow him, launched them at full speed in loose order through the camp. He found it full of our allies: Portuguese, Swiss and Bavarian infantry; some of whom, scattered by the very effect of their victory, were seeking to reassemble, while others were collecting the plunder which the Russians had abandoned. Of these, the Guards killed and wounded a good many, until they began to retreat: at first in disorder, soon in panic-stricken flight. In such cases soldiers mistake those of their own side who are running up to join them for the enemy; and in a cloud of dust the number of pursuers, often only a handful of men, appears immense. This was what happened here.

The Gentlemen Guards, scattered over a wide space and always coming on without looking behind them, looked to the fugitives like a huge body of cavalry; so that the disorder spread until it reached a Swiss battalion in the midst of which General Saint-Cyr had taken refuge; and by the pressure of the crowd, he and his horse were overturned into a ditch. In his plain blue overcoat, with no mark of his rank, the General lay prostrate on the ground, and made no movement when the Guards drew near; and they, thinking him dead, or taking him for some non-combatant official, passed on over the plain in pursuit. There is no knowing where this chaos would have ended had not General Berckheim, with equal boldness and good sense, hurried up at the head of the 4th Cuirassiers and charged the Russian horsemen. They defended themselves bravely but were nearly all killed or taken, their valiant major being among the slain. If the charge executed by this handful of men had been properly supported it would have been very effective; and this fine feat of arms performed by the Gentlemen Guards proved afresh that an attack by cavalry has the best chance of success when it is unexpected.

General Saint-Cyr, having been picked up by our *cuirassiers*, at once ordered all his infantry divisions forward and attacked the Russians before they had recovered from their disorder. Success was not for a moment doubtful: the enemy were beaten with the loss of many men and guns. While this infantry action was taking place before Polotsk, the fortunes of the left wing of our army in the meadows along the Dwina were as follows. As soon as the first cannon-shot gave the signal for action, our cavalry regiments, headed by Castex's brigade,[10] moved rapidly to meet the enemy's squadrons which were advancing upon us.

A serious engagement appeared imminent, and General Castex kindly remarked to me that though I had been able, in spite of my wound, to command my regiment at Sivoshina and the Swolna, when I had only to face infantry and artillery fire, it did not follow that I could do so now, when we should be engaged with cavalry. I might find myself involved in a charge without the means of defending myself, since, as I could only use one arm, I could not hold both sabre and bridle; and he advised me, therefore, to stay for the moment with the infantry division posted in reserve. I felt that I could not accept this good-natured offer, and expressed so strongly my objection at being away from the regiment that the General yielded; but he had six of the bravest troopers placed close in rear of me, commanded by the intrepid Sergeant Prud'homme. Further, I had beside me the two adjutants, the regimental staff-sergeants, a trumpeter, and Fousse, my orderly, one of the best men in the regiment. Thus surrounded, and riding in front of a centre squadron, I was pretty well protected; and in the case of urgent necessity I could drop my reins and take up my sword, which hung to my wrist by its knot.

The meadow being large enough to hold two regiments in line, the 23rd and 24th formed the first line, General Corbineau's[11] brigade, consisting of three regiments, forming the second, and the *cuirassiers* following as reserve. The 24th, which was on the left, had in front of it a regiment of Russian dragoons; my regiment was facing the Cossacks of the Guard, known by their red coats and the beauty of their horses. These, though they had arrived only a few hours before, seemed in no way fatigued. We advanced at a gallop and as soon as we were in striking distance General Castex gave the word to charge. His brigade fell upon the Russians and at the first stroke the 24th broke the dragoons opposed to them. My regiment met with more resistance from the Cossacks – picked men of large stature – and armed with lances fourteen feet long, which they held very straight. I had some men killed and a good many wounded; but when, at length, my troopers had pierced the bristling line of steel, all the advantage was on our side. In a cavalry fight the length of a lance is a drawback when their bearers have lost their order and are pressed closely by adversaries armed with swords which they can handle easily. So the Cossacks were constrained to show their backs and my troopers did great execution and took many excellent horses.

As we were about to follow up our success, our attention was drawn by a great uproar to our right, and we saw the plain covered with fugitives: it was just then that the Gentlemen Guards were making their charge. General Castex, deeming it unwise to advance further while our centre seemed to be retreating in confusion, ordered the recall to be sounded and the brigade halted. But it had hardly re-formed, when the Cossacks, emboldened by what was taking place in the centre and anxious to avenge their first defeat, returned to the charge and dashed madly on my squadrons, while the Grodno Hussars attacked the 24th. Repulsed at all points by Castex's brigade, the Russians brought up in succession their second and third lines, while General Corbineau supported us with the 7th and 20th Chasseurs and the 8th Lancers. A grand cavalry engagement ensued, in which each side experienced varying fortunes. Our *cuirassiers* were just coming up to take part in it, and the Russian *cuirassiers* were advancing also, when Wittgenstein, seeing that his infantry was beaten, ordered his cavalry to retire. The latter were, however, too closely engaged to be able to effect a retreat easily. Indeed, Generals Castex and Corbineau – sure of the support from our *cuirassiers* – were launching their brigades alternately at the Russian horsemen, who, being thrown into great confusion, were losing heavily. General Saint-Cyr, meanwhile, having got beyond the forest where our victorious divisions were collected, and seeing that night was coming on, stopped the pursuit; and the troops returned to Polotsk and the bivouacs which they had left a few hours before.

During this bustling cavalry action my wound had caused me severe pain, especially when I had to put my horse into a gallop. My inability to defend myself often put me in a very awkward position, from which I should not have escaped had I not been surrounded by brave men who never let me out of their sight. One time, when I was pushed by the combatants on to a section of Cossacks, I was obliged, in self-defence, to let go my reins and take my sword. However, I had no need to use it, for the men who escorted me, seeing their commander in danger, furiously attacked the Cossacks by whom I was surrounded, made many of them bite the dust, and put the rest to flight. My orderly, Fousse, killed three; Adjutant Joly, two. I returned, therefore, from this great fight safe and sound. I had wished to be present at it in person in order to put still more dash into my regiment and to show that, so long as I could sit on a horse, I felt bound in honour to command it in the hour of danger.

When cavalry meets cavalry the slaughter is much less than when it is opposed to infantry. Moreover, the Russian troopers are generally awkward in handling their weapons and their leaders are not very competent in handling their men. Thus, although at Polotsk my regiment had to fight the Cossacks of the Guard – reputed to be among the best troops in the Russian service – its losses were not heavy. I had eight or nine killed and some thirty wounded. Among the latter was Major Fontaine. This excellent and valiant officer was in the thick of the scuffle when his horse was killed. He was trying, with the help of some of the men, to get his feet disentangled from the stirrups, when a confounded Cossack officer, galloping into the middle of the group, leaned carefully over and aimed a terrible blow at Fontaine, destroying his left eye, injuring the other, and splitting his nose. As, however, the Russian officer was galloping off, proud of his exploit, one of our men broke his back with a pistol-shot at six paces' distance, thus avenging his major. I had Major Fontaine attended to as soon as possible, and he was placed in the Jesuit convent at Polotsk. Visiting him that evening, I was much struck with the brave soldier's resignation. With an eye quite destroyed, he was patiently enduring all the pain and inconvenience resulting from the almost total loss of sight. He was never again fit for active service, which was a great loss to the 23rd Chasseurs.

You will think I have described in too much detail the various actions in which II Corps was concerned; but I repeat what I have said before, that I enjoy the reminiscences of the great wars in which I took part; and I speak of them with pleasure. I seem to be in the field, in the midst of my gallant companions, most of whom, alas, have now left this world.

But to return to the Russian campaign. Anyone but Saint-Cyr, after such heavy fighting, would have reviewed his troops, complimented them on their courage, and enquired into their wants: but that was not his way. The last shot had hardly been fired when Saint-Cyr went and shut himself in the Jesuit convent, where he spent all his days and part of his nights in – what do you suppose? Playing the fiddle! This was his master-passion, and nothing but the necessity of marching against the enemy could draw him from it. He left the task of placing the troops to Generals Laurencez and Wrede, who posted two divisions of infantry and the *cuirassiers* on the left bank of the Dwina. The third French and the two Bavarian divisions remained at Polotsk, where they were set to throw up a vast entrenched camp to serve as a base for the troops, who from this important point covered the left and rear of the Grand Army in its march towards Smolensk and Moscow. Corbineau's and Castex's brigades of light cavalry were placed two leagues in advance of the great camp on the left bank of the Polota, a small stream which joins the Dwina at Polotsk. My regiment was to bivouac near a village called Luchonski, the colonel of the 24th fixing himself a quarter of a league in rear of us. We stayed there two months, during the first of which we never went far away.

On hearing of Saint-Cyr's victory[12] the Emperor sent him his marshal's bâton. But instead of visiting his troops, the new marshal lived – if possible – more apart than ever. No one could approach him: whence the soldiers nicknamed him 'the Owl'. The numerous rooms of the convent would have been of great service to the wounded, but he would live there alone, and thought that he had conceded a great deal when he allowed wounded field officers to be put in the outbuildings. Even they were only allowed to remain forty-eight hours, after which they had to be moved into the town. The cellars were overflowing with provisions but the Marshal kept the keys and not even the hospitals could get anything. I had much trouble in getting two bottles of wine for Major Fontaine. Strange to say, Saint-Cyr was most abstemious and used scarcely any of the stores for himself. Two months later, when the French had to leave the place – after setting town and convent on fire – all these provisions which the Marshal would not distribute became the prey of the Russians or of the flames.

16 Blood Calls For Blood

Retreat From Russia,
December 1812–January 1813

The longer the retreat continued, the more
ghastly became the sight of the fugitives. In the
most frightful cold men could be seen toiling
along the road without fur or overcoat, dressed
only in a light suit, the frost visibly
overpowering them. Their limbs gradually
stiffened, they fell, picked themselves up
painfully, staggered on a few paces, and fell once
more never to rise again.

Lieutenant H.A. Vossler[1]

*After the Battle of Polotsk, Saint-Cyr converted the town into
an armed camp from which to cover the left flank and rear of
Napoleon's main column as it advanced on Moscow. As the
soldiers of II Corps settled down into camp life, Marbot spent
much of his time improving the lot of his men: he had the local
watermills repaired in order to provide bread; he gathered
together hundreds of abandoned beasts to form a regimental
herd for meat and milk; he persuaded the local Jesuits to distil
brandy for the troops; and compelled his men to find sheepskin coats for the coming winter. By his care and attention
Marbot kept his regiment in excellent condition: 'we were well
off from a material point of view, but very uneasy about what*

was going on in the direction of Moscow, and we seldom got news from France. At length, I received a letter from my dear Angélique, in which she announced that she had given birth to a boy. Great as was my joy it was mingled with sadness, for I was far from my family and, though I did not foresee all the dangers to which I was shortly to be exposed, I could not hide from myself that there were great obstacles in the way of our meeting again.'

Meanwhile, bowing to public pressure, Alexander gave overall command of his army to the elderly Field Marshal Kutusov, who made a stand at Borodino, sixty miles west of Moscow. At last Napoleon had got his battle. But instead of outmanoeuvring his enemy, as in times past, he merely ordered a frontal assault against Kutusov's position and the two armies slogged it out in one of the bloodiest battles of the period. Eventually the Russians made an orderly withdrawal and Napoleon claimed the victory, though his army was in no condition to pursue.[2] Kutusov retreated through Moscow, evacuating the city and ordering incendiaries to set it alight. He then withdrew to the south-east, to await reinforcements.

Napoleon entered Moscow on 14 September as the city fell prey to a conflagration which lasted for three days. He later described the scene as 'the most grand, the most sublime, the most terrifying sight the world ever beheld'.[3] He expected Alexander to sue for peace; but the Tsar obstinately refused any contact and put his faith in 'General Winter' to defeat the French for him. Indeed, Russian officers, fraternizing with Murat's troopers at the outposts, warned them that their courage and military prowess would be no match for the coming cold. By 19 October, with Russian armies threatening his lines of communication, Napoleon decided to abandon Moscow and retreat to Smolensk. He hoped to be able to avoid the route of his incoming march, which had been devastated, and to pass through the fertile region around Kaluga. He was, however, frustrated in this by the wily

Kutusov, who blocked his path at the Battle of Maloyarosla-vets. The Grand Army was then herded by the Russians back onto its original line of march. Deliberately avoiding a pitched battle, Kutusov was content merely to pursue and harass: the retreat became a rout.

Saint-Cyr, meanwhile, had been forced to abandon Polotsk after a second clash with Wittgenstein. The Marshal, having been wounded in the foot, gave up his command, whereupon Marshal Oudinot promptly returned to duty. He was escorted back to his command by Marbot and the troopers of his regiment. Shortly afterwards, Marbot received his longed-for promotion to colonel: 'If you consider that as major I had received a wound at Znaim in Moravia, two at Miranda de Corvo in Portugal, one at Jakubovo, had served four campaigns with that rank, and that I had been in command of a regiment ever since the French entered Russia, you will perhaps think that I had pretty well earned my new epaulettes.'

On 4 November the first snow of winter fell and the roads were soon icebound. Discipline dissolved and within the space of ten days 10,000 horses had perished: 'Every day the Cossacks burst out with shouts on the road but as our men were armed, they dared not approach us; they merely stationed themselves along the road to see us pass. But they slept in good quarters and we on the snow.'[4] By the time Napoleon reached Smolensk, the army had virtually ceased to exist as a cohesive unit, becoming instead a freezing sea of stragglers. At Smolensk discipline broke down among the Imperial Guard, whose soldiers helped themselves to rations intended for the whole army. Napoleon decided that the retreat must go on and headed for the River Beresina, the last major obstacle before the frontier. Oudinot was ordered to secure the main bridge at Borisov but arrived to find it in the hands of the Russians, who set it ablaze on his approach.

Napoleon was within three days' march of the Beresina when the news arrived from Oudinot that a Russian army under Admiral Chichagov had already reached the river and was threatening to cut off his line of retreat. Wittgenstein's army, meanwhile, was bearing down upon him from the north-east and Kutusov, with 80,000 men, was approaching from the rear. The most devastating piece of news, however, was that the Beresina, due to an unseasonal thaw, was not frozen as Napoleon had expected, but was in full flow. As he had himself ordered the destruction of the pontoon train only days before in order to lighten the men's load, it now looked as though the Grand Army was stranded, while the net closed around it.

The Emperor's luck, however, was about to turn: General Eblé of the engineers had, contrary to Napoleon's orders, saved his tools and field-forge; while General Corbineau found a ford to the north of Borisov at the village of Studenka. Everything was in place for an engineering miracle as the French, working for hours on end in the freezing water, built two temporary bridges at the site of the ford, using timber from the nearby village. Between 27 and 28 November the remains of the Grand Army crossed these extemporized bridges while Marshals Victor, Oudinot and Ney beat off the Russian armies of Wittgenstein and Chichagov (Oudinot picking up another wound, this time in his side). Fortunately for the French, Kutusov maintained his leisurely pace and Napoleon, having once again achieved the impossible, escaped his clutches. On 29 November the bridges were burned, leaving 10,000 stragglers who had refused to make the crossing during the night on the opposite bank: they were massacred by Cossacks. By early December Kutusov gave up his pursuit and the survivors of the Grand Army crossed into the comparative safety of Prussia. Their losses for the campaign were approximately 400,000. The Russians later claimed to have dragged 36,000 bodies from the Beresina alone. Perhaps the biggest casualty of the campaign, however, was Napoleon's reputation: from now on he would be fighting not for territory or political domination, but for survival.

SINCE MARSHAL OUDINOT and General Legrand had been wounded, General Maison had been in command of II Corps, which in spite of its heavy losses was the most numerous in the whole army, so that the task of beating off the Russians usually fell to it. We kept them at a distance during 30 November and 1 December; but on the 2nd they pressed us so close with powerful forces that some serious fighting took place, in which I received a wound that was all the more dangerous from the fact that there were that day 25° of frost.[5] I ought, perhaps, to say no more than that I received a lance wound, without entering into the details, for they are so shocking that I still shudder when I think of them; but I have promised to tell you the whole story of my life, so you shall hear what happened at the action of Plechenitzi.

In order to put you in a position to understand my story, I must tell you, to begin with, that a Dutch banker named Van Berghem – of whom I had been an intimate friend at the college of Sorèze – had at the beginning of the campaign sent me his only son, who, having become a Frenchman by the inclusion of his country in the Empire, had, though hardly sixteen years old, enlisted in the 23rd.[6] This young man had many good qualities and much intelligence. I took him for my secretary and he always marched fifteen paces behind me with my orderlies. On the day of which I speak he was in his place when, as we were crossing a wide plain, II Corps saw hastening towards it a large body of Russian cavalry, which in a moment overlapped it and attacked it on all sides. General Maison arranged his troops so well that our infantry squares beat off all the charges of the Russian regular cavalry. As, however, they brought into action a host of Cossacks, who came insolently up, spearing the French officers in front of their troops, Marshal Ney ordered General Maison to drive them away by sending at them all that was left of the *cuirassier* division, as well as Corbineau's and Castex's brigades.

My regiment, which was still strong, found itself in front of a 'pulk' of Cossacks from the Black Sea, wearing tall astrakhan caps, and much better dressed and mounted than Cossacks usually are. We charged them; but as Cossacks never fight in line they wheeled about and galloped away. Being, however, strangers to the locality, they went in the direction of an obstacle which is very uncommon in these wide plains, and were brought to a dead stop by a deep and broad ravine, which the perfect evenness of the ground made it impossible to see from a distance. Finding it out of the question to cross with their horses and forced to face my regiment – which was on the point of catching them – the Cossacks turned and, closing up, met us bravely with their lances. The ground was covered with ice and was very slippery, so that our tired horses could not gallop without tumbling. There was, therefore, no shock, and my line reached the motionless mass of the enemy at a trot.

Our sabres touched the lances but as these were thirteen or fourteen feet long, it was impossible for us to reach our adversaries, who, on their side, dared not advance to meet our swords, nor to retreat for fear of falling over the precipice. We watched each other, therefore, until the following scene took place in less time than it takes to tell it. In haste to get done with the enemy I called out to my men that they must catch hold of the lances with their left hand, turn them aside, and push into the middle of the crowd, where our short weapons would give us a great advantage over their long poles. In order to be better obeyed, I thought I would set the example, and putting some lances aside, I actually succeeded in getting within the front ranks of the enemy. My adjutants and orderlies followed me, and all the regiment presently doing the same, a general scuffle ensued. But at that moment an old white-bearded Cossack, who, being in the hinder ranks, was separated from me by other combatants, bent forward and pointing his lance adroitly between his comrades' horses, struck me with his sharp steel, which passed clean through below the knee-pan of my right leg.

Feeling myself wounded, I was pressing forward to revenge myself on the man for the sharp pain which I experienced when I saw before me two youths of eighteen or twenty years in a rich costume: the sons of the chief of the 'pulk'. An elderly man accompanied them as mentor, having no sword in his hand, nor did the younger of the two lads use his; but the elder charged bravely and attacked me furiously. He seemed so undeveloped and so weak that I merely disarmed him, and taking him by the arm, passed him behind me and told Van Berghem to look after him. The next moment, however, I felt a hard object laid against my left cheek, a double report rang in my ears, and a bullet went through the collar of my cloak. Turning sharply, I saw the young Cossack officer with a brace of double-barrelled pistols in his hands. He had just fired treacherously on me from behind and now he blew poor Van Berghem's brains out. Beside myself with rage, I dashed on the madman, who was taking aim at me with his second pistol. But as he met my eye he seemed fascinated and cried out in good French, 'Oh God! I see death in your eyes! I see death in your eyes!' 'Aye, scoundrel, and you see right!' And he dropped.

Blood calls for blood. The sight of young Van Berghem stretched at my feet, the excitement of battle, and perhaps also the frightful pain of my wound, all combined to throw me into a state of feverish agitation. I made towards the younger of the Cossack officers, caught him by the throat, and was in the act of raising my sword, when the old governor, seeking to protect his ward, bent over my horse's neck in such a way as to prevent me from using my arm, and cried in a tone of entreaty, 'For your mother's sake, pardon this one, who has done nothing!' On hearing him invoke that revered name my mind

– overwrought by the surroundings – was struck with hallu-
cination: I thought I saw a well-known white hand laid upon
the young man's breast (which I was on the point of piercing)
and I seemed to hear my mother's voice saying 'Pardon!
Pardon!' My sword dropped, and I had the youth and his
governor taken to the rear.

So great was my emotion after this incident that I could not
have given any word of command if the fight had lasted much
longer; but it was soon at an end. A great many of the
Cossacks had been killed and the rest, leaving their horses,
had slid down the ravine, where most of them perished in the
snowdrifts which the wind had heaped up there. On other
sides, too, the enemy was beaten off.

During the evening I questioned my prisoner and his atten-
dant and learned that the two youths were the sons of a
powerful chief who had lost his leg at Austerlitz and in
consequence vowed such fierce enmity to the French that,
as he could fight them no longer, he had sent his two sons to
the war. I could see that the cold and his grief would soon
make an end of the junior, so I took pity on him and his old
mentor, and set them at liberty. As the old man took leave of
me he said: 'When she thinks of her elder son, these lads'
mother will curse you; but when she sees the younger she will
bless you and your mother, for whose sake you spared her
only remaining child.'

The vigorous repulse with which the Russian troops had
met in the recent action damped their ardour, so that we saw
nothing more of them for two days, and our retreat to
Molodechno was secured. But if the enemy left us a moment's
peace, the frost waged bitter war with us, for the thermometer
fell to 27° of cold. Men and horses were dropping at every
step: many never to rise again. Still I remained with the
fragments of my regiment, bivouacking in their midst every
night in the snow. Where, indeed, should I have been any
better off? My officers and men, who looked upon their

colonel as a living flag, made it a point of honour to save me, and took all the care of me that our terrible situation allowed. The wound in my knee prevented me from riding astride, so that I had to put my leg on the horse's withers and sit quite still, which made me very cold; my pain, meanwhile, was intolerable: but what could I do?

The way was strewn with dead and dying; our march slow and silent. The remains of the infantry of the Guard formed a small square, within which went the Emperor's carriage. He had Murat beside him. On 5 December, after issuing his twenty-ninth bulletin,[7] which threw France into a state of dismay, Napoleon left the army at Smorgon, and set out for Paris.[8] At Ochmiana he was nearly carried off by Cossacks. His departure produced a great effect on the troops: some blamed him for deserting them; others approved the course as the sole means of saving France from civil war and invasion by our so-called allies, most of whom were only awaiting a favourable moment to declare war against us. They would not dare to stir when they heard that Napoleon had re-entered his realm and was organising a new army. This was the view which I shared and events showed the justice of it.

The Emperor, at his departure, entrusted the command of his shattered army to Murat,[9] who showed himself unequal to the task: one as difficult, it may be admitted, as can be imagined. Everyone's faculties of mind and body were paralysed by the cold, and disorganisation prevailed throughout. Marshal Victor refused to relieve II Corps, which had been acting as rearguard from the Beresina, and Ney had much trouble in making him do so. Every morning we left thousands of corpses in our bivouacs. Then I congratulated myself on having in September made my troopers set themselves up with sheepskin coats: a precaution to which many of them owed their lives. Likewise the victuals with which we had supplied ourselves at Borisov, for without these we should have had to fight for dead horses with the famished multitude.

On this point I may say that Monsieur de Ségur exaggerates when he says that the poor wretches were driven by the pangs of hunger to eat human flesh.[10] The road was so lined with dead horses that no one needed to consider cannibalism. Further, it would be a great mistake to suppose that provisions were altogether lacking in the district. They only ran short in the places actually on the road, since the neighbourhood of these had been drained when the army was on its way to Moscow; but it had swept by like a torrent without spreading laterally, and the harvest had since been gathered, so that the country had in some measure recovered. I made arrangements, therefore, with several colonels to organise armed foraging-parties. These returned always not only with bread and some head of cattle, but bringing sledges laden with salt meat, flour and oats, obtained in the villages which the peasants had not deserted. This showed that if the Duke of Bassano and General Hogendorf, who had been entrusted with the management of Lithuania, had done their duty while they were at Vilna, they might with ease have established large stores. But they attended only to provisioning the town, and took no thought for the troops.

On 26 December the cold got far more intense and that day was even more fatal than the preceding, especially for the troops who had not become gradually acclimatised. Among these was Gratien's division, consisting of conscripts to the number of 12,000, which had left Vilna on the 4th and come to meet us. The abrupt change from warm barracks to a bivouac with 29° of frost caused the death of nearly all these poor fellows within forty-eight hours. Still more terrible was the effect produced on 200 Neapolitan troopers of Murat's guard. They also had stayed a long time at Vilna when they came to meet us; but the first night which they passed on the snow killed them all. Those who were left of the Germans, Italians, Spaniards and other foreigners whom he had brought into Russia saved their lives by a means repugnant to the

222

French: they deserted, took refuge in the villages near the road, and waited until the enemy came up.

This often did not occur for several days, for, strange as it may seem, the Russian soldiers (accustomed as they are to pass winter in houses where draughts are always excluded and stoves are always lighted) are far more sensitive to cold than those of any other country; and the heavy losses which the enemy incurred from this cause explained the slackness of the pursuit. We did not understand why Kutusov and his generals merely followed us with a weak advance guard, instead of hurling themselves on our flanks, overlapping us, and thus cutting off our retreat. But this manoeuvre, which would have completed our ruin, was impossible for them, seeing that the greater number of their soldiers – no less than of ours – died on the roads and in the bivouacs. So intense was the cold that we could see a kind of vapour rising from men's ears and eyes. Condensing on contact with the air, this vapour fell back on our persons with a rattle such as grains of millet might have made. We had often to halt and clear away from the horses' bits the icicles formed by their frozen breath.

Thousands of Cossacks, meanwhile, attracted by the hope of plunder, endured the inclemency of the weather, and kept alongside our columns, having even the audacity to attack at points where they saw the baggage. A few shots, however, were enough to drive them away. Finally, in order to give us trouble without any danger to themselves – since we had been obliged for want of teams to leave all our artillery behind – the Cossacks placed light guns on sledges, and with these fired at our men until they saw a detachment coming in their direction, when they made off with all speed. These partial attacks, which did us, indeed, little harm, became very disagreeable by continued repetition. Many of our sick and wounded were taken and plundered by these marauders, some of whom acquired immense booty. Even from the ranks of our allies, the desire for wealth raised up new enemies for us: I refer to the Poles.

Marshal Saxe, the son of one of their own kings, said rightly that the Poles are the greatest plunderers in the world, and would not respect even their fathers' goods. You may judge whether those who were in our service respected their allies' goods. On the march and in the bivouac they stole all they could see; but as people began to distrust them, and petty larceny became difficult, they decided to go to work on a large scale. To this end they organised themselves into bands, threw away their helmets, and put on peasants' caps; and slipping out of the bivouacs after dark, they assembled at an appointed place, and came back to the camp shouting the Cossacks' war cry of 'Hourra!' thus terrifying the weaker men, many of whom fled, leaving their effects behind. Then the pretended Cossacks, after pillaging all round, went off and returned before daylight to their places in the French column, where they resumed the title of Poles, with liberty to become Cossacks again the next night.

Attention having been called to this atrocious brigandage, several generals and colonels resolved to punish it. General Maison had such a good lookout kept in the bivouacs of II Corps, that one fine night our outposts surprised some fifty Poles just as they were making up to play their part of sham Cossacks, and were on the point of giving their 'Hourra!' as pillagers. Seeing themselves surrounded on all sides, the brigands had the impudence to say that they had meant to play a practical joke; but as it was neither the place nor the time for joking, General Maison had them all shot then and there. It was some time before we saw any more robbers of that sort, but they did reappear later on.

On 9 December we reached Vilna, where there were still some stores, but the Duke of Bassano and General Hogendorf had retired to the Niemen and there was no one to give orders. There, as at Smolensk, the commissaries required, before giving out provisions and clothing, that regular receipts should be handed to them; a thing which, in the disorganised state of all the regiments, was impossible to do, and thus precious time was lost. General Maison had several storehouses broken open, and his troops got some food and clothing, but the rest was taken the next day by the Russians. Soldiers from the other corps went about the town in the hope of being taken in by the inhabitants, but the people who, six months before, had been longing for the French closed their houses as soon as they saw them in trouble. The Jews alone received those who could pay for this fleeting hospitality.

Thus repulsed alike from the stores and from private houses, the great majority of the starving soldiers made their way to the hospitals, which were soon crammed to overflowing, although there was not enough food there for all the poor people; but at least they were sheltered from the cold. Yet this precarious advantage decided more than 20,000 sick and wounded – among them 200 officers and eight generals – to go no further: they were utterly exhausted in mind and body. Lieutenant Hernoux, one of the stoutest and bravest officers in my regiment, was so distracted by what he had seen in the last few days that he laid himself down on the snow and, no persuasions being able to make him rise, died there. Many soldiers of all ranks blew out their brains to put an end to their misery.

In the night of 9 December, with 30° of frost, some Cossacks came and fired shots at the gates of Vilna. Many people thought that it was Kutusov's whole army and in their terror left the town precipitately. I regret to have to say that King Murat was among the number. He departed without leaving any orders but Marshal Ney remained and organised the retreat as best he could. We evacuated Vilna on the morning of the 10th, leaving there a great number of men, a park of artillery, and a portion of the treasure. Scarcely were we out of Vilna when the infamous Jews threw themselves on the French, whom they had taken into their houses to get out of them what little money they had, stripped them of their clothing, and pitched them naked out of the window. Some officers of the Russian advanced guard, who were entering at the moment, were so angry at this atrocity that they had many of the Jews killed.

In the midst of this tumult Marshal Ney had taken all whom he could set in motion along the road to Kovno, but he had hardly gone a league when he came to the heights of Ponari. This hill, which in ordinary circumstances the column would have crossed without noticing it, became a serious obstacle, since the ice had made the road so slippery that the horses were unable to drag the wagons up it. What remained of the treasure was therefore on the point of falling into the hands of the Cossacks, when Marshal Ney gave orders to have the chests opened and to let the men help themselves. This prudent step, the motive of which Monsieur de Ségur probably did not know, led him to say that the troops plundered the imperial treasure. In the *Spectateur Militaire* of the period I have also noted the following expression used by Monsieur de Ségur: 'After the Emperor's departure, most of the colonels of the army, who had up until then gone on marching admirably with four or five officers or soldiers around their eagle, no longer took any orders save from themselves. There were men who went 200 leagues without turning their heads.' I may add that Marshal Ney, having seen the colonel and the major of a regiment which contained only sixty men fall in one fight, perceived that losses of this kind would only stand in the way of reorganising the army, and gave orders that no more field officers should be retained in presence of the enemy than were in proportion to the number of the troops.

Some days before our arrival at Vilna, many horses of my regiment having died from the intense cold, while it was impossible to mount those that remained, all my troopers marched on foot. I should have been very glad to be able to do the like, but as my wound did not allow of this, I got a sledge and harnessed one of my horses to it. This gave me the idea that I might by the same means save my sick, who now were numerous, and as in Russia a sledge can be found in the poorest house, I soon had a hundred, each of which (drawn by a troop-horse) brought away two men. General Castex thought this manner of travelling so convenient that he authorised me to put all the other troopers in sledges. Major Monginot, who had become colonel of the 24th Chasseurs since Monsieur A—— had been promoted to general, received the same permission and all that remained of our brigade harnessed its horses and formed a caravan which marched in perfect order. You may think that by travelling thus we destroyed our power for defence, but you must know that on the ice we were much stronger with the sledges – which could go anywhere, and in which the horses had the support of shafts – than if we had remained mounted on animals which tumbled down at every step.

The road was covered with muskets which had been thrown away and our troopers took two apiece and a plentiful stock of cartridges, so that when the Cossacks ventured too near they were met by a brisk fire which quickly drove them off. When necessary, our men fought on foot; and in the evening we formed the sledges into a square and lit our fires inside it. Marshal Ney and General Maison often came to pass the night there, finding it a safe place so long as we were pursued only by Cossacks. Doubtless it was the first time that a rearguard had gone on sledges; but owing to the frost it was the only practicable method, and it answered.

Thus we continued covering the retreat until 13 December when we at length saw once more the Niemen and Kovno, the last Russian town. Five months before we had entered the Empire of the Tsar at the same spot. What a change had since then taken place in our fortunes and what had been the loss of the French army! When the rearguard entered Kovno, Marshal Ney found a weak battalion of 400 Germans doing duty as the only garrison. With these he joined such troops as were left to him, in order to defend the place as long as possible and enable the sick and wounded to get away into Prussia. On hearing that Ney was coming, Murat went away to Gumbinnen.

On the 14th, Platov's[11] Cossacks, followed by two battalions of infantry and some guns, all drawn on sledges, attacked Kovno at several points; but Ney, helped by General Gérard, beat them off and held the town until night. Then he bade us cross the Niemen on the ice and was himself the last to leave Russian soil.

We were now in Prussia, among allies. But Ney, worn out with fatigue, unwell and, moreover, considering that the campaign was over, left us at once and joined the other marshals at Gumbinnen. Thenceforth the army had no longer a commander and the remains of each regiment marched independently through Prussia. The Russians, being at war with that country, had the right to follow us on to its territory; but content with having reconquered their own, and not knowing whether they should appear in Prussia as allies or enemies, they thought it best to await orders from their government, and halted at the Niemen. Their hesitation gave us time to reach the towns of Prussia proper.

Germans are for the most part humane and many of them had friends or relations in the regiments which had gone with the French to Moscow. They received us well and I must admit that – after sleeping for five months under the stars – it was delightful to find myself in a warm room and a good bed. But this rapid transition from an icy bivouac to comforts so long forgotten made me seriously ill. Nearly all the army suffered from the same cause; and we lost many, including Generals Eblé and Lariboisière of the artillery.

For all the decent reception which they gave us, the Prussians had not forgotten Jena, and the manner in which Napoleon had treated them in 1807, when he dismembered their kingdom. They hated us in secret and at a signal from their King would have disarmed us and made us prisoners. General Yorck, commanding the Prussian corps which the Emperor had so imprudently employed as the left wing of the Grand Army, being in cantonments between Riga and Tilsit, was already making terms with the Russians[12] and had sent Marshal MacDonald away, though he had enough shame left to refrain from arresting him. All classes in Prussia applauded General Yorck's treachery; and as the provinces through which the French soldiers were just now passing, sick and disarmed, were full of Prussian troops, it is probable that the inhabitants would have tried to get hold of us, had they not been restrained by fear for their King, who was at Berlin, surrounded by a French army under Marshal Augereau. This fear and a disavowal on the part of the King – the most honourable man in the kingdom – of General Yorck's conduct, to the point of having him tried and condemned to death for high treason,[13] prevented a general rising against the French. We took advantage of its absence to get away and reach the banks of the Vistula.

My regiment crossed that river near the fortress of Graudenz, which we had passed on our way to Russia. This time the crossing was very dangerous, for, as a thaw had taken place some leagues higher up, the ice was a good foot deep in water, and ominous crackings were heard foretelling a general break-up. The order to cross instantly reached me, moreover, in the middle of a dark night; for the General had just learned that the King of Prussia had left Berlin and fled into Silesia, that the people were getting uneasy, and there was reason to fear that they would rise against us as soon as the break-up of the ice prevented us from crossing the Vistula. It was, therefore, absolutely necessary to face the danger. This was very great, for the river is wide opposite Graudenz and the ice was full of wide cracks which could only be seen with difficulty by the light of fires kindled on both banks.

As it was useless to think of taking sledges across we left

them behind; and leading the horses, preceded by men with poles to notify the cracks, we began our perilous crossing. We were up to mid-leg in half-frozen water, which made things worse for the sick and wounded; but bodily pain was nothing to the fear caused by the cracking of the ice, which threatened to give way under our feet. A servant of one of my officers fell into a hole and never reappeared. At last we reached the other bank, where we passed the night warming ourselves in fishermen's huts. Next day we saw the Vistula thaw completely, so that if we had delayed a few hours we should all have been made prisoners. From the spot where we crossed the Vistula my regiment proceeded to the little town of Sweld, where it was cantoned before the war and there I began the year 1813. That which was just over had surely been the most painful of my life.

17 Brave Hearts

The Retreat From Leipzig, October 1813

> The grief of having lost a great and bloody
> battle, the frightful prospect of a morrow that
> might perhaps be still more wretched, the guns
> raging at every point of our unhappy lines, the
> defection of our cowardly allies, and lastly the
> privations of every kind that had for days been
> crushing us: all these ills, all these causes taken
> together, made me reflect bitterly indeed upon
> war and its vicissitudes!
>
> Jean-Baptiste Barrès[1]

*Napoleon had sown the seeds of his own destruction by his
disastrous invasion of Russia, in which he lost both his army
and his reputation; while Tsar Alexander, having once been
Napoleon's friend and ally, became the Messianic leader of a
new coalition dedicated to his downfall. This new alliance,
born in the summer of 1812, eventually included most major
European states: Prussia joined in February 1813, declaring a
War of German Liberation against the French; Bernadotte,
the former marshal turned crown prince, joined in July,
commanding his Swedish troops in person; Austria finally
declared for the Allies the following month; Britain, once
again, was the paymaster.*

In the spring of 1813 Napoleon went to war against this

231

Sixth Coalition with a new army, hastily cobbled together in a matter of weeks: sailors, marines, policemen and teenagers all being drafted in. It was an administrative miracle; but the French lacked adequate training, experienced officers and sufficient horses (a staggering total of 180,000 having been lost in Russia). The war was fought in, and for control of, Germany: Napoleon's aim was the subjugation of Berlin; the Allies' the liberation of Germany from French domination (and eventually the seizure of Paris – a little piece of revenge on Alexander's part for Napoleon's occupation of Moscow). Despite early French successes at Lützen (2 May), Bautzen (20–22 May) and Dresden (27 August), Austria's entry into the war on 12 August tipped the scales heavily in favour of the Coalition; and on 16 October Napoleon found himself hemmed in at the Saxon city of Leipzig. The stage was set for the climax of the campaign: a three-day trial of strength which came to be known as the Battle of Nations.

'Hardly had we arrived when the thousand gun battery burst forth simultaneously. All the armies of northern Europe had met together on the ground about Leipsic.'[2] Confronted by a quarter of a million Coalition troops – thus being outnumbered by more than two to one – the French were eventually forced (after much heroism and hard fighting) to withdraw through Leipzig and over the only bridge spanning the River Elster. The Allies assaulted the town and bitter street-fighting broke out, as the French soldiers were fun- nelled through the town to the Lindenau bridge, their escape route to the west. Napoleon gave the job of covering the retreat to the newly appointed Marshal Poniatowski and his Polish Corps;[3] but in the chaos which followed the Allied assault, a panic-stricken corporal blew the bridge too soon, leaving 20,000 Poles stranded on the enemy bank: Ponia- towski drowned trying to swim the Elster, his troops were massacred. Meanwhile in the market square, Alexander of Russia, Frederick William of Prussia, Bernadotte and an

assortment of Allied field marshals gathered to savour the moment of victory.

Napoleon's army, although beaten, managed an orderly retreat south-westwards to the safety of Frankfort. A Bavarian army under General von Wrede (the same von Wrede who had fought at Polotsk under Saint-Cyr) tried to block its path at Hanau on 30 October, but was was beaten off. The Allies had won a great victory at Leipzig (at a total cost of around 150,000 lives for both sides), and with the subsequent collapse of the Confederation of the Rhine, Napoleon's hold over Germany was broken: the following year would see the invasion of France proper.

Marbot was stationed in Germany at the beginning of 1813: General Castex had left to join the Imperial Guard, and General Corbineau had become the Emperor's aide-de-camp, leaving General Exelmans in charge of the brigade. With the wound in his knee still giving him a good deal of pain, Marbot was recalled to the regimental dépôt at Mons, Belgium (then still part of the French Empire), to organize new recruits and remounts. He was joined there by his wife and child: 'After a year of separation and all that danger, it was a great pleasure to see my wife again, and for the first time to kiss our little Alfred, now eight months old. It was one of the happiest days of my life.'

He remained at Mons until the end of June; but was back at the front in time for the débâcle at the Katzbach River in August, where Marshal MacDonald was defeated by the Prussians, under Field Marshal Blücher, losing 15,000 men and 100 guns: 'It has been truly said that in the later campaigns of the Empire the fighting was seldom well managed when Napoleon did not direct it in person. It is to be regretted that the great captain did not realise this, and put so much trust in his lieutenants, many of whom – though, as we had plenty of evidence, had no lack of self-confidence – were not up to their work.' On 28 September Napoleon made Marbot a *baron and an officer of the Legion of Honour; while at Leipzig, he received a somewhat unusual wound: being struck in the thigh by an arrow, fired from the bow of a Russian backwoodsman.*

WHILE THE EMPEROR and the divisions from Leipzig were halted at Markranstadt came the disastrous news of the destruction of the Lindenau bridge. The army had lost by this nearly all its artillery, half the troops were left as prisoners, and thousands of our wounded comrades handed over to the hostile soldiery: hounded on by its infamous officers to the slaughter. Grief was universal, for each man had a relation or a friend to mourn. The Emperor appeared overwhelmed; but he ordered Sébastiani's cavalry to return as far as the bridge for the protection of individuals who might succeed in crossing the river at one point or another. My regiment and the 24th, being the best mounted, were ordered to lead the column and to go at full trot. General Wathiez being unwell, it fell to me, as senior colonel, to command the brigade. Hardly had we traversed half the distance when we heard frequent shots, and as we drew near the suburb we could distinguish the despairing cries of the unhappy French, who, unable to retreat, and without cartridges, were being hunted from street to street and butchered in a cowardly manner by Prussians, Badeners and Saxons.

The fury of my two regiments was indescribable. Every man breathed vengeance and regretted that vengeance was almost impossible, since the River Elster, with its broken bridge, lay between us and the assassins. Our rage increased when we met about 2,000 French, mostly without clothing and nearly all wounded, who had only escaped death by leaping into the river and swimming across under the fire from the other bank. Among them was Marshal MacDonald,[4] who owed his life to his bodily strength and his practice in swimming. He was completely naked and his horse had been drowned. I hastily got him some clothes and lent him my led horse, which allowed him to rejoin the Emperor at once and report the disaster he had witnessed; one of the chief episodes in it being the death by drowning of Prince Poniatowski.

The remainder of the French who had crossed the river, having to get rid of their weapons in order to be able to swim, were without the means of defence; they were running across the fields to escape from some 400 or 500 Prussians and others, who, not content with the bath of French blood which they had had in the town and suburbs, had laid planks across the pieces of the exploded bridge and had come over to kill such of our soldiers as they could overtake on the road to Markranstadt. When I caught sight of this band of murderers I ordered Monsieur Schneit, Colonel of the 24th, to make a combined movement with my regiment, by means of which we enclosed these brigands in a vast semicircle. Then I gave the order to sound the charge. The effect was terrible. The bandits, taken by surprise, offered only a feeble resistance and there was a very great slaughter, for no quarter was given. So enraged was I, that before the charge I had vowed to run my sabre through all who came within my reach. Yet when I was in the thick of them and saw that they were drunk, in disorder, and with no commanders but two Saxon officers, who trembled before the approaching vengeance, I saw that it was no case of fighting, but an execution, in which it did not become me to take part. I dreaded lest I might actually find pleasure in killing some of the scoundrels with my own hand. So I sheathed my sword and left the task of exterminating the assassins to my troopers. Two-thirds of them fell on the spot; the rest, among them two officers and several men of the Saxon guards, fled towards the bridge in the hope of recrossing the river by the planks. But as they could only go in single file and our men were pressing them hard, they made for a large inn close by, whence they set to work to fire on my people: some Badish and Prussian pickets on the further bank aiding.

As it was probable that the noise of the fight might attract large forces towards the bridge, who, without crossing the river, could destroy my two regiments by musketry and artillery fire, I resolved to lose no time. I ordered most of my men to dismount and, taking a good supply of cartridges, to attack the inn in rear and set fire to the stables and haylofts. On this, the assassins, finding themselves about to be caught by the flames, made an effort to escape; but as fast as they appeared at the gates the *chasseurs* shot them down. In vain did they send one of the Saxon officers to me: I refused to treat the monsters who had butchered our comrades as soldiers who surrendered honourably. The Prussian, Saxon and Badish assassins who had crossed the footbridge were therefore all exterminated. I announced the fact to General Sébastiani and he halted the the other brigades halfway. The fire which we had kindled soon reached the neighbouring houses. A great part of the village of Lindenau was burnt and the reconstruction of the bridge and passage of the enemy's troops in pursuit of the French army thereby delayed.

Our expedition ended, I brought the brigade back to Markranstadt, as well as the 2,000 French who had escaped the disaster at the bridge. Among them were officers of all ranks. The Emperor questioned them as to what they knew regarding the explosion of the mine and the massacre of the French prisoners by the Allies. It is probable that the sad tale made Napoleon regret that he had not followed the advice which had been given him that morning to secure the retreat of the army and prevent any attack from the enemy by setting fire to the suburbs; and even, if necessary, to the town of Leipzig. I may say that nearly all the inhabitants had left the place during the three days' battle.

In our counter-attack at the bridge of Lindenau, only three men in my brigade had been wounded and only one of my regiment; but he was one of my bravest and best non-commissioned officers, named Foucher. In the attack on the inn a bullet had made four holes in him, passing through both his thighs. In spite of this severe wound, the brave Foucher went through the retreat on horseback, refused to go into hospital at Erfurt, and accompanied the regiment into France. His comrades and all the troopers of his section took particular care of him, and in all respects he deserved it.

After crossing the Saale Napoleon thanked and bade farewell to the officers and some troops of the Confederation of the Rhine who, whether from honourable feeling or for want of an opportunity to desert, were still in our ranks. He carried his magnanimity so far as to allow these soldiers to retain their arms, although, as their sovereigns had joined his enemies, he had the right to detain them as prisoners. The French army continued its retreat to Erfurt with no event except the combat of Kosen, where a single French division beat an Austrian army corps and took its commander, Count Gyulai, prisoner.

Always beguiled by the hope of returning to the attack of Germany, in which case the fortresses which he was compelled to leave would be of great service to him, Napoleon established a strong garrison at Erfurt. He had left 25,000 men under Saint-Cyr at Dresden, 30,000 under Davout at Hamburg, while the various fortresses on the Oder and the Elbe were garrisoned in proportion to their importance. These were additional to those which Danzig and the other places on the Vistula had already cost us. Napoleon left in the fortresses of Germany 80,000 soldiers, not one of whom saw France again before the fall of the Empire; which they might – perhaps – have prevented if they had been united on our frontiers.

Our artillery repaired its losses in the arsenal of Erfurt. The Emperor, who up until then had borne his reverses with stoic fortitude, was affected by the desertion of his brother-in-law.[5] Under the pretext of going to defend his kingdom of Naples, Murat left Napoleon, to whom he owed everything. Formerly so brilliant in war, he had done nothing remarkable during this campaign. It is certain that while he was still among us he had been keeping up a correspondence with Metternich,[6] and the Austrian minister, placing before his eyes the example of Bernadotte, had, in the name of the Allied sovereigns, guaranteed him the preservation of his kingdom if he would take his place among Napoleon's enemies. Murat left the French army at Erfurt and no sooner had he reached Naples than he prepared to make war upon us.

At Erfurt also the Emperor heard of the audacious manoeuvre of the Bavarians – his former allies – who, after betraying his cause, had joined an Austrian corps and marched (under the command of General Wrede) with the intention not only of opposing the passage of the French army, but of taking it and the Emperor prisoners. Wrede marched for two days parallel with our army and was already at Würzburg with 60,000 men. He detached 10,000 towards Frankfort and with the remainder proceeded towards the small fortress of Hanau, with a view of blocking the road of the French. He had been with us on the Russian campaign and thought to find the French army still in the wretched state to which cold and hunger had reduced it when it reached the Beresina; but we soon showed him that, in spite of our misfortune, we still had some troops in good condition, and quite enough to beat the Austrians and Bavarians.

Not knowing that beyond Erfurt the Allied troops whom we had fought at Leipzig had been following us only at a considerable distance, Wrede had become very enterprising and thought to catch us between two fires. This he could not do; still, as several of the enemy's corps were seeking to outflank our right by way of the Franconian Mountains, while the Bavarians met us in front, our situation might become critical. Then Napoleon, rising to the height of the danger, marched briskly on Hanau, the approaches to which are covered by thick forests and especially the famous defile of Geluhausen, through which the Kinzig flows. This stream, the banks of which are very steep, runs between two mountains where there is only a narrow passage for the river, beside which a very fine road has been hewn out of the rock, going from Fulda to Frankfort-am-Main, by way of Hanau.

Sébastiani's cavalry, which had acted as advance guard from Weissenfels to Fulda, ought at that point where the road enters the mountains to have been replaced by infantry. I have never known for what reason that grand principle of war was not followed on this occasion; but to our surprise, Exelmans' light cavalry division continued to march in front of the army. My regiment and the 24th were at the head and I commanded the brigade. We learned from the peasants that the Austro-Bavarian army was already at Hanau, and that a strong division was coming to meet us to dispute our passage through the defile.

My position as commander of the advance guard now became very ticklish. How was I, without a single foot soldier and with my cavalry shut in between lofty hills and an impassable torrent, to attack infantry whose scouts could climb the rocks and shoot us down at point-blank range? I at once sent to the rear of the column to let the General know, but Exelmans was not to be found. So, as my orders were to advance and I could not stop the divisions behind me, I marched on, until at an elbow in the valley my scouts reported that there was a detachment of the enemy's hussars in front. The Austrians and Bavarians had made the same mistake as our leaders. We had to attack with cavalry a long and narrow defile in which not more than ten or twelve horses could walk abreast; and they were sending cavalry to defend a place which a hundred light infantry could have held against any number of horse. I was rejoiced to see that the enemy had no infantry, and as I knew by experience that when two columns meet in a narrow place the advantage is always with the side that makes the charge: I sent my picked company ahead at full speed.

Only the first section could touch the enemy, but it did it so thoroughly that the Austrian column was thrown into disorder, and my troopers had only to hold their sabres straight.

We pursued for more than an hour. The enemy were Ott's regiment and I never saw finer hussars. They were just from Vienna and their uniforms – handsome, if a little theatrical – were as new and smart as you could wish. You might have thought they came from a ballroom or a theatre. Their brilliant costume contrasted strangely with the more than modest get-up of our *chasseurs*, many of whom were still wearing the clothes, stained with smoke and dust, in which they had bivouacked for a year and a half past; but brave hearts and sturdy limbs were inside them. The white jackets of Ott's hussars were soon terribly blood-stained and the trim regiment lost more than 200 killed and wounded. Not one of ours was touched, as the enemy never had a chance of turning round. Our men took a number of excellent horses and gold laced jackets. So far all had gone well; but as I galloped after the stream of pursuers I was not without anxiety as to the end of this curious fight. The hills on each side of the stream were falling away and it was clear that we were approaching the end of the valley. There we should probably find a plain full of infantry and might have to pay dearly for our success. Happily it was not so. On issuing from the defile we saw nothing but the cavalry, including the main portion of Ott's hussars, whom we had just handled so roughly, and who now drew along some fifteen squadrons with them in their headlong retreat on Hanau.

Then General Sébastiani made his three divisions of cavalry debouch. These were soon supported by the infantry under Victor and MacDonald, with several batteries. The Emperor and part of the Guard presently appeared and the remainder of the army followed. It was the evening of 21 October. We bivouacked in a neighbouring wood, at not more than a league from Hanau and the Austro-Bavarian army.

During the night the Emperor relieved the army very materially by sending all the baggage off to Koblenz, escorted by some battalions of infantry and the cavalry of Lefebvre-Desnouettes and Milhaud. On the morning of the 30th he had with him only MacDonald's and Victor's infantry, 5,000 bayonets in all, and Sébastiani's cavalry.

The side by which we approached Hanau is covered by a great forest, through which the road passes; the trees of which are large enough to allow scarcely impeded movement. The town of Hanau is on the further bank of the Kinzig. General Wrede, who as a rule was not devoid of military talent, had committed the huge blunder of posting his army with the river in its rear; thereby depriving it of the support offered by the fortifications of Hanau. His only means of communication and retreat was by the bridge of Lamboy. No doubt the position which he occupied barred the road to Frankfort and to France and he thought himself well able to stop us.

At daybreak on 30 October the battle began. It was like a great hunting expedition. A few rounds of grape, the fire of the infantry skirmishers, and a charge in loose order by Sébastiani's cavalry dispersed the enemy's first line, awkwardly posted on the edge of the wood. But when we had advanced a little further, our squadrons could only act in the few clearings, and the light infantry pursued the Bavarians singly, driving them from tree to tree till they got out of the wood. Then they were brought up by the enemy's line, 40,000 strong, with eighty guns in its front. If the Emperor had then had all the troops whom he brought away from Leipzig, a vigorous attack would have mastered the bridge and General Wrede would have paid dear for his rashness; but the corps of Mortier, Marmont and Bertrand, and the great convoy of artillery had been delayed by the defiles, and Napoleon had only 10,000 combatants at his disposal. The enemy should have seized the opportunity for a brisk charge; but they did not venture it and their hesitation allowed time for the artillery of the Guard to come up. As soon as General Drouot, who commanded it, had fifteen pieces on the field, he opened fire; and his line increased gradually, until it showed fifty guns. These he caused to advance firing, though he had few troops to support him; but owing to the smoke of so great a battery, the enemy did not find out. At last, just as a puff of wind drove the smoke away, the *chasseurs* of the Guard appeared.

At the sight of the *chasseurs'* bearskins the Bavarian infantry recoiled in consternation. Wishing to check the disorder at any cost, General Wrede made all the cavalry at his disposal charge our guns, and in a moment the battery was surrounded by a cloud of horsemen. But at the voice of their intrepid chief who, sword in hand, was setting the example of a valiant resistance, the French gunners seized their muskets and remained immovable behind the carriages, whence they fired on the enemy at close quarters. Numbers would, however, have triumphed but that – at the Emperor's order – the whole of Sébastiani's cavalry and that of the Guard: grenadiers, dragoons, *chasseurs*, Mamelukes, lancers, all dashed furiously on the enemy, killing a great number and scattering the rest. Then, flying upon the squares of Bavarian infantry, they broke them with heavy loss and the routed Bavarian army fled towards the bridge and the town of Hanau.

General Wrede – being a brave man – determined, before owning himself beaten by a force of half his own strength, to make a fresh effort. Assembling all his available troops, he attacked us unexpectedly. The musketry fire suddenly drew near to us; again the forest re-echoed with the roar of the cannon, the balls whistled through the trees, bringing great branches down with a crash. The wood was too deep for the eye to penetrate; through the shade cast by the thick foliage of the huge beeches, one could barely see the occasional flashes of the guns. On hearing the noise of this attack, the Emperor sent off in that direction the grenadiers of his Old Guard, under General Friant. These soon repulsed this last effort of the enemy, who quickly left the field of battle and rallied under the shelter of the fortress of Hanau. During the night they abandoned this also, leaving a great number of wounded and the French occupied the place.

We were only two short leagues from Frankfort, where there is a stone bridge over the Main. Now, as the French army had to march along this river to reach the French frontier at Mainz, Napoleon sent forward General Sébastiani's corps with a division of infantry to occupy Frankfort and destroy the bridge; he himself with the main army bivouacking in the forest. The high road from Hanau to Frankfort passes close along the right bank of the Main. My friend General Albert, who commanded the infantry which accompanied us, had been married some years before at Offenbach – a pretty little town on the left bank – exactly opposite the spot where, having emerged from the forest of Hanau, we rested our horses in the wide plain of Frankfort. Finding himself so near his wife and children, General Albert could not resist the desire to get news of them, and still more to reassure them of his safety after the battles of Leipzig and Hanau. To this end he exposed himself perhaps to more danger than in those sanguinary engagements. Advancing in uniform and on horseback to the edge of the stream, in spite of all we could say, he hailed a boatman who knew him. While he was talking to this man, a Bavarian officer, coming up at the head of an infantry picket, ordered them to make ready and was about to fire on the French General. However, a number of inhabitants and boatmen placed themselves in front of the muskets and stopped the soldiers from firing, for Albert was much beloved at Offenbach. As I looked at that town where I had just been fighting in my country's service I little thought that I should one day take refuge there from the proscription of the French government, and should pass three years in exile.[7]

The Emperor, on leaving the forest of Hanau, had scarcely gone two leagues on the road to Frankfort when he learned that the battle had begun again behind him. The Bavarian General, who had feared after his defeat that the Emperor would stick to his heels until he had made an end of him, when he saw that the French army cared more about reaching the Rhine than about pursuing him, plucked up courage and made a smart attack on our rearguard. But the corps of MacDonald, Marmont and Bertrand, who had occupied Hanau during the night, received his army with the bayonet and overthrew it with great slaughter. General Wrede was severely wounded, and his son-in-law, the Prince of Oettingen, was killed. The command of the enemy's army devolved on the Austrian General Fresnel, who gave orders for a retreat, while we continued our march to the Rhine unmolested, crossing it on 2 November, after a campaign in which brilliant victories had been mingled with depressing reverses. The cause of these last was Napoleon's mistake in quarrelling with Austria instead of making peace after his victories in the month of June. All Germany followed and Napoleon soon had the whole of Europe against him.

After our return to France the Emperor stayed only six days at Mainz and then went to Paris: a prompt departure with which the army found fault. It was admitted that there were strong political reasons calling him to the capital; but it was thought that the duty of reorganising the army also had claims on him, and that he should have gone to and fro between it and Paris, for experience might have taught him that when he was absent little or nothing was ever done.

The last cannon-shots which I heard in 1813 were fired at the Battle of Hanau; and that day went very near to being the last of my life. My regiment charged five times: twice upon infantry squares, once upon guns, and twice on Bavarian cavalry; but the greatest danger which I ran arose from the explosion of a wagon full of shells, which took place close to me. The Emperor ordered the cavalry to make a general charge at a very difficult moment. Now, in such a case, it is not enough for a commanding officer – and especially when he is engaged in a forest – to send his regiment straight forward, as I have seen many do; he must cast a quick glance over the ground to which his squadrons are coming, so that he does not lead them into swampy places. I marched, therefore, some paces in front, followed by my regimental staff and having beside me a trumpeter who signalled (as I bade) the obstacles which my men would find in front of them.

Although the trees stood wide apart, the passage through the forest was difficult for cavalry because the ground was piled with men and horses – killed or wounded – and with weapons, guns and wagons which the Bavarians had left. It is easy to see that it is difficult in such a case for a colonel, as he gallops amid bullets and cannon-balls, to examine the ground and at the same time take any thought for his own personal safety. I had to leave this to the intelligence and nimbleness of my excellent horse, Azolan; but the small group which followed me close had been greatly thinned by a discharge of grape, which had wounded many of my orderlies, and I had only my trumpeter near me, when suddenly, from the whole line I heard shouts of 'Colonel! colonel! look out!' and ten paces from me I saw a Bavarian artillery wagon which one of our shells had just set on fire. A huge tree which had been cut down by the cannon-balls barred the road in front of me. To go round would have taken me too long. I called to the trumpeter to stoop, and lying flat over my saddle-bow, I took my horse at the jump. Azolan made a long leap but not long enough to clear all the branches, and his legs got caught among them. Meantime the wagon was blazing and the powder would take fire in a moment. I gave myself up for lost when my horse – as though he had understood our common danger – began bounding four or five feet high, always getting further from the wagon, and as soon as he was clear of the branches he went off at such a stretching gallop that he was literally *ventre à terre.*[8]

I shivered when the explosion took place; but I must have been out of the reach of the bursting shells, for neither my horse nor I was touched. It was otherwise with my young trumpeter, for when the regiment resumed its march after the explosion, they saw the poor fellow dead and horribly mutilated by the splinters. His horse was also blown to pieces. My brave Azolan had saved me already at the Katzbach,[9] and now I owed him my life a second time. I caressed him and, as though to show his joy, the poor animal whinnied aloud. There are moments when one is led to believe that some creatures have far more intelligence than is generally thought.

I keenly regretted my trumpeter, who was beloved by the whole regiment. He was the son of a professor at the college of Toulouse; had been through his course there and took great delight in spouting Latin. An hour before his death the poor lad, having observed that nearly all the trees in the forest of Hanau were beeches, and that their spreading branches formed a kind of roof, found it a suitable occasion to repeat the Eclogue of Virgil which begins with the verse: *Tityre, tu patulæ recubans sub tegmine fagi.*[10] Marshal MacDonald, who happened to pass at this moment, laughed heartily, exclaiming, 'There's a little chap whose memory isn't disturbed by his surroundings! It is certainly the first time that anyone has recited Virgil under the fire of the enemy's guns.'

'He who takes the sword shall perish by the sword,' says the Scripture. If this saying does not apply to all soldiers, it did to many of them under the Empire. Monsieur Guindet, who in October 1806 had killed Prince Louis of Prussia at Saalfeld,[11] was himself killed at the Battle of Hanau. The remnants of the French army expected, when they crossed the Rhine, that their hardships would be at an end as soon as they were on their native soil; but they were greatly mistaken. The government and the Emperor himself had so reckoned on our success that no arrangements had been made to receive the troops at the frontier and reorganise them. On the very day of our entry into

Mainz, the men and horses would have had no food if they had not been billeted about in the neighbouring towns and villages. The inhabitants, however, had had no experience of feeding soldiers since the old Revolutionary Wars. They complained loudly and in fact the charge fell too heavily on the communes.

The sick and wounded were established as well as circumstances permitted in the hospitals of Mainz, and in order to watch the line of the Rhine from Basle to Holland, all able-bodied men joined the nuclei of their regiments, and the divisions and army corps, sadly weakened, were distributed along the river. My regiment, with what was left of Sébastiani's corps, went down the Rhine by easy marches. The weather was splendid, and the country lovely; but we were all heartbroken, foreseeing as we did, that France was going to lose these fair countries and that her misfortunes would not stop there.

After passing some time at Cleves and Urdingen, we went on to Nijmegen. On the further bank we could see the Dutch and German population tearing the French flag from their towers and replacing those of their old sovereign. Amid our melancholy thoughts, the colonels did their best to reorganise their few remaining troops; but we could do little for want of supplies. Moreover, the necessity of feeding the army forced the Emperor to keep it scattered; while in order to organise it, it should have been concentrated. Meanwhile our enemies required time to recover from the rough handling we had given them, and were in no condition to cross the Rhine. They left us alone, therefore, throughout November and December, and I passed those months chiefly on the banks of the Rhine with the phantom of an army corps commanded by MacDonald.

18 Soldiers May Never Surrender Without a Fight

Mons, January–April 1814

After the battle of Champ Aubert, the emperor
was under such a delusion as to his situation,
that while supping with Berthier, Marmont, his
prisoner General Alsufieff, and others, he said,
'Another such a victory as this, gentlemen, and I
shall be on the Vistula.' Finding that no one
replied, and observing by the countenances of
the marshals that they did not share his hopes, 'I
see how it is,' he added, 'everyone is growing
tired of war; there is no longer any enthusiasm.
The sacred fire is extinct.'

Louis Antoine Fauvelet de Bourrienne[1]

*Following their victory at Leipzig, the Allies offered peace to
Napoleon on the condition that France returned to her 'natural' boundaries of the Rhine, the Alps and the Pyrenees: he
refused and the war continued with an invasion of France in
January 1814. Although the situation was desperate, Napoleon refused to compromise with his enemies. Instead, he
marshalled his meagre resources, breathed fire into his army
of boys,[2] and turned on a dazzling display of generalship: 'The
campaign of 1814 has been greatly admired, and has even*

249

been held up as the greatest effort of the Emperor's genius.'[3]
So wrote the French historian F. Loraine Petre, a century after
Napoleon's 'Campaign of Miracles'. But not even an experienced miracle-worker like Bonaparte could squeeze more men
from a France bled white by over twenty years of war; or
rescue the thousands of French troops besieged in German
fortresses and garrison towns. As for the Marshals: Lannes,
Bessières and Poniatowski were dead; Berthier and Oudinot
were wounded; Saint-Cyr and Davout were trapped in Germany; Augereau and Masséna were in disgrace, or semi-
retirement; and Murat had deserted. Those who remained
with Napoleon were jaded, war-weary, and incapable of
winning battles without him. Having had honours and wealth
heaped upon them they were no longer willing to risk their
lives, desiring instead peace; and a chance to grow old quietly.
France was exhausted; and Paris, the very heart of the Empire,
was ripe for revolution. War had gone out of fashion.

Meanwhile treachery was in the air, personified by Talleyrand,[4] Napoleon's ex-foreign minister. Having despaired of
his master's endless wars and boundless ambition, Talleyrand
had resigned his post after Tilsit in 1807 and entered into
secret negotiations with the Tsar and the exiled heir to the
Bourbon throne, the Comte de Lille (later Louis XVIII). When
Napoleon learned of Talleyrand's machinations he merely
subjected him to a verbal drubbing, calling him – amongst
other things – 'shit in silk stockings'. The artful ex-minister
continued to sell his services to the Allies.

By January 1814 three Allied armies had entered France:
Prince Schwarzenberg of Austria – in overall command –
attacked from Switzerland; Blücher from Lorraine; and Bernadotte from the Netherlands (the British had already crossed
from Spain into southern France and were engaged in a
successful campaign against Marshal Soult).[5] Although the
Allies enjoyed overwhelming numerical superiority, their
forces were divided; and starting on 10 February Napoleon

hit each one in turn, in what came to be known as the Six Days' Campaign. Within the space of a week, Napoleon marched his army eighty miles, inflicted 20,000 casualties upon the Allies, and won a series of astonishing victories: Champaubert, Montmirail, Château-Thierry, and Vauchamps: followed up by Montereau on the 18th. Desperate to stop the Allies from uniting their forces and driving on Paris, Napoleon, 'with his handful of men, made supernatural efforts; taking advantage of every good position that presented itself, and attacking the enemy upon several points upon the same day'.[6]

Further offers of peace were made by the Allies – only to be rejected – until, on 9 March, the Coalition agreed on a common front: Bonaparte was to be beaten by force and France reduced to her pre-revolutionary boundaries. The race for Paris began: 'So this war might be compared to the battles of the ravens and the eagle in the Alps. The eagle kills them by hundreds, every stroke of his beak is the death of an enemy, but still the ravens return to the charge and press upon the eagle, until he is literally overwhelmed by the number of his assailants.'[7]

Napoleon was marching to the aid of the capital when the battle for the city began on 30 March. Joseph Bonaparte and the Empress Marie-Louise[8] watched the fighting rage around Montmartre, before joining the stream of refugees heading south. Paris fell the following day with the surrender of Marshal Marmont. The victors entered the city and Cossacks camped on the Champs Élysées. Talleyrand, having made a pretence of leaving, remained behind to welcome Tsar Alexander. Napoleon was at Fontainebleau, thirty-six miles southeast of the capital when the news of its capitulation reached him. Plans to march to the city's relief were dropped when General Souham deserted to the enemy with the 11,000 men of Marmont's corps. Then the marshals, headed by Ney, refused to continue the fight; and Napoleon found himself

251

alienated, his abdication being demanded by all sides (the Allies had cleverly isolated Napoleon politically by declaring him to be the only obstacle to peace, not France or the French people). Momentarily deluded that he was the only man capable of saving France in her hour of need, the truth gradually began to sink in: all parties were claiming to be saving France – from him! In his despair he drank the poison which he kept in a phial around his neck; but it was too old to be effective and on 13 April the fallen Emperor abdicated in favour of his infant son.[9]

But any question of a Bonaparte dynasty was soon quashed by the Tsar, who, influenced by Talleyrand, demanded the return of the Bourbon monarchy in the bodacious person of Louis XVIII (referred to by a British soldier of his escort as 'a bloated poltroon').[10] *Napoleon, meanwhile, boarded a British warship to be ferried to his new home, the island of Elba, ten miles off the Italian coast. As the island's new 'sovereign' he was permitted an army of 400 guards, and allowed to design his own flag. Once installed in Paris, the Bourbons reneged on their promise to supply the former Emperor with a pension; and settled down to plot his abduction – or worse.*

At the end of 1813 Marbot had been ordered back to his regimental dépôt at Mons: 'There I saw the eventful year 1813 out – a year in which I had borne many toils and incurred many dangers.' At that time, however, the Low Countries were on the brink of revolt against their French masters, having declared for the young Prince of Orange. The situation was extremely volatile, especially when the Allied advance began, and in the confusion which ensued Marbot found himself not only responsible for his regiment and dépôt, but also the whole department of Jemappes.

I BEGAN the year 1814 at Mons. Physically, I ran no dangers that year equal to those of its predecessors; but I underwent far greater moral suffering. All my troopers who were still mounted having remained at Nijmegen, I found at the dépôt only men in want of horses. These I was trying to supply from the Ardennes, when the course of events interfered. On 1 January, after nearly three months' hesitation, the enemy crossed the Rhine at several points. The two most important were Caub, between Bingen and Koblenz, close to the Lurlei; and Basle, where the Swiss violated their neutrality by throwing open the bridge: they have a way of insisting on or renouncing their neutrality according to the interests of the moment.

The number of the invading troops was reckoned at 500,000–600,000. France was exhausted by twenty-five years of war; more than half her soldiers were prisoners in foreign lands, and many of her provinces were ready to break away on the first opportunity; among them that to which Mons, the capital of the department of Jemmapes, belonged. This broad and rich country, annexed at first to France de facto by the war of 1792 and then *de jure* by the Treaty of Amiens,[11] had grown so accustomed to the union that it had distinguished itself after the Russian disaster by the zeal which it displayed in helping the Emperor to restore his army to its former footing, and the willingness with which it complied with all kinds of requisitions. But our losses in Germany had taken heart out of the Belgians and I found the spirit of the population changed. There was regret for the old paternal government of Austria and a keen desire for separation from France, and the perpetual wars which were ruining commerce and industry. In short, Belgium was only awaiting the opportunity to revolt; and owing to her position in rear of the weak army corps which we had on the Rhine, nothing could have been more dangerous for us. The Emperor accordingly sent troops to Brussels under General Maison, a man of ability and solid character.

After visiting various departments he found that that of

Jemmapes, and especially the town of Mons, was deeply disaffected. People talked openly of taking men against the weak garrisons; nor could the commandant, General O——, gouty, old and indolent, as a native of Belgium and afraid of compromising himself in the eyes of his countrymen, have done anything to hinder it. General Maison relieved him of his command and appointed me commandant of the department of Jemmapes. It was a difficult duty, for next to the men of Liège, those of Mons and its district are the boldest and most turbulent in all Belgium; while to keep them in check I had only a battalion of 400 recruits, some *gendarmes*, and 200 dismounted troopers of my own regiment: fifty of whom were natives of those parts. All I could really count on, therefore, were the remaining 150 *chasseurs*, who, being French by birth, and having all fought under me, would have followed me anywhere. The officers were good; and those of the infantry – especially the major – were perfectly willing to back me up. Yet I could not but see that if we came to blows the odds would be great. From my hotel I could see every day 3,000–4,000 peasants, armed with big sticks, assembling in the square and listening to the talk of certain retired Austrian officers. These men, all wealthy and of good family, had left the service when Belgium was joined to France, and now preached against the Empire, which had loaded them with taxes, carried their children off to the wars, and so forth. This talk found all the readier listeners for being addressed by great landowners to their tenants and persons whom they employed and over whom they had great influence.

Every day brought news of the enemy's advance from Brussels, driving before them the remnants of MacDonald's corps. All French officials left the department to take refuge at Valenciennes and Cambrai. Finally, the mayor of Mons, Monsieur Duval de Beaulieu, felt bound in honour to warn me that I and my small garrison were no longer safe amid the excited populace, and that I had better evacuate the town. No hindrance would be offered, as the regiment had lived on perfectly good terms with the inhabitants. This proposal came, I was aware, from a committee of ex-Austrian officers; and they had sent it through the mayor in the hope of intimidating me. Therefore I determined to show my teeth and begged Monsieur Duval to summon a meeting of the town council and notables, when I would reply to the proposal he had made.

Half-an-hour later my garrison was under arms; and as soon as the town council – accompanied by the wealthier inhabitants – appeared in the square, I mounted my horse so that all could hear; and having told the mayor that before talking to him and the council I had an important order to give my troops, I imparted to them the proposal which had been made to me: that we should leave without a fight the town which had been given into our keeping. They were indignant and said so plainly. I added that no doubt the ramparts were broken down in many places and had no guns so that it would be difficult to defend them against regular troops; but that if – contrary to the laws of nations – the civil population of the district rose against us, we need not confine ourselves to the defensive, but should treat them as rebels and attack them by every means in our power. I therefore ordered my men to take possession of the belfry and thence, after half-an-hour's delay and three summons by beat of drum, to fire on the crowd in the square; while patrols were to clear the streets, shooting down especially the country people, who had left their work to make trouble for us. Lastly, I ordered that, fighting once begun, the town was to be set on fire to occupy the inhabitants, and that in order to prevent the flames from being extinguished, the men were to keep firing on the burning quarters.

This speech will seem to you pretty brutal; but think of my critical position. With only 700 men – few of whom had seen any fighting – I was surrounded by a multitude which increased every moment; and the officer in command on the tower told me that all the roads leading to the town were covered with dense masses of colliers from the mines of Jemmapes, making their way to Mons. If I did not act with energy my little band was in danger of being crushed.

The nobles who had promoted the rising and the inhabitants of the town felt the force of my discourse and began to withdraw; but the peasants did not stir; so I ordered up two wagons of ammunition and distributed a hundred cartridges to each soldier. Then I gave the order to load, and bade the drums beat the three rolls which were to precede a volley. At the dreaded signal the crowd fled in disorder into the nearest streets and in a few moments the leaders of the Austrian party, with the mayor at their head, came to shake me by the hand and implore me to spare the town. I agreed on condition that they would instantly order the colliers and workmen to return home. They accepted eagerly and the young men of fashion (who had the best horses) galloped out at every gate, met the crowds, and sent them back without any demur to their villages. This ready obedience confirmed my belief that the movement had powerful leaders and that I and my garrison would soon have been prisoners had I not frightened the promoters by threatening to use all means – even arson – rather than to give in to insurgents.

The Belgians are great musicians. That evening there was to be an amateur concert, to which my officers and I, as well as the prefect of the department, were invited. We settled to go as if nothing had happened and we did rightly; for so far as appearances went, we were perfectly well received. As we chatted with the leaders of the movement we pointed out to them that the fate of Belgium was to be decided not by the population in rebellion, but by the belligerent armies, and that it would be madness to excite labourers and peasants to fight and shed blood in order to hasten by a few days a decision for which they should wait.

An old retired Austrian general, a native of Mons, then told his fellow townsmen that they had been very wrong in plotting the capture of the garrison. It would have brought calamity on the town, since soldiers may never surrender without a fight. All admitted the justice of this and from that day garrison and townsfolk lived on the same good terms as before. A few days later the people of Mons gave us a striking proof of their loyalty under the following circumstances. As the Allied army advanced, a crowd of vagabonds – chiefly Prussians – got themselves up like Cossacks, and urged by the lust for plunder, fell upon everything which had been official property during the French occupation, seizing even without scruple the property of individuals not belonging to the army. A strong band of these pretended Cossacks made their way even to the gates of Brussels and looted the château of Tervueren, carrying off all the horses of the stud which the Emperor had formed there. Then, breaking up into detachments, they went marauding all over Belgium. Coming into the department of Jemmapes, they tried to bring about a rising, and when this did not succeed, they thought it was owing to the fact that Mons was deterred from pronouncing for them by the fear which the colonel commanding there had inspired among the people. They determined, therefore, to carry me off or kill me; but in order not to arouse my suspicions by employing too many men on that service, they sent only 300.

The leader of these partisans must have had good information, for, knowing that I had too few people to guard properly the old gates and half-demolished ramparts, he brought his horsemen close to the town on a dark night, and the greater part of them, dismounting, made their way in silence through the streets in the direction of the Hôtel de la Poste, where I had at first lodged. But since hearing that the enemy had crossed the Rhine, I had taken to going every evening to the barracks and passing the night with my troops. It was lucky I did, for the German Cossacks surrounded the hotel, rummaged all the rooms, and in their rage at finding no French officers, fell out with the landlord. They ill-treated him, plundered him, and got drunk – men and officers alike – on his best wine.

A Belgian named Courtois, formerly a corporal in my regiment, for whom (as one of my best soldiers) I had obtained the Legion of Honour, entered the hotel at that moment. He had lost a leg in Russia in the previous year, and I had been fortunate enough to save his life by procuring for him the means of returning to France. For this he was so grateful that while I was at Mons in the winter of 1814 he often came to see me, on those occasions wearing his old uniform of the 23rd Chasseurs. Now it happened that on the night in question, Courtois, being on his way back to the house of a relation with whom he was staying, saw the enemy's detachment making for the Hôtel de la Poste. Although the brave corporal knew that I no longer stopped there, he wished to make sure that his colonel was not in any danger, and boldly walked into the hotel, taking his relation with him. At the sight of the French uniform and the decoration the Prussians were infamous enough to assault the poor maimed man and try to tear the cross from his breast. The old soldier tried to defend his medal; but the Prussians killed him, dragging his body into the street, and continued their orgies.

In proportion to my weak garrison, Mons was so large that I had fortified myself in the barrack and concentrated my right defence on that point, forbidding my soldiers to go in the direction of the great square. I had been informed that the enemy were there, but I did not know their strength and feared that the inhabitants might join with them. But as soon as the people heard of the murder of their compatriot Courtois, a man esteemed by all the neighbourhood, they resolved to avenge him; and forgetting for the moment their grudge against the French, they deputed the brother of Courtois to ask me to put myself at their head and drive the Cossacks out. No doubt the excesses which had been committed in the hotel made every citizen fear for his own family and house: they would, I suppose, have acted very differently if regular troops had entered the town instead of marauders and assassins. Nevertheless, I thought it my duty to profit by the goodwill of the townspeople and, taking part of my force, I went to the square. Meanwhile the infantry major, who knew the town well, went with the remainder and formed an ambuscade near the breach by which the Prussian Cossacks had got into the place.

At the first shots which our people fired on the scamps the hotel and the square were in a tumult. Those of the enemy who were not killed on the spot made off as fast as their legs would carry them, but a good many lost their way in the streets and were polished off in detail. As for those who got as far as the place where they had left their horses – fastened to the trees on the promenade – they found the major there and were received by a volley at close quarters. When day came, we counted more than 200 of the enemy dead, while we had not lost a single man: for our adversaries were too stupefied by wine and strong drink to be able to defend themselves. Such of them as survived the surprise, slipped along the ruins of the old ramparts and made off into the country. There they were all captured or killed by the peasants, who were furious at hearing of the death of poor Courtois. He was regarded as the glory of the neighbourhood; the people called him 'Woodenleg', and he was as dear to them as another wooden-leg, General Daumesnil, was to the people of the Paris suburbs.

I passed another month at Mons in perfect friendship with the inhabitants; but the advance of the enemy's armies became so serious that the French had to leave not only Brussels but all Belgium and re-enter the frontiers of France proper. I was ordered to bring the dépôt of my regiment to Cambrai, where, with the horses which we had taken from the Prussian Cossacks, I was able to replace in the ranks 300 good troopers returned from Leipzig. I thus formed two fine squadrons, which, under Major Sigaldi, were shortly sent to the army which the Emperor had assembled in Champagne. They attracted notice there and sustained the credit of the 23rd Chasseurs, particularly at the Battle of Champaubert, where Captain Duplessis was killed.

The regimental dépôts being obliged to move to the left bank of the Seine to avoid falling into the hands of the enemy, mine went to Nogent-le-Roi. We had a good number of troopers but scarcely any horses. The government was making great efforts to collect some at Versailles, where a central cavalry dépôt had been created under the command of General Préval. Like his predecessor, General Bourcier, he understood the details of organisation much better than war, of which he had seen very little. He discharged his duties very well; but as he could not improvise horses or equipments, and was particular about not sending any but well-organised detachments, they went off very slowly.

I groaned over this, but no colonel could join the army without an order from the Emperor; and to economise his resources, he had forbidden any more officers to be sent to the war than were proportionate to the number of men that they had to command. In vain, therefore, did I beg General Préval to let me go to Champagne: he fixed my departure for the end of March, at which date I was to join the army with a so-called 'marching' regiment composed of mounted men from my dépôt and some others. Until then I was allowed to reside at Paris with my family; for my lieutenant colonel, Monsieur Caseneuve, could command and organise the 200 men who were still at Nogent-le-Roi, and I could always inspect them in a few hours.

In Paris, therefore, I spent most of the month of March, one of the saddest times of my life; although I was with those who were dearest to me. But the imperial government to which I was attached and which I had so long defended at the cost of my blood, was crumbling on all sides. From Lyons the enemy's armies occupied a great part of France and it was easy to see that they would soon reach the capital.

It is impossible to give any idea of the agitation which prevailed. Few of the inhabitants had foreseen an invasion; and as for me, who had expected it and had seen the horrors of war so near, I was in great trouble to know where I could place my wife and little child in safety. The kind old Marshal Sérurier offered them shelter at the Invalides, of which he was governor, and I was calmed by the thought that as the French had always respected the places where old soldiers lived, the enemy would do the same. So I took my family there, and left Paris before the Allies entered. I reported myself to General Préval at Versailles and he put me in command of a small column formed of troopers from my own regiment and from the 9th and 12th Chasseurs, with orders to rendezvous the same day at Rambouillet. There I found my horses and outfit and took the command of my squadrons.

As soon as Napoleon had learned that Paris had capitulated and that the two small corps of Marmont and Mortier were withdrawing to join him, he ordered them to take up a position at Essones, halfway between Paris and Fontainebleau. He went himself to the latter town as the heads of the columns returning from Saint-Dizier were reaching it: this shows that his intention was to march on Paris. The enemy's generals have since admitted that if the Emperor had attacked them, they would not have dared to accept battle. Behind them was the Seine and Paris with its million inhabitants, who might rise during the battle, barricade the streets and bridges, and cut off their retreat. They had, therefore, determined to retire and encamp on the heights of Belville, Montmartre and Chaumont, which command the right bank of the Seine and the road to Germany.

But fresh events detained them in Paris. Monsieur de Talleyrand, once a bishop, now married, had been to all appearance most devotedly attached to the Emperor, who had made him Prince of Benevento, Grand Chamberlain, and so on. But his pride was hurt at being no longer Napoleon's first confidant and director of his policy, and he had, since the disastrous Russian campaign, put himself at the head of the smothered opposition, set up by the malcontents of all parties, and especially the aristocracy of the Faubourg Saint-Germain. In the days of his prosperity they had submitted to and even served Napoleon; now they were his enemies and without openly compromising themselves, attacked him by all available means.

The chiefs were such men as the Abbé de Pradt, Archbishop of Malines, Monsieur de Chateaubriand, Monsieur Laisné, and others; all able men who, directed by Talleyrand – the ablest intriguer of them all – had for some time been looking out for a chance of upsetting Napoleon. They saw that they would never have one more favourable than the present. But though Napoleon was at the moment greatly weakened, he was not quite beaten. Besides the army which had just done wonders under him, there was Suchet's force between the Pyrenees and the Garonne, numerous troops under Soult, and two fine divisions at Lyons. The Army of Italy was still formidable; and thus, though the English were in occupation of Bordeaux, Napoleon could still collect a large force and prolong the war indefinitely if he raised the population, whom the enemy's requisitions had exasperated.[12]

Monsieur de Talleyrand and his party saw that if they allowed the Emperor time to bring up all these troops to Paris, he might beat the Allies in the streets, or retire to the loyal provinces and continue the war until he tired the enemy into making peace. The government must be changed: but there was the difficulty! They wanted to restore the Bourbons, while part of the nation wished to leave Napoleon on the throne, or call his son to it. There was the same difference of opinion among the Allies: the Kings of England and Prussia being on the side of the Bourbons, while the Emperor of Russia – who never liked them – was disposed to support the interests of Napoleon's son.

In order to settle the question by taking the first step and, as it were, to force the hand of the Allied sovereigns, Talleyrand caused a score of young aristocrats to appear on horseback on the Place Louis XV wearing white cockades.[13] Led by Viscount Talon, an old comrade of mine, from whom I have the details, they made their way towards the Emperor Alexander's hotel. loudly shouting, 'Long live Louis XVIII! Down with the tyrant!' At first the bystanders were merely stupefied; presently the crowd began to threaten and the most resolute members of the cavalcade wavered. The first outburst of royalism had misfired, but they repeated the scene at various points. Sometimes they were hooted, sometimes applauded. The Parisians required a cry to arouse them, and that which Talon and his friends had started resounded all day in the ears of the Emperor Alexander. In the evening Talleyrand was able to say to him, 'Your Majesty can judge for yourself with what unanimity the country desires the restoration of the Bourbons.' From that moment, though Napoleon's partisans – as the events of the next year showed – were many more than those of Louis XVIII, his cause was lost.

Epilogue

June 1815–November 1854

Had I died at Moscow I should have left behind
me a reputation as a conqueror without parallel
in history. A ball ought to have put an end to
me there. To die at Borodino would have been
to die like Alexander: to be killed at Waterloo
would have been a good death – perhaps
Dresden would have been better – but no, better
at Waterloo. The love of the people, their
regret . . .

Napoleon[1]

*The victorious Allied leaders were at Vienna, redesigning the
map of Europe, when the shocking news of Napoleon's escape
'. . . struck the world with astonishment. France hailed him
back with all its wild enthusiastic pride of military fame. His
former companions in arms crowded to his standard, and
from the Pyrenees to the Alps, from the Mediterranean to the
Atlantic, all were in motion.'[2] Galvanized by reports of Louis
XVIII's unpopularity, Bourbon plots against his person, and
Talleyrand's plans to have him moved further from France,
Napoleon gave his captors the slip on 26 February 1815 (the
governor of Elba being on the Italian mainland, visiting his
mistress). He landed at Golfe Juan in the south of France on 1
March. The army flocked to him almost en masse, whole*

regiments exchanging their white Bourbon cockades for the tricoleur and joining the triumphant march on Paris. Marshal Ney, sent by Louis to arrest Bonaparte, deserted the King and threw in his lot with the Emperor: Louis fled the country and Napoleon entered the capital on 20 March.

Napoleon needed time to consolidate his position and proffered peace; but his old adversaries refused to countenance a deal with the 'upstart' and promptly formed the Seventh Coalition. They mobilized their armies and France grimly prepared for war. Napoleon – who was far from having the support of the whole country – had to act quickly. His goal (if indeed it could be achieved) was no longer foreign conquest, but political survival. Gathering together an army of 72,000 veterans, he planned to inflict a decisive defeat upon his enemies in order to bring them to the bargaining table. He needed to find a way of splitting – or at least undermining – the Coalition before it could concentrate the bulk of its forces prior to an invasion of France. The only Allied units within his reach were those of Wellington (67,000 Belgian, British, Dutch and German troops – mainly raw and inexperienced) and Blücher (84,000 Prussians) over the border in Belgium. Napoleon proposed, therefore, to isolate these two armies, defeating each one in turn. The occupation of Brussels would follow and, he hoped, a favourable peace.

But Bonaparte was no longer at the peak of his powers; his Grand Army of Austerlitz, Jena, Eylau and Friedland had perished in the snows of Russia; and as for the surviving marshals, those who were not wounded, sick, or suffering from battle-fatigue, had, for the most part, elected to stay at home. No longer a latter-day Charlemagne, he was, in fact, a gambler, pinning his hopes on a single throw of the dice. Despite an early victory over the Prussians at Ligny, Napoleon's luck finally ran out on Sunday 18 June. In a battle which raged all day and claimed a total of 50,000 casualties, the armies of Wellington and Blücher effected a junction on the field of Waterloo, ten miles south of Brussels, and defeated the French in detail.

By 8 p.m. *the Emperor's army had dissolved into a mass of fugitives, mercilessly pursued by Blücher's Prussians; while the exhausted British – having doggedly held the ridge of Mont St Jean against successive French attacks – slept on the field of slaughter. As for Napoleon, declared an outlaw by the Bourbons and dubbed the 'disturber of the world'[3] by the Allies, he abdicated for a second time on 22 June; subsequently surrendering to the Captain of HMS* Bellerophon. *He hoped – somewhat optimistically – to obtain asylum in Britain or the United States; but was sent to St Helena (a tiny speck in the South Atlantic), his final place of exile, arriving there on 15 October 1815. The following month the Second Peace of Paris concluded the two decades of war to which he gave his name.*

The Allies wisely offered France generous terms: the aim being to establish a balance of power within Europe which would guarantee a lasting peace. This aim was more or less realized, and peace reigned in Europe for almost a hundred years. Napoleon, meanwhile, marked time in a melancholy fashion, bickering with his British gaoler, Sir Hudson Lowe; rewriting the history of his campaigns; and playing cards or chess: 'What a delightful thing rest is. The bed has become for me a place of luxury. How fallen am I. Once my activity was boundless; my mind never slumbered; I sometimes dictated to four or five secretaries, who wrote as fast as words could be uttered. But then I was Napoleon. Now I am nothing. I am sunk into a stupor, I can hardly raise my eyelids, my faculties forsake me. I do not live; I merely exist.'[4] A medley of morose generals waited upon him, each one angling for favouritism and recording his every utterance for posterity.

His health quickly deteriorated and he died on 21 May 1821. The subsequent autopsy gave stomach cancer as the cause of death; but later tests on locks of hair revealed the presence of an abnormally high level of arsenic, giving rise to an assortment of theories: including that of poisoning at the hands of a Bourbon assassin.[5] Whatever the cause, Napoleon Bonaparte suffered a slow, agonizing and squalid death. On 15 October 1840 his coffin was exhumed and his remains returned to Paris for interment.

Marbot's memoirs end with Napoleon's first abdication of April 1814. Upon the restoration of the Bourbon monarchy, he was given command of the 7th Hussars; but like so many other officers of the First Empire, he took his regiment over to Bonaparte upon the latter's return from Elba: his loyalty was rewarded by promotion to major general, though this order never took effect. At the Battle of Waterloo, Marbot's regiment formed part of the 1st Cavalry Division of d'Erlon's I Corps. Posted on the far right of the French line, Marbot and his men were sent in search of Marshal Grouchy's expected reinforcements;[6] but instead bumped into the advancing Prussian IV Corps. Marbot captured some prisoners and sent them back to the Emperor, only to be told that the Prussians with whom he was heavily engaged were mere stragglers, driven before Grouchy's advance, and that he should continue to push forward! After fierce fighting, Marbot's hussars fell back, only to find themselves entangled with Wellington's troops near Frischermont, where Marbot received yet another wound. The confusion surrounding these events are described by him in a bitter letter dated Laon, 26 June.

I CANNOT get over our defeat. We manoeuvred like so many pumpkins. I was with my regiment on the right flank of the army almost throughout the battle. They assured me that Marshal Grouchy would come up at that point; and it was guarded only by my regiment with three guns and a battalion of infantry: not nearly enough. Instead of Grouchy, what arrived was Blücher's corps. You can imagine how we were served. We were driven in and in an instant the enemy were in our rear. The mischief might have been repaired but no one gave any orders. The big generals were making bad speeches at Paris; the small ones lose their heads and all goes wrong.[10] I got a lance-wound in the side; it is pretty severe, but I thought I would stay to set a good example. If everyone had done the same we might yet get along; but the men are deserting and no one stops them. Whatever people may say, there are 50,000 men in this neighbourhood who might be got together; but to do it we should have to make it a capital offence to quit your post, or to give leave of absence. Everybody gives leave and the coaches are full of officers departing. You may judge if the soldiers stay. There will not be one left in a week unless they are checked by the death penalty. The Chambers can save us if they like; but we must have severe measures and prompt action. No food is sent to us and so the soldiers pillage our poor France as if they were in Russia. I am at the outposts before Laon; we have been made to promise not to fire. All is quiet.

After Napoleon's second abdication Marbot quit France for the safety of Germany. It was while in exile that he began writing on military matters: penning a criticism of General Roignart's 'Considérations sur l'Art de la Guerre', which had attacked Napoleon's handling of the Essling campaign of 1809. Napoleon later rewarded this effort in the form of a legacy of 100,000 francs, left to Marbot in his will: 'I bid Colonel Marbot continue to write in defence of the glory of the French armies, and to the confusion of calumniators and apostates.'[7]

Marbot returned to France in 1818 and was put on half-pay. After the fall of the Bourbons in the July Revolution of 1830, and the subsequent coronation of Louis Philippe, Marbot was finally made the rank of major general and

269

became aide-de-camp to the Duke of Orléans. He received his final wound at the age of fifty-nine, on the Medeah expedition, during the French subjugation of Algeria.[8] Hit by a bullet in the left knee, he managed a joke as he was carried to the rear. 'This is your fault, sir,' he said to Orléans. 'How so?' said the Duke. 'Did I not hear you say, before the fighting began, that if any of your staff got wounded, you could bet it would be Marbot? You see you have won!'[9] This worthy warrior was laid to rest in November 1854.

Glossary

Battalion A unit of infantrymen, usually consisting of around 1,000 soldiers. One or more battalions might constitute a regiment or brigade.

Blockade The Royal Navy operated two types of blockade, 'open' and 'close'. The former method involved the observation of an enemy port, while keeping a battle-fleet out to sea, as an intercepting force: thus inviting battle. The latter method was designed to prevent enemy ships from either entering or leaving the blockaded port.

Brigade A unit of cavalry or infantry, usually made up of several regiments or battalions acting together.

Caisson A four-wheeled ammunition wagon.

Cannister An artillery shell consisting of a tin container packed with lead musket-balls.

Cantinière A female camp-follower selling food and drink to the troops.

Carabinier A 'heavy' cavalryman supplied with helmet and body-armour.

Carbine A short-barrelled cavalry musket, usually clipped to a broad belt slung over the shoulder.

Chasseur-à-cheval A 'light' cavalryman. The name roughly translates as 'huntsman' and their uniform was, appropriately, dark green.

Congreve Rocket Named after its inventor, Sir William Congreve. In 1813 Congreve took an artillery company armed with his rockets abroad, fighting at the Battle of Leipzig.

Corps A sub-division of an army into a smaller, self-contained force of all arms. The French perfected this system, each corps being commanded by a marshal. The system afforded great flexibility and after successive defeats at the hands of Napoleon, most European armies adopted the fashion.

Cossacks Irregular cavalrymen in the service of the Tsar of Russia.

Cuirassier A 'heavy' cavalryman wearing a *cuirass*, or breastplate. French *cuirassiers* wore both breast- and backplates.

Debouch The deployment of troops into open ground.

Defile A narrow opening or way through which troops must march in file.

Division A body of troops, usually several thousand in number, and supported by guns.

Dragoon Originally an infantryman who rode into battle before deploying. By the Napoleonic period they had become 'medium' cavalry.

Eagle Napoleon presented these regimental standards to most army units. They were supposed to embody the 'spirit' of the regiment: the soldiers nicknamed them 'cuckoos'. The original pattern, based on the Roman imperial eagle, was designed by the sculptor Chaudet in 1804. The eagle weighed approximately four pounds and was mounted on a pole six feet in length.

Enfilade Gunfire designed to rake a line of troops from end to end.

Epaulette An ornamental shoulder-piece, usually fringed.

Escalade The scaling of fortified walls by the use of ladders.

Grapeshot A short-range artillery shell, being a bag full of musket-balls designed to scatter through the ranks of the enemy.

Grenadier A picked infantryman, supposedly over five feet eight inches tall. Often having élite status, their combat role was as shock-troops.

Howitzer A short-barrelled artillery-piece used for high-angled firing.

Hussar 'Light' cavalry based on Hungarian irregular horsemen. Acting primarily as scouts, they were the eyes and ears of the army: leading the advance guard in an offensive; and bringing up the rear in the case of a retreat. Noted for their extravagant uniforms and their role as troubleshooters, General Lasalle observed that any hussar who *wasn't* dead by the time he was thirty was 'a black-guard'.

Imperial Guard   Originally Napoleon's bodyguard but effectively an army within an army. Eventually sub-divided into Old, Middle, and Young, according to length of service, they were all veterans. In battle, the Emperor usually kept them in reserve, the mere threat of their deployment often being enough to demoralize the foe: this earned them the nickname of 'the Immortals' among the less pampered line regiments.

Jäger   German light troops, literally, 'huntsman'.

Lancers   Light cavalry armed with lances. The original lancers in Napoleon's army were Polish; but later additions came from France, Germany and Holland. The latter, in their distinctive scarlet uniforms, were – along with the Poles – included in the Guard.

Legion of Honour   Wanting to introduce a system of rewards for acts of loyalty, Napoleon instituted *La Légion d'Honneur* on 19 May 1804. Recipients were awarded a medal in the form of a five-pointed white star; and financial support in the form of an annuity.

Line of communication   The link between an army on campaign and its source of supplies.

Line of march   The direction of an army on campaign.

Mamelukes   Oriental horsemen brought back by Bonaparte from Egypt and later taken into the Imperial Guard. Armed to the teeth and wearing the most exotic of outfits, they were usually brigaded with the *chasseurs-à-cheval*.

Outpost   A lookout, or outlying sentry-post.

Pelisse   A hussar's fur-lined jacket. Usually heavily braided and festooned with buttons.

Picket   A sentry-post (see outpost).

Round-shot   Most common form of artillery ammunition. A solid sphere of metal designed to cut a swathe through densely packed troop formations.

Shako   A cylindrical cap, usually peaked. Often decorated with cords and plumes, they usually bore a metal plate identifying the wearer's regiment.

Shrapnel   An artillery shell, being a hollow sphere crammed with explosives and musket-balls. Detonated by a fuse, it was designed to explode in mid-air, thus showering the enemy with its deadly contents.

Glossary

Uhlan   A German lancer.
Vedette   A cavalry scout.
Voltigeur   A light infantryman, supposedly able to keep pace with a trotting horse.

Notes and Sources

Preface (pp. vii–ix)

1 Doyle, Sir Arthur Conan, *Through the Magic Door*, London 1907.
2 Butler, A.J., *Memoirs of Baron de Marbot*, London 1900.

Chapter 1 (pp. 1–9)

1 Ségur, Count Philippe de, *An Aide-de-Camp of Napoleon*, London 1895 (Ed. Patchett-Martin, H.A.).
2 Augereau, Pierre François Charles, Duke of Castiglione (1757–1816). This swashbuckler of the *Ancien Régime* was one of the original marshals created by Napoleon in 1804. Often portrayed as a vulgar bandit, he was, in fact, a generous man, a devoted husband, and beloved by his men. His later career was dogged by ill-health and a fall from grace for daring to criticize Napoleon's handling of the Battle of Eylau.
3 Bonaparte left Egypt on 23 August and returned to French soil on 9 October. Despite Bernadotte's calls for his arrest for breaking the quarantine laws, he was greeted as a saviour by the people. He arrived at Lyons on or around 13 October on his way to Paris.
4 Bonaparte, Louis, King of Holland (1778–1846). Napoleon's younger brother and ADC who was bullied by him: firstly into an unhappy marriage to Hortense, Josephine's daughter; and

secondly, onto the throne of Holland. Determined to be a good king and loyal to the interests of his subjects, Louis refused to join Napoleon's Continental System: Napoleon simply annexed Holland and Louis abdicated.

5 Berthier, Louis Alexandre, Duke of Valangin, Prince of Neuchâtel, Prince of Wagram (1753–1815). Nicknamed 'the Emperor's Wife' by the troops, this tubby, jolly man, as Napoleon's chief-of-staff, was his constant companion. Bonaparte called him his 'Chief Clerk'; he was, in fact, one of the greatest staff officers of all time.

6 Lannes, Jean, Duke of Montebello (1769–1809). Nicknamed 'the Roland of the Army', Lannes was a brave and outspoken ex-grenadier. A personal friend of Bonaparte's, he was the first of the marshals to be mortally wounded in action.

7 Murat, Joachim, Prince of the Empire, Grand Duke of Berg and Cleves, King of Naples and the Two Sicilies (1767–1815). The son of an innkeeper who became a king, thanks to his marriage to Caroline, Napoleon's sister. Charismatic, recklessly brave, and impossibly vain, he was promoted far above his natural abilities: a dashing captain of cavalry masquerading as a king. As Napoleon's star began to wane, the desire to keep power led both Murat and Caroline to betray Napoleon, only to be betrayed in their turn by the Allies, Murat ending up a fugitive. A foolhardy attempt to regain the Neapolitan throne in 1815 led to Murat's arrest by the Italian authorities: half-an-hour later he was executed. Vain to the last, he requested the firing squad to aim for his heart, thereby sparing his face.

8 Roustam Raza (1780–1845). A Mameluke slave-boy presented to Bonaparte by Sheik El-Bekri in 1799. Napoleon took him as his bodyguard, sparing no expense for his exotic outfits. He deserted the Emperor prior to his first abdication and later published his unfaithworthy memoirs.

Chapter 2 (pp. 11–23)

1 Gonneville, Colonel de, *Recollections of Colonel de Gonneville*, London 1875 (Ed. Yonge, Charlotte M.).

2 After Nelson had blasted the French fleet out of the water at Aboukir on 1 August 1798, the Army of the Orient was effectively stranded. Following Bonaparte's departure, the French fought both Ottoman and British forces, eventually surrendering to the latter on 31 August 1801.

3 *Les Deux Philiberts* by L.F. Picard, a popular comedy first produced in 1815.

4 These locks were the hussar's beloved *cadanettes*, the hair being plaited at the temples and weighted down with pistol balls!

5 Count Ladislaw de Bercheny, a Hungarian nobleman, raised a regiment of hussars for French service in 1720. The Bercheny Hussars gained a fearsome reputation during the Wars of Polish and Austrian Succession. In 1791 they became the 1st Regiment of Hussars.

6 On 22 September 1792 the French Republic adopted a new calendar. The months were renamed *Vendémaire, Brumaire, Frimaire, Pluvôise, Ventôse, Germinal, Floréal, Prairial, Messidor, Thermidor, Fructidor*; and 1792 became year 1. Napoleon abolished the system in 1805, returning France to the old Gregorian calendar.

7 The Ligurian Republic was a French satellite, established at Genoa in 1797.

8 A league was roughly equivalent to three English miles.

9 The Kingdom of Sardinia-Piedmont consisted of the island of Sardinia and the Italian lands between Nice and the River Ticino.

Chapter 3 (pp. 25–33)

1 Wheeler, Harold F.B., *The Mind of Napoleon: As Revealed in his Thoughts, Speech and Actions*, London 1910.

2 The French term is *sous*-lieutenant, literally meaning underlieutenant. As there is no corresponding rank in the British army, Butler borrowed the Royal Navy rank, sub-lieutenant. I have seen no reason to change this.

Chapter 4 (pp. 35–50)

1 Thiébault, General A.C., *The Memoirs of Baron Thiébault*, London 1896 (Ed. Butler, A.J.).

2 Masséna, André, Duke of Rivoli, Prince of Essling (1758–1817). Bonaparte's 'Spoilt Child of Victory', Masséna was a hero of the Revolutionary Wars and one of France's ablest generals. His reputation was later tarnished, however, by his love of plunder and his inability to defeat Wellington in the Peninsula.

3 Soult, Nicholas, Jean de Dieu, Duke of Dalmatia (1768–1851). One of Napoleon's most talented marshals, he was showered with honours, titles and wealth: none of which stopped him from looting Europe's art treasures for his private collection.

4 Oudinot, Nicholas Charles, Duke of Reggio (1767–1847). Made a marshal after the Battle of Wagram, he was not one of Napoleon's brighter lieutenants, though he was undoubtedly the toughest, surviving twenty-two serious wounds.

5 Village in north-west Italy on the Gulf of Genoa. On 6 April 1800 the Austrians began their campaign to take Genoa with this victory.

6 Thiébault kept a journal of the siege which he read aloud to Masséna every night, as the General took his bath.

7 On 6 December 1745 the Genoese rose up in defiance of their Austrian garrison. After five days of fighting the Austrians quit the city, having sustained 5,000 casualties.

8 The Peace of Amiens, an Anglo-French treaty signed on 25 March 1802, promised much but delivered a mere fourteen months of peace.

9 Haiti was once a prized French colony. In 1801 Bonaparte sent an expedition to put down a slave rebellion led by Toussaint L'Ouverture. Yellow fever wiped out the French force, the survivors surrendering to the British Royal Navy in 1803.

10 The Battle of Marengo, fought on 14 June 1800, was almost a disaster for the French. Outnumbered initially by the Austrians, only the timely arrival of General Desaix with reinforcements saved the day. Bonaparte's official account of the battle later claimed that all had gone according to his master-plan.

Chapter 5 (pp. 51–64)

1 Coignet, Captain Jean-Roch, *The Notebooks of Captain Coignet*, London 1928.

2 Wheeler, *The Mind of Napoleon.*

3 Bernadotte, Jean Baptiste Jules, Prince of Pontecorvo, later Charles XIV of Sweden (1763–1844). An early rival of Bonaparte and arch-plotter against his régime, his neck was usually saved by his marriage to Désirée Clary, Joseph Bonaparte's sister-in-law. His military performance was, to say the least, patchy; and an exasperated Napoleon dismissed him from the army on the field of Wagram. The sequel to his fall from grace, however, was an invitation from the Swedish government to become crown prince to the ailing and heirless King Charles XIII. Bernadotte accepted, changing his name, his religion and his allegiance: the dynasty he founded survives to this day.

4 The Battle of Hohenlinden, fought on 3 December 1800, was a decisive victory for Moreau's Army of the Rhine over the Austrians; and brought the War of the Second Coalition to a close.

5 The *chasseurs-à-cheval* of the Imperial Guard provided Napoleon's personal escort and were regarded as something of an élite within an élite.

6 Larrey, Dominique-Jean, Baron (1766–1842). The son of a shoemaker, Larrey entered the army as a surgeon in 1792. His devotion to the wounded won him Napoleon's recognition, and he became chief surgeon to the Imperial Guard.

7 Although there had been a kingdom of Galicia in north-western Spain, there was also a Polish province of the same name. Once a possession of the Austrian Empire, it became part of the Grand Duchy of Warsaw in 1809.

Chapter 6 (pp. 65–76)

1 Wheeler, *The Mind of Napoleon.*

2 Atteridge, A.H., *Marshal Murat, King of Naples*, London 1911.

3 In 1817 Napoleon gave this portrait of the Prussian King: 'He

was a tall, dry-looking fellow and would give a good idea of Don Quixote. He attached more importance to the cut of a dragoon or hussar uniform than would have been necessary for the salvation of a kingdom.' Herold, J. Christopher, *The Mind of Napoleon: A Selection from his Written and Spoken Words*, New York 1955.

4 The Prussians invaded Saxony on 6 September 1806.

5 Davout, Louis Nicholas, Duke of Auerstädt, Prince of Eckmühl (1770–1823). The youngest of the marshals created in 1804, he found fame at Austerlitz and, more especially, at Auerstädt, where he took on virtually the whole Prussian army – and won. Bald, bespectacled, brusque, he was the complete opposite of *beau sabreurs* like Murat. Nicknamed 'the Iron Marshal', he was stern, capable and efficient.

6 In the pursuit which followed the French victory, Bernadotte accepted the surrender of a Swedish contingent at Lübeck, belatedly sent to aid the Prussians. His chivalrous treatment of these prisoners persuaded the Swedes to adopt him as crown prince.

Chapter 7 (pp. 77–90)

1 Barrès, Jean-Baptiste, *Memoirs of a Napoleonic Officer*, London 1925 (Ed. Miall, Bernard).

2 Coignet, *Notebooks*.

3 Coignet mentions the cemetery at Eylau and the fate of the 14th Regiment in his *Notebooks*: 'This cemetery was the burial-place of a great number of French and Russians. We held on to the position. But to the right, in front of us, the 14th of the Line was cut to pieces; the Russians penetrated their square and the carnage was terrible.'

4 Advancing deeper into Poland, by late December the French had crossed the Vistula and had reached the River Bug and its tributary, the Wkra. Colonel Savary, determined to be the first across, was killed by a Cossack who, galloping out of the nearby woods, plunged a lance into his heart.

5 Augereau's country estate where, according to Marbot, 'he lived in fine style.'

6 Marbot's brother Felix died while still at military school when a wound caused by duelling with a fellow pupil reopened.

7 Marbot was decorated for his bravery at Eylau on 29 October 1808 by Napoleon on Augereau's recommendation.

8 Present-day south-western Poland.

Chapter 8 (pp. 91–8)

1 Johnson, David, *The French Cavalry 1792–1815*, London 1989.

2 Now the Russian town of Kaliningrad.

3 Mortier, Édouard Adolphe Casimir Joseph, Duke of Treviso (1768–1835). A big man, half-English, and very popular. He was killed on the parade ground by a bomb intended for King Louis Philippe.

4 Ney, Michel, Duke of Elchingen, Prince of the Moscowa (1769–1815). Nicknamed 'the Bravest of the Brave' by Napoleon for his super-human efforts as rearguard commander in Russia. It was Ney, however, who demanded Napoleon's abdication in 1814; and who promised Louis XVIII to bring the ex-Emperor back to Paris in an iron cage after his escape from Elba in 1815. Napoleon's magnetism proved too much for him, however, and he betrayed the Bourbons. For this he was eventually tried for treason and executed, living up to his sobriquet by commanding his own firing squad.

5 Marbot may be quoting from official figures, often exaggerated for public consumption.

Chapter 9 (pp. 99–118)

1 Gonneville, *Recollections*.

2 Ferdinand, Prince of the Asturias, later Ferdinand VII of Spain (1784–1833). Plotted against his father, King Charles IV, and was later forced by Napoleon to renounce his right to the throne. Kept in semi-imprisonment at Valençay, he steadfastly refused to be rescued, while the Spanish people rallied to his cause: thus igniting the Peninsular War. On Napoleon's fall he returned to claim his crown; but proved to be a tyrant, provoking a popular

uprising in 1820 (ironically, he was only saved by French intervention).

3 Clarke, Henri Jacques Guillaume, Duke of Feltre (1765–1818). Born in France of Irish descent, Clarke attached himself to Bonaparte on the eve of the latter's coup of November 1799. He was later rewarded with a dukedom and the tenancy of the War Office.

4 Labédoyère hero-worshipped Napoleon. Upon the Emperor's escape from Elba, he set off with his troops to join him. After Waterloo, Labédoyère returned to Paris, still espousing the Bonapartist cause: the Bourbons had him shot.

5 Butler used the term 'busby' to denote Marbot's hussar-cap; but as this derives from W. Busby of the Strand, supplier to the British army, I have seen fit to replace it with the more descriptive term, 'bearskin'.

6 The Spanish *guerrilleros* fought a savage war against the French between 1808 and 1814. Fear of guerrilla attacks tied down large numbers of troops for escort duty: a courier was often escorted by as many as two hundred troopers.

7 As the Battle of Tudela was fought on 23 November, this is an obvious error: the date inferred is the 24th.

8 On 19 May 1804 Napoleon introduced the Legion of Honour, a system to reward the brave and the faithful. Recipients received a medal and a gratuity. (See also Glossary.)

Chapter 10 (pp. 119–31)

1 Rocca, Albert Jean Michel de, *Memoirs of the War in Spain*, London 1815.

2 The British, under Sir Arthur Wellesley (the future Duke of Wellington), landed at Mondego Bay between 1 and 8 August; after clashes at Obidos, and Roliça, they decisively defeated the French at Vimiero on the 21st. By November, command having passed to Sir John Moore, the British had advanced from Lisbon to Salamanca, approximately 100 miles north-west of Madrid.

3 On 29 December the British scored a notable success at Bena-

vente, drubbing the *chasseurs* of the Imperial Guard and capturing their commander, Lefebvre-Desnouettes who was 'attacked by a private of the Tenth [Hussars], to whom he surrendered after receiving a slight wound'. Gordon, Captain Alexander, *The Journal of a Cavalry Officer in the Corunna Campaign*, London 1913.

4 Soult caught up with Moore at La Coruña on 15 January 1809. He attacked the next day, hoping to prevent the British from escaping; but gave up after meeting stiff resistance: Moore was mortally wounded in the final moments of the battle.

5 Palafox attempted to rescue Ferdinand; but he was quite happy cutting out paper patterns and doing embroidery.

6 After the abortive and bloody revolt in Madrid on 2 May, Murat assured Napoleon that all Spanish resistance to the French occupation was over: 'Napoleon was not displeased with the news. It was his theory that nothing strengthened a Government so much as an abortive insurrection. He could not foresee that the *Dos de Mayo* was the first wild flicker of a flame that would soon set Spain ablaze from the Pyrenees to Tarifa.' Atteridge, *Marshal Murat, King of Naples*.

7 'If these people had known how to fight as well as they know how to die, we should not have crossed the Pyrenees so easily.' Rocca, *Memoirs of the War in Spain*.

8 Total losses can never truly be known: the Spanish garrison probably lost around 18,000 killed, 12,000 captured or surrendered; the Spanish population approximately 34,000 through war, sickness and starvation; French losses from fighting and sickness were about 10,000.

Chapter 11 (pp. 133–47)

1 Wheeler, *The Mind of Napoleon*.

2 Napoleon's ascendancy in Germany forced Francis to renounce his title of Holy Roman Emperor on 6 August 1806, thus becoming simply Francis I of Austria.

3 Austria had backed a popular uprising in the Tyrol against

Bavarian occupation, led by Andreas Hofer. After the French victory at Wagram the insurrection foundered, Hofer being executed on Napoleon's orders.

Chapter 12 (pp. 149–67)

1 Cohen, Louis, *Napoleonic Anecdotes*, London 1925.
2 Wife of Louis Bonaparte and Queen of Holland.
3 Bessières, Jean Baptiste, Duke of Istria (1768–1813). A trusted friend of Napoleon's who commanded the cavalry of the Imperial Guard. A popular commander, he was killed by a canonball at Lützen in 1813.
4 On hearing of Lannes' awkward situation, Augereau paid the deficit out of his own purse.
5 A reference to Marbot's adventure at Mölk on 7 May 1809, when he was sent on a hazardous intelligence-gathering mission across the Danube by Napoleon himself. Needless to say, Marbot accomplished his mission and once again was promised the rank of major.
6 The village of Aspern, four miles east of Vienna, was of great strategical importance and it was taken and retaken ten times over the two days of fighting. Troops were constantly fed in, only to become casualties, making it (on a percentage basis) one of the bloodiest battles in history.
7 The Austrian Emperor also held the title of King of Hungary; as such he fielded an imperial and royal army composed of many ethnic groups.
8 Beauharnais, Eugène de (1781–1824). Josephine's son by Alexandre de Beauharnais. Napoleon adopted him and Eugène proved to be a loyal and capable lieutenant.

Chapter 13 (pp. 169–80)

1 Johnson, David, *Napoleon's Cavalry and its Leaders*, New York 1978.
2 An unsuccessful plot against Bonaparte led by Bernadotte from his headquarters at Rennes.

3 Joseph Bonaparte married Julie Clary on 1 August 1794. Her sister, Désirée, married Bernadotte four years later.
4 They had been kept too long under artillery fire and had lost their nerve.
5 On 2 July 1809 Masséna was injured in a fall from his horse and thereafter took to his carriage.
6 The familiar as opposed to the formal mode of address.

Chapter 14 (pp. 181–92)

1 Kincaid, Captain Sir John, *Adventures in the Rifle Brigade*, London 1830.
2 As Marbot later mentions 'slings', I take this item to be a sabretache: a kind of pouch suspended from the sword-belt and used for storing maps, despatches, etc.
3 Casualties for the two armies 3rd–14th March were pretty even. However, Wellington had lost 130 men at Casal Novo when, advancing in thick fog, they found themselves on top of the French guns.
4 The name of this skirmish varies in the literature of the period; but Wellington correctly referred to this hamlet in central Portugal as Foz d'Arouce.
5 Although Marbot's description of the action roughly tallies with British accounts, Sir Charles Oman has pointed out certain errors: Ney counter-charged at the head of the 69th Regiment, not the 27th, as Marbot states; and although French casualties amounted to almost 250, the British and Portuguese lost only nine killed and about sixty wounded: the combat was, therefore, an Allied victory, rather than the draw which Marbot's account might suggest.
6 Ney appears not to have been punished for his insubordination: after spending a few weeks at his château, he was appointed commandant of the camp at Boulogne.
7 The sister in question was Napoleon's favourite, Pauline. Married first to General Leclerc and then to Prince Borghese, Pauline had a string of affairs and scandalous liaisons. A noted beauty with a penchant for nude-modelling, she was loyal only to Napoleon, whom she adored.

8 The Duke of Lauzun was a high-society soldier of the eighteenth century. A regular visitor to London, he had been both friend to King George III and mentor to his son, the Prince Regent.

9 The name given by the French to the Battle of Borodino, 5–6 September 1812.

Chapter 15 (pp. 193–211)

1 Bourrienne, F. de, *Memoirs of Napoleon Bonaparte*, London 1905.

2 On 10 January 1810 Napoleon's marriage to Josephine was annulled. He had married her in 1796, when still a general, and had crowned her Empress with his own hands in 1804; but she had failed to produce the heir which he so desperately wanted. On 11 March 1810 Napoleon married Marie-Louise, daughter of Francis, Emperor of Austria.

3 Nicolson, Nigel, *Napoleon 1812*, London 1985.

4 Gouvion Saint-Cyr, Laurent, Marquis de (1764–1830). A failed artist and actor, Saint-Cyr was, however, an able and talented general. Cool and aloof, he disapproved of looting, political intriguing, and the dynastic ambitions of generals: thus putting himself at odds with almost everyone from the Emperor down. The troops called him 'the Owl' and, although often maligned, he was, in fact, an honourable soldier and devoted husband.

5 Moreau, Hoche, Kléber and Desaix were heroes of the Revolutionary Wars.

6 On 19 May 1804 Napoleon created eighteen marshals of the Empire. Mainly of humble origins, these career soldiers became the Emperor's new aristocracy.

7 Sources vary as to numbers involved, but approximately 23,000 Russians and 33,000 French and Bavarians were engaged.

8 Elsewhere in his memoirs Marbot mentions this weapon: 'The Russian artillery is far from being as good as ours, but on campaign it employs pieces called *unicorns*, the range of which was longer than that of any French guns of the period.'

9 The Gentlemen Guards were aristocratic volunteers who provided their own horses and equipment.

10 General Castex commanded the 5th Light Cavalry Brigade, composed of the 23rd and 24th Chasseurs.

11 General Corbineau was in overall command of II Corps' cavalry.

12 'Polotsk was hardly a glorious victory, St Cyr having some 35,000 men on the field against Wittgenstein's 23,000 or 24,000 at most, but it had important results in freeing Napoleon from anxiety for his left flank.' Foord, Edward, *Napoleon's Russian Campaign of 1812*, London 1914.

Chapter 16 (pp. 213–30)

1 Vossler, Lieutenant H.A., *With Napoleon in Russia 1812*, London 1969.

2 Borodino cost Napoleon forty-three generals and 110 colonels among the 30,000 French casualties: he had already lost 150,000 on the campaign prior to the battle.

3 Herold, J. Christopher, *The Mind of Napoleon, A Selection From His Written and Spoken Words*, New York 1955.

4 Coignet, *Notebooks*.

5 Presumably centigrade, this being –13° Fahrenheit.

6 Marbot was thirty years old in 1812; it seems unlikely, therefore, that he would have had a school friend with a son sixteen years of age.

7 The infamous 29th Bulletin, which detailed the destruction of the Grand Army while omitting its terrible sufferings, closed by informing a stunned Paris that 'His Majesty's health has never been better.' Often quoted as an example of supreme callousness, Napoleon needed both to play down the disaster and to quash the rumours of his death.

8 Napoleon set out from Smorgon during the night of 5 December. Accompanied by the minimum of attendants, he travelled in secret, under the pseudonym of Count Gérard de Reyneval. Driving non-stop, he reached Paris in two weeks.

9 Napoleon probably chose Murat to lead the army because of his ability to inspire the troops. When the news of the Grand Army's total disintegration reached the Emperor, however, he reproached Murat for having 'lost the army': a harsh judgement

in the circumstances. Murat, who had already complained to Davout that Napoleon was 'a maniac', became even more disaffected.

10 Marbot had little time for de Ségur's history of the campaign, which was published in 1825: 'More than one survivor of that campaign was distressed by the spirit of the work, and even our enemies called it a military romance . . .'

11 General Platov gained fame as the colourful leader of the Don Cossacks.

12 On Christmas Day 1812 General Yorck found his small Prussian army cut off and surrounded by the Russians. After five days of talks Yorck – at best an unwilling ally of the French – signed the Convention of Tauroggen, whereby the Prussians quit the Grand Army.

13 Although Frederick William initially disapproved of Yorck's action at Tauroggen, it was the first step in Prussia's eventual defection to the Allies. General Yorck, far from being executed, went on to play a leading role in the war against Napoleon.

Chapter 17 (pp. 231–47)

1 Barrès, *Memoirs*.

2 Barrès, *Memoirs*.

3 By 1795 Poland had been swallowed up by Russia, Prussia and Austria. Many Poles registered their dissatisfaction by enlisting in the French service. When Napoleon created the Grand Duchy of Warsaw in 1809 it provided him with perhaps his most loyal foreign soldiers.

4 MacDonald, Jacques Étienne Joseph Alexandre, Duke of Taranto (1765–1840). Born in France, the son of a Scottish Jacobite exile, he received his marshal's bâton on the field of Wagram. An able commander under Napoleon's hand, his performance was poor when left to his own devices. He deserted the Emperor in 1814 and remained loyal to the Bourbons, being rewarded with a peerage and command of the army.

5 On 24 October, while at Erfurt with Napoleon, Murat secretly

agreed to join the Allies in return for a (worthless, as it happened) guarantee that he should remain King of Naples.

6 Metternich-Winneburg-Beilstein, Prince Clemens Wenzel Lothar, von (1773–1859). One of the most influential politicians of his day, Metternich guided Austrian policy with great skill. Unlike many other Allied statesmen, he was not a rabid anti-Bonapartist, but merely a pragmatist: binding Austria to whichever alliance best served the Habsburgs' interests.

7 Upon the second Bourbon restoration many officers who had remained loyal to Napoleon fled abroad. After a couple of years the political situation had cooled sufficiently to allow most of them to return.

8 To run flat out.

9 At the Battle of the Katzbach River in August 1813, the victorious Prussians pushed the French down the steep banks and into the river, swollen by heavy rains: Marbot was saved by the 'pluck and cleverness of my Turkish horse. He went along the precipice like a cat on a roof and saved my life, not for the only time.'

10 The opening words of Virgil's First Eclogue: *Tityrus, lying back beneath the shade of the spreading beech tree.*

11 On 10 October 1806 at the Battle of Saalfeld, Prince Louis Ferdinand, nephew to the King of Prussia, led a desperate charge against the French centre: he was cut down by Quartermaster Guindet of the 10th Hussars.

Chapter 18 (pp. 249–63)

1 Bourrienne, *Memoirs*.

2 As Napoleon's misfortunes increased, so the average age of his soldiers decreased and by 1814 French conscripts were in their middle teens: they were nicknamed 'Marie-Louises' after the Emperor's young wife.

3 Petre, F. Loraine, *Napoleon at Bay*, London 1914.

4 Talleyrand-Perigord, Charles-Maurice, de, Prince of Benevente (1754–1838). Of noble birth, a childhood accident left him crippled in one foot. Unfit for military service, he joined the

Church, becoming Bishop of Autun in 1789. Following the Revolution, he resigned his clerical post and entered politics as a diplomat, becoming foreign minister in 1797. Initially a supporter of Bonaparte, he became disaffected with the Empire and resigned in 1807. Turning to treachery, he began secret negotiations with both the Allies and the exiled Bourbons, preparing the way for their restoration in 1814.

5 Wellington's war ended on 10 April 1814 with his victory at Toulouse.

6 Gronow, *Reminiscences and Recollections of Captain Gronow*, London 1900.

7 Bourrienne, *Memoirs*.

8 Chosen by Napoleon to succeed Josephine for dynastic reasons, she bore him a son on 20 March 1811. After her husband's abdication she returned to Vienna: she never saw him again.

9 Napoleon-François Joseph-Charles Bonaparte, King of Rome, Duke of Reichstadt, Prince of Parma (1811–32). Napoleon's only legitimate son, he became the ward of his grandfather, Francis of Austria, upon his father's abdication. He died of tuberculosis on 22 July 1832.

10 Liddell Hart, B.H., *The Letters of Private Wheeler*, London 1951.

11 After the War of Spanish Succession in 1714, Belgium came under Austrian rule. During the Revolutionary Wars the French invaded, and Belgium was ceded to France by the Treaty of Lunéville, being formally annexed in October 1795. In March 1802 the Treaty of Amiens confirmed French domination of Belgium, Holland, Luxembourg and all German territory west of the Rhine. The French were finally removed from Belgium by the Allies of the Sixth Coalition in 1814: the settlement which followed bolted Catholic Belgium and Protestant Holland together as the short-lived Kingdom of the United Netherlands.

12 Although the Prussians mistreated the French and plundered their property, the British won the hearts and minds of the locals in the south by paying for all requisitions.

13 The white cockade was a royalist symbol.

Epilogue (pp. 265–70)

1 Wheeler, *The Mind of Napoleon*.
2 Anton, James, *Retrospect of a Military Life*, Edinburgh 1841.
3 Thornton, Michael John, *Napoleon After Waterloo*, Standford 1968.
4 Wheeler, *The Mind of Napoleon*.
5 See Weider, Ben, and Forshufvud, Sten, *Assassination at St Helena*, Vancouver 1978.
6 After his victory over Blücher on 16 June, Napoleon sent Grouchy with 33,000 troops in pursuit of the retreating Prussians. Bad weather and blunders caused Grouchy to lose touch with the Prussians who, he assumed, were retreating into Germany. Blücher, however, had reorganized his army and was marching to Wellington's aid at Mont St Jean. The morning of the 18th saw Grouchy twelve miles distant from Napoleon, enjoying an early lunch, and resisting the entreaties of his staff to march toward the sound of guns, coming from the direction of Waterloo.
7 Butler, *Memoirs of Baron de Marbot*.
8 France invaded Algeria in 1830, intent on making it a white settler colony. In 1832 an insurrection led by Sultan Abd Al-Qadir was met by force, and the French subjugation of Algeria began in earnest: the territory was annexed by France in 1870.
9 Butler, *Memoirs of Baron de Marbot*.
10 Although thousands of French troops deserted after Waterloo, Napoleon still had 120,000 men with which to defend Paris, plus 170,000 conscripts still in training. But he was exhausted; and no longer wielded sufficient political clout to organize a counterstroke. While government ministers manoeuvred and intrigued to save their own skins, the Chamber of Representatives, led by police chief Joseph Fouché, demanded the Emperor's second abdication.

Select Bibliography

Many works have been consulted in the preparation of this book. The following list represents those upon which I have relied most; and I acknowledge my debt to their authors.

Belchem, John and Price, Richard, *Penguin Dictionary Of Nineteenth-Century History*, London 1996.

Butler, A.J., *Memoirs of Baron de Marbot*, London 1900.

Chandler, David G., *Dictionary of the Napoleonic Wars*, London 1979.

Coignet, Captain Jean-Roch, *Note-Books of Captain Coignet*, London 1928, re-issued 1998.

Davis, Paul K., *Encyclopedia of Invasions and Conquests*, Oxford 1996.

Haythornthwaite, Philip J., *Napoleonic Source Book*, London 1990.

Who Was Who in the Napoleonic Wars, London 1998.

Horricks, Raymond, *Napoleon's Elite*, New Brunswick 1995.

Johnson, David, *Napoleon's Cavalry and its Leaders*, New York 1978.

Laffin, John, *Brassey's Battles*, London 1986.

Palmer, Alan, *Encyclopaedia of Napoleon's Europe*, London 1984, re-issued 1998.

Rogers, Colonel H.C.B., *Napoleon's Army*, London 1974.

Schom, Alan, *Napoleon Bonaparte*, New York 1997.

Smith, Digby, *Greenhill Napoleonic Wars Data Book*, London 1998.

Select Bibliography

Wheeler, Harold F.B., *The Mind of Napoleon: As Revealed in his Speech and Actions*, London 1910.

Windrow, Martin and Mason, Francis K., *Concise Dictionary of Military Biography*, London 1990.